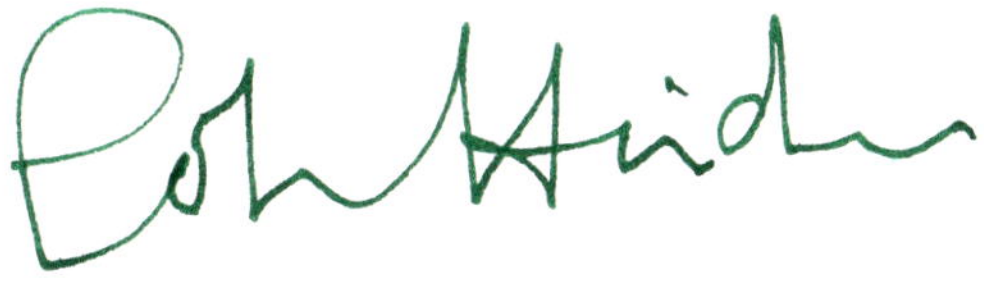

Second Print 2022 : First Print 2021

www.colinhindle.co.uk

A PICTORIAL GUIDE TO THE BEST
LAKELAND VIEWS

an illustrated account of the history of the English Lake District

by

Colin Hindle

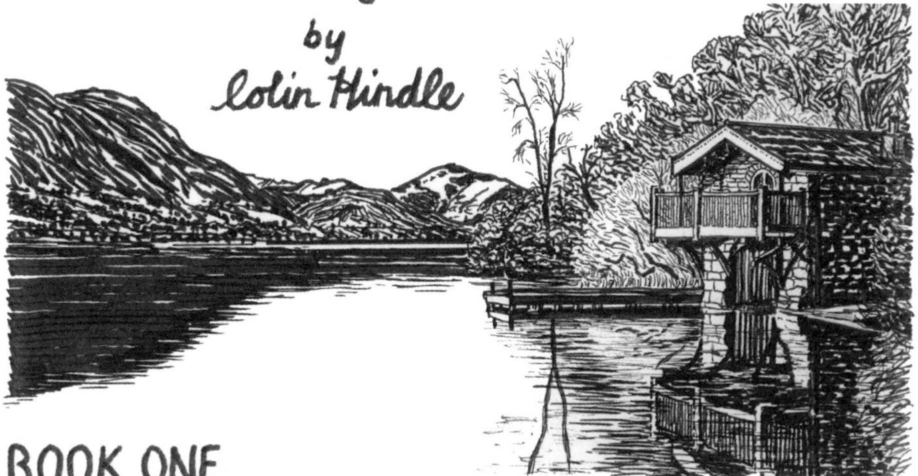

BOOK ONE

ULLSWATER · BROTHERSWATER · HAWESWATER

Printed by H&H Reeds
Penrith 2021

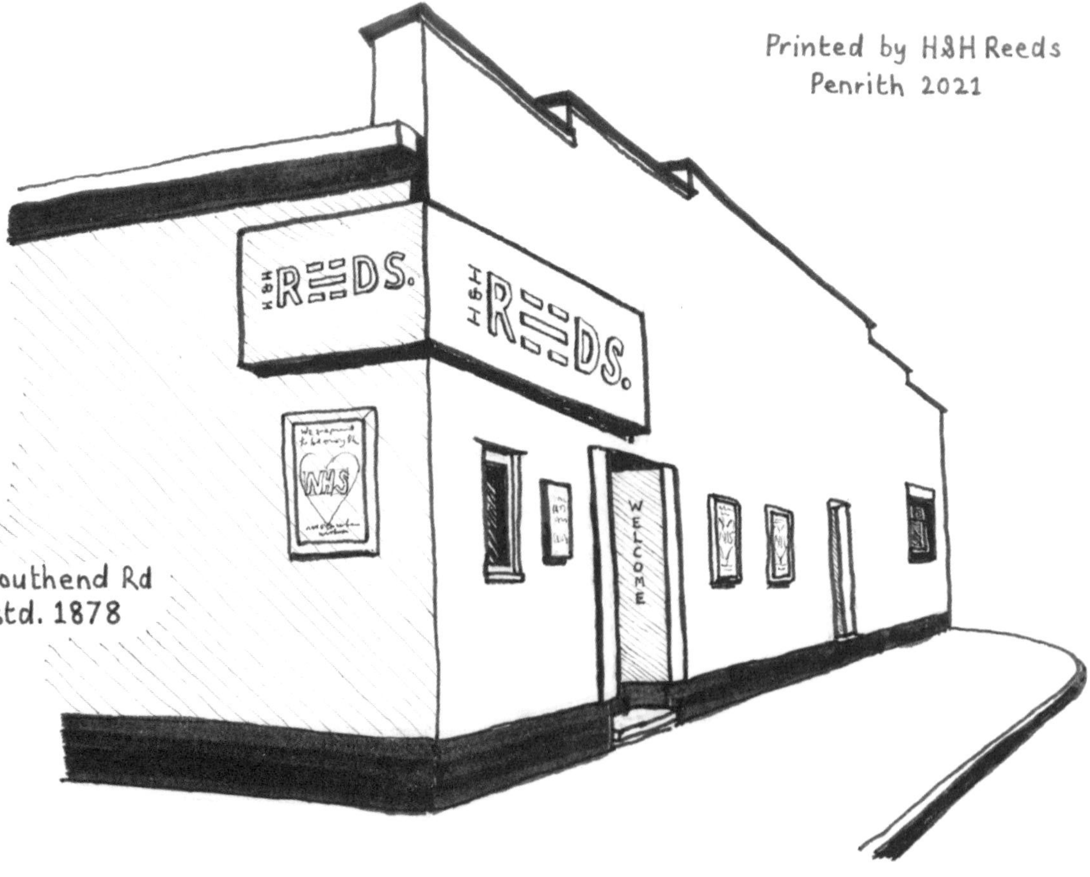

H&H Reeds, Southend Rd
Penrith Estd. 1878

ISBN 978-0-9933864-5-9

Foreword

In 2015 a great friend of mine (let's call him Dave B) decided to walk the 214 Wainwrights in one year to fundraise for a cancer charity in memory of his mother. On reaching many of the summits with him I felt a sense of deflation; there was no view, or a compromised view, or the view was better earlier or later on the walk.

Despite owning the Wainwright Pictorial Guides for a decade it wasn't until reading Hunter Davies' excellent biography of him that I realised every page was designed as a complete entity so the reader never had to turn over on a windy fell to find the information they needed. Additionally how he had rewritten the first 120 pages of Book One in order to justify the right hand margins; and how frustrated he was in trying to achieve perfection, eventually accepting no matter what he did there would always be errors. His books are objects of beauty in themselves, and it was this framework that inspired me to make this guide to the best views in Lakeland as a supplement to his epic work.

However, this guide is not a slavish copy of his format and content; the area covered in this guide is equivalent to most of Wainwright's Books One and Two; here, fells are omitted if there is no view, many views included are from the valley bottom or a lake shore path, and through the book I try to give the reader a sense of the history of how the view has come to be.

As a teenager in Darwen, Lancashire, I remember seeing Eric Robson's TV interviews of Wainwright on the BBC, taking him up Darwen Tower and to the centre of the pitch at Blackburn Rovers Ewood Park, both places of great meaning in my life. Forty years later I found that I used to ride my bike to school past Wainwright's first home on Audley Range in Blackburn; my parents had grown up there too, but were born a few years after Wainwright moved to Kendal in 1941.

I know there are hundreds of guide books to the Lake District, but only Wainwright's that I am aware of that is hand drawn and hand written. Pen and ink provides the reader with consistent clear presentation, whereas photography filled guide books always vary in their depiction, depending

Foreword

on the weather, light and time of day. The drawings of the views have been created from photos taken on my mobile phone, all without the use of zoom, editing or special effects; and all are included because of the feeling of joy, pleasure or huge interest from when I came across them.

So, thank you AW for the inspiration, I hope this iteration of your legacy is up to scratch.

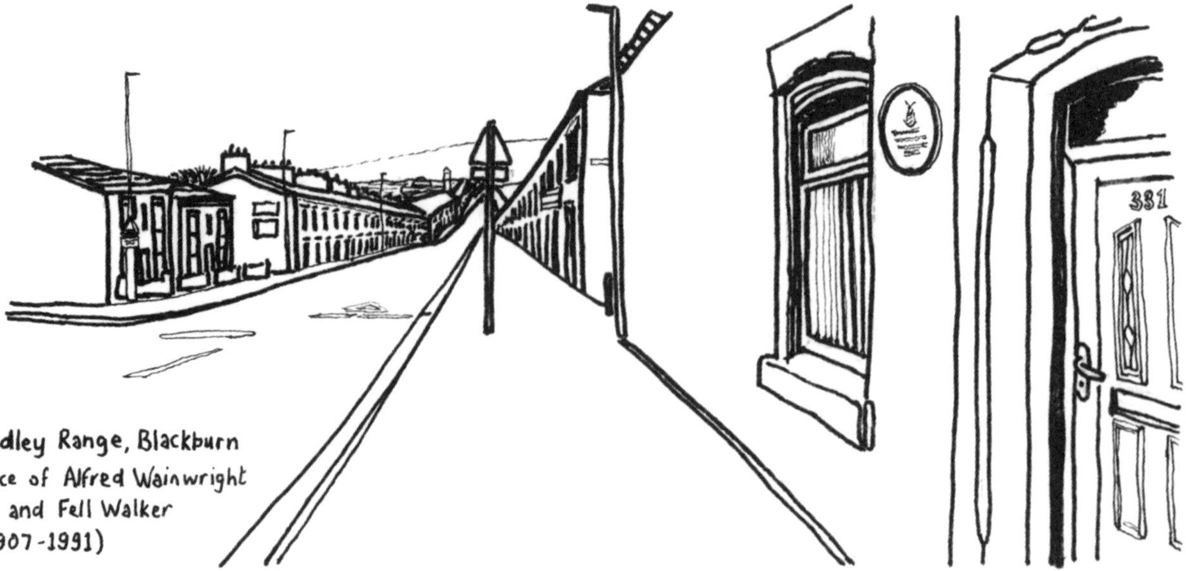

331, Audley Range, Blackburn
Birthplace of Alfred Wainwright
Author and Fell Walker
(1907-1991)

Contents

Introduction

"WOW!" ... so many times this word has tumbled from my lips at a world class view. An unexpected 'WOW' is a great pleasure; coming around a corner, a cliff edge, summitting or simply happening on a scene.

The world class views in this book have been found on lake shores, on roadsides, on footpaths, in woodland, on the fell tops and in intimate scenes where man and the elements have interacted for millennia. The fells are amazing; you give your effort once and they repay you with memories that last a lifetime. Every drawing in this book stirs the mind's eye and takes me back to who I was with and when. This book hopes to achieve two things; the first to be beautiful in its own right; the second, to encourage the reader to explore and savour the world class scenery in this corner of the Lake District.

Introduction

The making of this book has given me permission to amble, bumble and bimble around in a bubble of absorption ... totally consumed, engaged and contented in wondrous surroundings. Music is in the air, history is all around; everything you see is the product of volcanoes, glaciers, invasion, migration, technology, war, man's response to war, and the conservation movement which started right here in the Lake District. All of these things have helped make the most achingly beautiful 800 square miles in the world.

This book will not guide you to the views, but will attempt to carry and caress you through the landscape, helping you truly see what is in front of you and what has gone before. The views in the book are arranged into four areas; there is a map at the start of each area showing roughly where to find the views in that area. The maps are deliberately decorative, and indicative only; when you are out exploring an Ordnance Survey Map or equivalent is essential. So, go forth, explore and find the 'WOWS!'- you will find many more of your own on the way too.

Four books are planned in this series covering the whole of the Lake District (good health and fortune willing); I hope that you can join me on the journey; I know it will be one that gives the greatest pleasure.

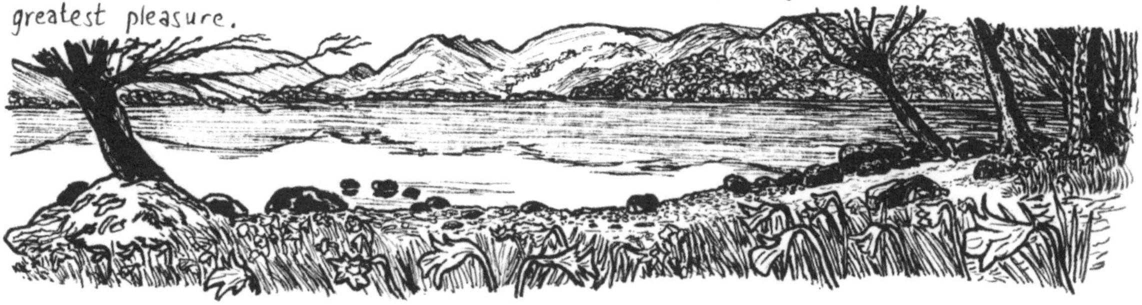

Daffodils on the shore of Ullswater

Introduction

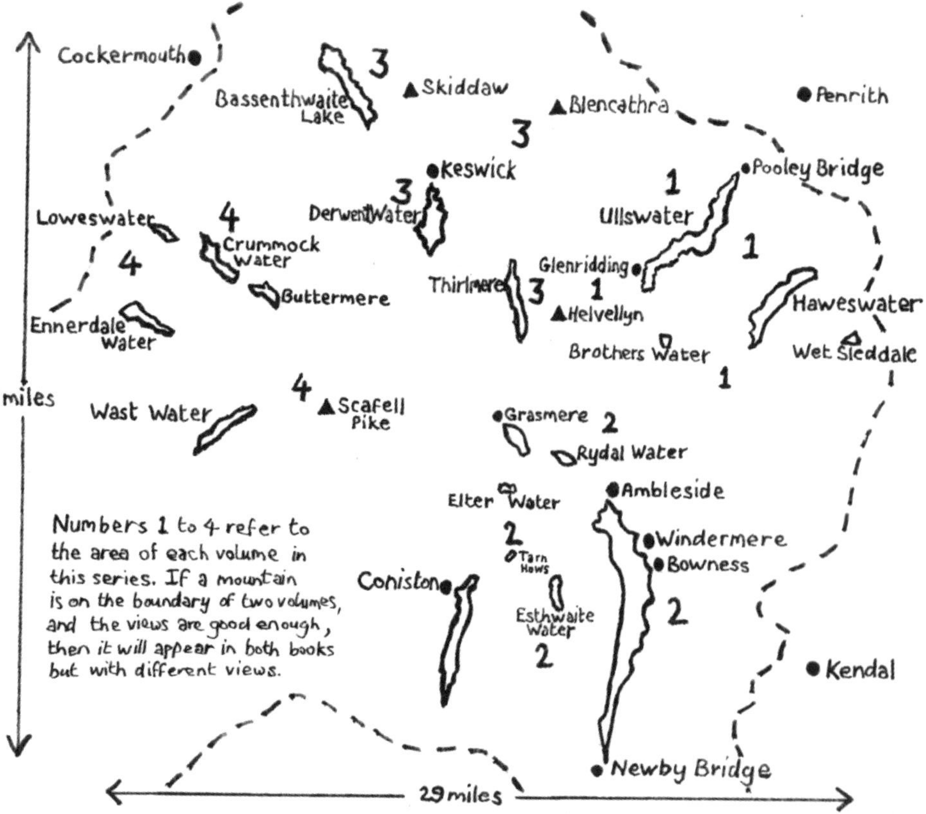

As the crow flies, the Lake District is just 29 miles across both west to east and north to south. It is an incredibly compact, discreet mountainous area with steep sided glacial valleys and finger lakes that radiate from the central massif.

All of this is held within the Lake District National Park boundary established in 1951.

- - - National Park Boundary

Introduction

Three elements contributed to UNESCO (United Nations Educational Scientific and Cultural Organisation) granting World Heritage status to the Lake District in 2017. First, the phenomenal geology; second, a thousand continuous years of farming with its own subculture and characteristics; and third, the Picturesque and Romantic movements that started the idea of landscape having a value and everyone having a right to enjoy it. The movement popularised the concept of scenic beauty uplifting body and soul; that landscape could create an emotional response, which in turn led to the start of the Conservation movement. UNESCO treated the Lake District as one property, creating a new category of 'Cultural Landscape' in order to confer the new status; deeming it of 'outstanding universal value, globally significant,' and of 'extraordinary beauty and harmony'.

William Wordsworth (1770-1850) was a poet, a gardener, a long distance walker, a campaigner, a guide book writer and probably the world's first conservationist. His legacy and influence cast a long shadow which is still felt today; the momentum he created led to the formation of the National Trust in 1895 and, in turn the Lake District National Park in 1951. In his best selling 'Guide to the Lakes' (printed in five editions from 1815 to 1835) Wordsworth helped the reader visualise the tight knit topography of the Lake District; no apology is made for the length of this magical paraphrased quote from him :

II Introduction

" place 'yourself' with me, in imagination, on top of a cloud hanging midway between Scawfell and Great Gavel (Gable) not many yards above their highest elevation; then we shall see at your feet eight valleys diverging like spokes from a wheel... first to the south east... Langdale will conduct the eye to the long lake of Winandermere, stretched nearly to the sea; or rather to the sands of the vast bay of Morcamb, serving here for the rim of this imaginary wheel; we next fix upon the vale of Coniston... running up from the sea to the nave of the wheel... to the west the vale of Duddon, in which there is no lake, but a copious stream... winding and terminating its course in the sands of the Duddon. The next is the Esk ... its stream passes Muncaster Castle and enters the sea below Ravenglass. Due west, the deep valley of Wastdale, with neat dwellings scattered upon a plain of meadow intersected with stone walls. Beyond this the narrow, stern, desolate lake of Wastdale; and level ground to the Irish Sea. Next, Ennerdale... its stream passes Egremont... the ruins of the castle... to the Irish Sea. The vale of Buttermere and Crummock-water next... we follow the Coker through the vale of Lorton, till it is lost in the Derwent below the noble ruins of Cockermouth Castle. Lastly Borrowdale... due north... nearly opposite the vale of Winandermere where 'we' began. 'We' then take a flight east to the ridge of Helvellyn, and look down upon Wytheburn (Thirlmere) and St. John's vale which are a branch of the vale of Keswick. Ullswater, due east and not far beyond the vale of Haweswater; lastly the vale of Grasmere and Ambleside, completing on the east the irregular figure of the wheel. "

Introduction

Wordsworth took us on an imaginary drone or helicopter flight from Scafell to Helvellyn; his love of the Lakes is summed up here:

"I do not know of any tract of country in so narrow a compass, may be found an equal variety in the influences of light and shadow upon the sublime or beautiful features of landscape."

One hundred and fifty years later Alfred Wainwright (1907–1991) used drone like perspectives in his maps in the unsurpassable series of seven 'Pictorial Guides to the Lakeland Fells'. First published 1955–66 they explored every route up the 214 fells which have become known as 'The Wainwrights'. In 1933 he made his first ever trip to the Lakes, having never ventured much beyond smoky industrialised Blackburn before; he arrived at Windermere and headed straight up Orrest Head:

"I saw mountain ranges, one after another, the nearer starkly etched, those beyond fading into the blue distance. Rich woodlands, emerald pastures and the shimmering waters of the lake below added to a pageant of loveliness, a glorious panorama that held me enthralled. I had seen landscapes of rural beauty pictured in the local art gallery, but here was no painted canvass; this was real. This was truth. God was in his heaven that day and I a humble worshipper."

The Lakes

There are 16 bodies of water which make up the Lake District. Bassenthwaite Lake is the only one with 'Lake' in its title, the others having 'mere' or 'water' in theirs.

Windermere

Windermere is the largest and longest natural lake in England at 11¼ miles in length. It is a ribbon lake formed by glaciers, the most recent being 14-17,000 years ago, gouging a trench 219' at its deepest. The Roman fort Galava (A.D.79) just south of Ambleside protected vital routes north to Carlisle and Brougham, west to Papcastle and Ravenglass and east to Kendal. It was known as 'Winandermere', after the Norse hero Winandr up until Wordsworth's time in the early 1800's. In 1847 the railway arrived at the village of Birthwaite; this sparked the development of tourism along the whole east shoreline as it became easily accessible for the massive urban population in the north west. By 1859 Birthwaite's identity had been subsumed by the station's name of Windermere; 'Birthwaite' disappeared from maps and common usage. The launch of the paddle steamer Lady of the Lake in 1845 was an instant hit, taking a cruise on the lake becoming 'the' fashionable Victorian pastime. The service today from Lakeside to Bowness to Ambleside is the most popular visitor attraction in the Lake District. Despite having three major villages on its shores, Windermere remains a stunning and elegant lake.

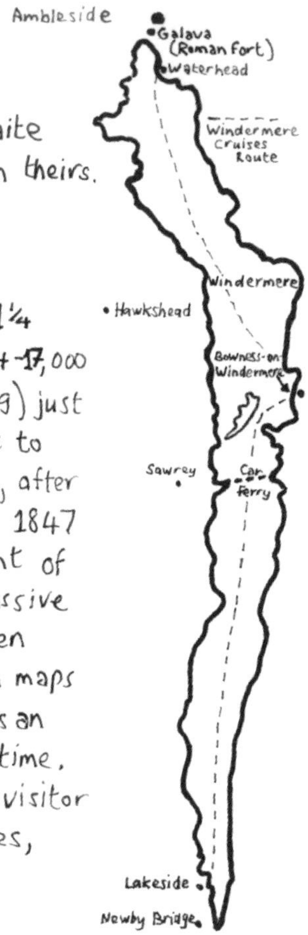

Ullswater

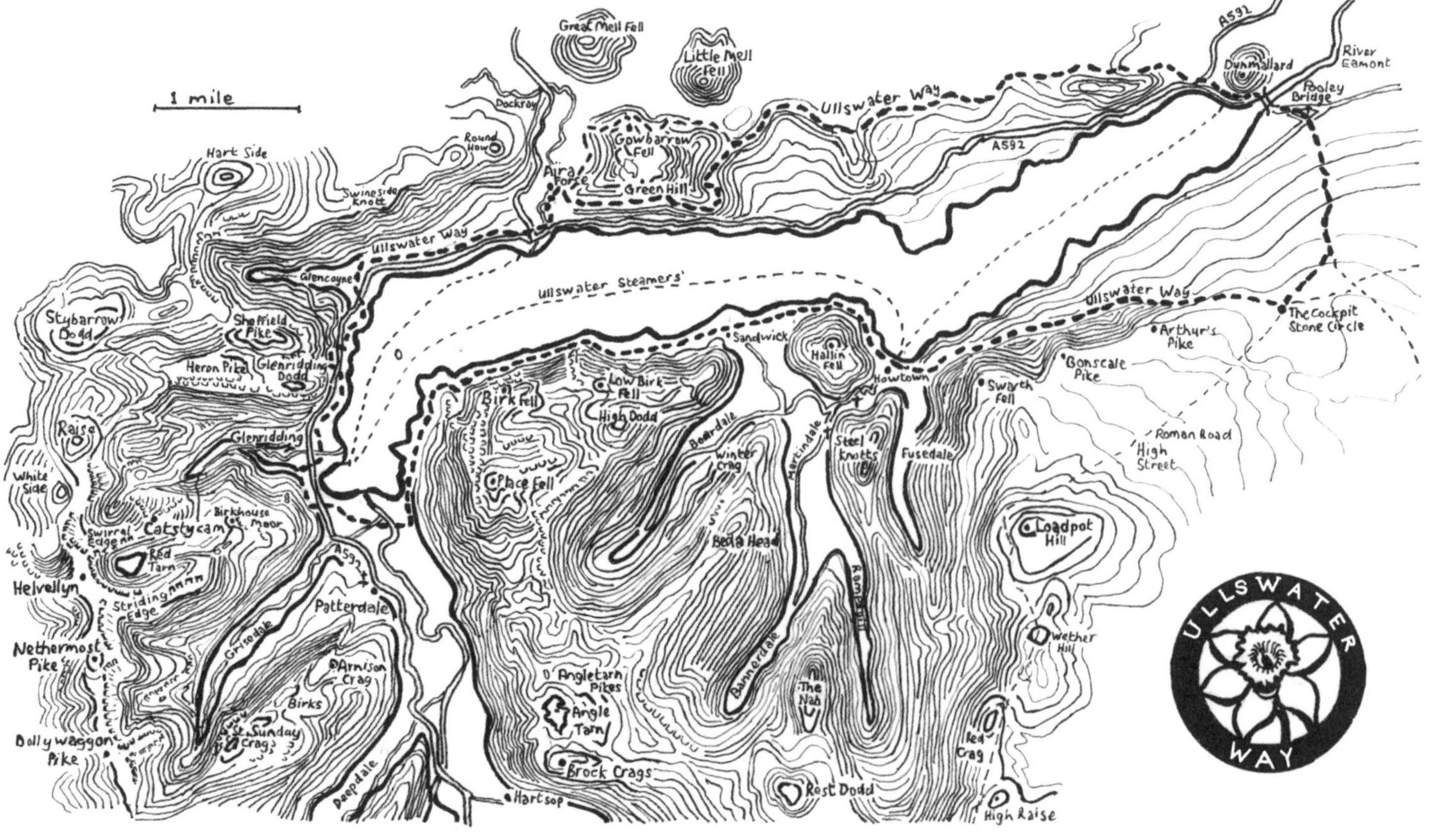
to Penrith
A592
River Eamont
Dunmallard
Pooley Bridge
Great Mell Fell
Little Mell Fell
1 mile
Ullswater Way
Dockray
Round How
Hart Side
Swineside Knott
Aira Force
Gowbarrow Fell
Green Hill
A592
Ullswater Way
Glencoyne
Ullswater Steamers'
Ullswater Way
The Cockpit Stone Circle
Stybarrow Dodd
Sheffield Pike
Heron Pike
Glenridding Dodd
Sandwick
Hallin Fell
Arthur's Pike
Bonscale Pike
Howtown
Low Birk Fell
Birk Fell
High Dodd
Swarth Fell
Raise
Glenridding
Boardale
Winter Crag
Martindale
Steel Knotts
Fusedale
Roman Road
High Street
White Side
Place Fell
Birkhouse Moor
Catstycam
Swirral Edge
Red Tarn
Beda Head
Loadpot Hill
Helvellyn
Striding Edge
A592
Patterdale
Rampsgill
Nethermost Pike
Grisedale
Arnison Crag
Wether Hill
Angletarn Pikes
Bannerdale
The Nab
Birks
Angle Tarn
Red Crag
Dollywaggon Pike
St. Sunday Crags
Brock Crags
Deepdale
Hartsop
Rest Dodd
High Raise
ULLSWATER WAY

Ullswater

Ullswater is the second longest and third deepest, but without doubt the most magnificent of the Lakes. Its three segments or 'reaches' form an elongated 'z' shape, the legacy of three separate glaciers carving out some of the most spectacular scenery on earth. In his final book of the pictorial guides Wainwright declared Ullswater "the most beautiful of the Lakes."

It is host to the best 'around the lake' walk in the district; the 21 miles long Ullswater Way, opened in 2016 and is punctuated with art installations celebrating the valley's artistic and cultural heritage. Wainwright again, "the lakeside path from Scalehow Beck, near Sandwick, to Patterdale (in that direction) is the most beautiful and rewarding walk in Lakeland". Since 1859, Ullswater Steamers' has transported people, post and lead ore up and down the lake; they now have four stops making it easy to do the Ullswater Way in sections.

The lake is absolutely surrounded with scenic vantage points, the fells ascending in height as they build toward the Helvellyn massif. The lake remains largely undeveloped, the natural barriers of Kirkstone Pass to the south, and the virtually impassable Stybarrow Crag on the west side meant that it was shielded from the first wave of Victorian tourism. Ullswater Steamers' were founded partly to transport lead ore from Greenside Mine above Glenridding down to Pooley Bridge; ironically the pollutants from the mine contributed to saving Ullswater from being dammed and turned into a reservoir. The railways stayed at arms length too, the nearest stations being four or five miles away at Yanwath and Penrith. A lakeshore road on the west side to Glenridding only opened in the 1890's after Stybarrow Crag was dynamited out of the way. By that time the conservation movement was organised, full of momentum and able to protect the splendour of Ullswater.

Haweswater

The remote valley head hamlet of Mardale was a handful of farms, a church and an Inn which served as a resting point on the pack horse route south to Windermere and Kendal via the Nan Bield Pass; connection with Shap to the east was made via the Old Corpse Road. After World War One Britain was battered and bruised, and Manchesters' demand for water was more than Thirlmere could supply.

Haweswater originally was two and a half miles long, a lake often separated into two bodies by a tongue of land at Measand; these were known as High Water and Low Water. There was public outcry at the flooding proposal, but no effective campaign from the conservation movement, So the Haweswater Act 1919 was passed, allowing the water level to be raised by 96 feet and the creation of a 4½ mile reservoir. Manchester received its first supplies via a 73 mile aqueduct in 1942. We are left with a valley with steeply raked banking and ugly tide marks around the perimeter. Despite this the horseshoe of wilderness from the Old Corpse Road around the southern shore to Kidsty Pike offers supreme tranquility, top walking, and tremendous tarn-dotted views.

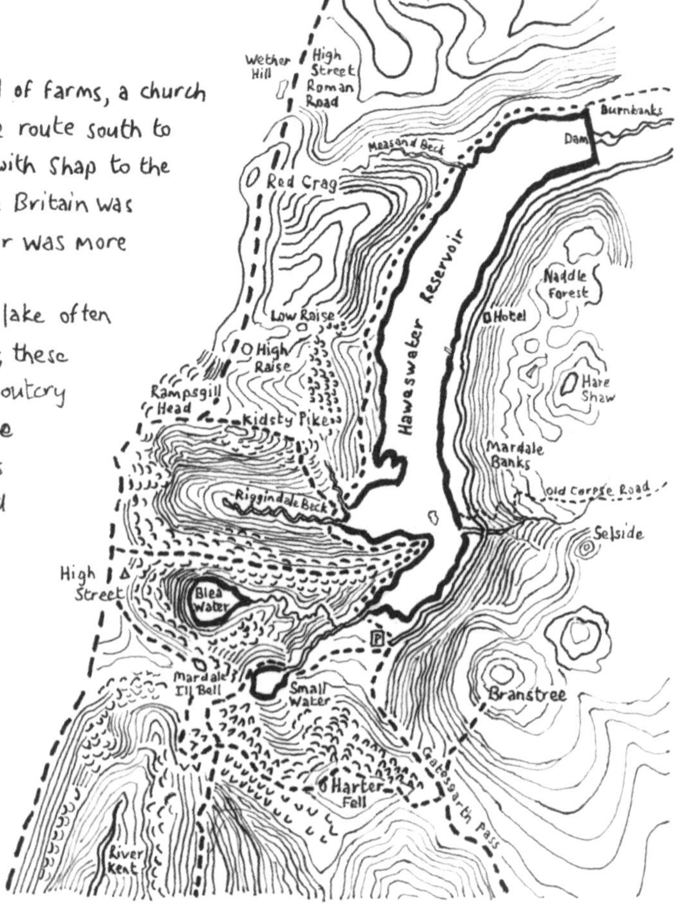

Coniston

Coniston runs parallel to Windermere's west for 5¼ miles. Its shores are virtually unspoilt, with Coniston village set well back in the majestic foothills of The Old Man of Coniston. Man has lived here since at least 2000 BC, Bronze Age agricultural life flourished.

The Romans began mining copper here, this continued for two thousand years; iron was smelted on the shores of the lake in Medieval times also. From 1123 to 1537 the lake and its surrounds were owned by Furness Abbey near Barrow; the monks used the fish from the lake for the Abbey.

From 1870 John Ruskin, artist, critic and philosopher made his home at Brantwood, whose beautiful gardens look across the water to the Old Man. Arthur Ransome's Swallows and Amazons series of novels is based on the setting of Coniston and Windermere, with Peel Island the inspiration for Wild Cat Island in the novels. Donald Campbell brought worldwide attention to the lake in the 1960's breaking seven world water speed records here until the water claimed him in 1967. In Records Week, usually early November, the 10 mph limit is lifted temporarily for new water speed record attempts. Since 1980 its sparkling waters have been crossed by the restored 1859 Venetian style steam gondola. It remains a tranquil haven.

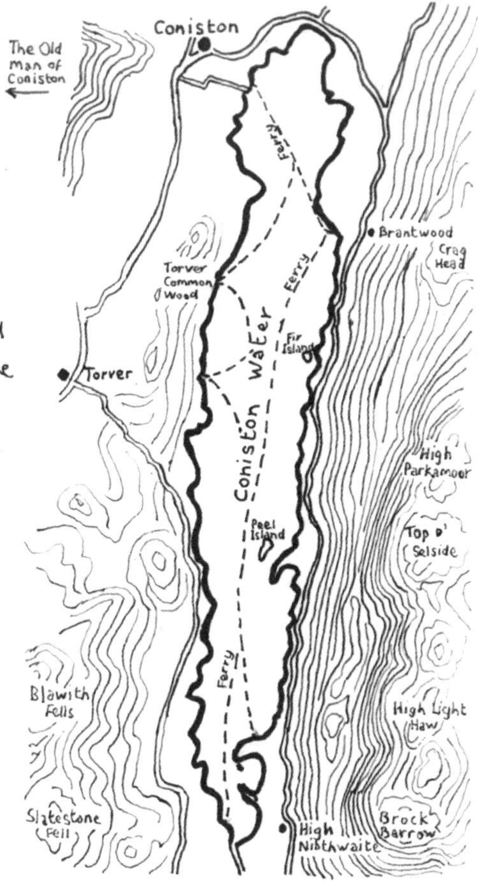

Bassenthwaite Lake

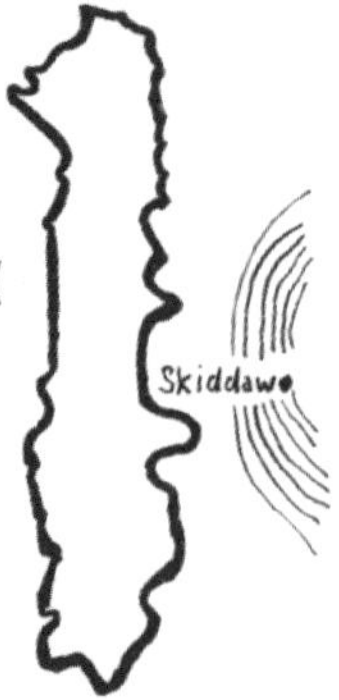

Bassenthwaite Lake is four miles long and shallow throughout. Stone Age man rightly valued the fertile soil which surrounds it and extends back to Derwent Water. The Skiddaw range forms a splendid backdrop to the east shore. Alas the west side is ruined as an amenity by the A66 dual carriageway thundering along its whole flank. After a century of absence Osprey were reintroduced into Dodd Wood in 2001; spotting them is now a very popular pastime.

Thirlmere

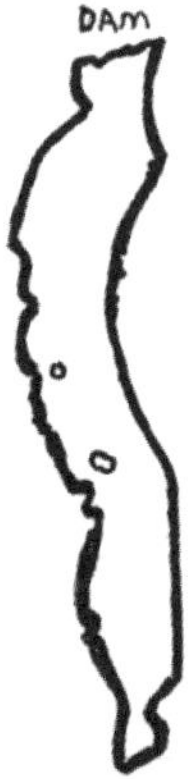

Originally Thirlmere was Leathes Water and Wythburn Water surrounded by farms. In the 1850's it was proven for the first time that clean water was essential for public health. The 'U' shaped valleys of igneous rock in the Lake District not only produced soft potable water not requiring any treatment, but also were relatively easy to dam. Manchester was the powerhouse of the industrial revolution and its needs prevailed over a haphazard conservation movement, enabling the 1879 Manchester Corporation Water Works Act to pass. It opened in 1894 as the Lake Districts first reservoir; gravity alone was enough to take the water on its 96 mile journey to the centre of Manchester. The valley it occupied has been forever blighted by inappropriate crenellated architecture; concreted becks; a permanently stained perimeter rim, and dense mono planting of conifers. The impact of the building of Thirlmere acted as a catalyst for those trying to preserve and protect the Lakes against the all pervasive spread of industrialisation.

Wast Water

Wast Water has WOW! factor. Wasdale Head includes the spectacular mountains Great Gable, Lingmell and Scafell; then the lake itself is flanked by 1800' high screes to the south and the upturned boat shape mountain of Yewbarrow to the North. This was voted 'Britain's Favourite View' in a 2007 national TV program. The lake is 3miles long; the screes pull the land under water for another 258', making it the deepest lake in England; its bottom is actually 50' below sea level. This is truly unspoilt magnificence; it is the Lake District at its finest. It is no accident that the Lake District National Park Authority use this view as their logo.

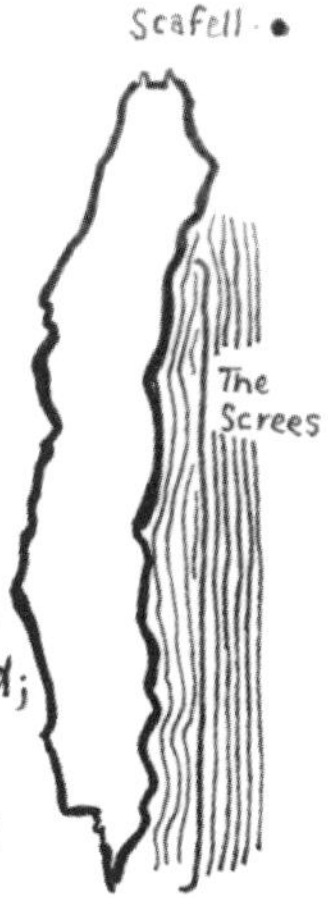

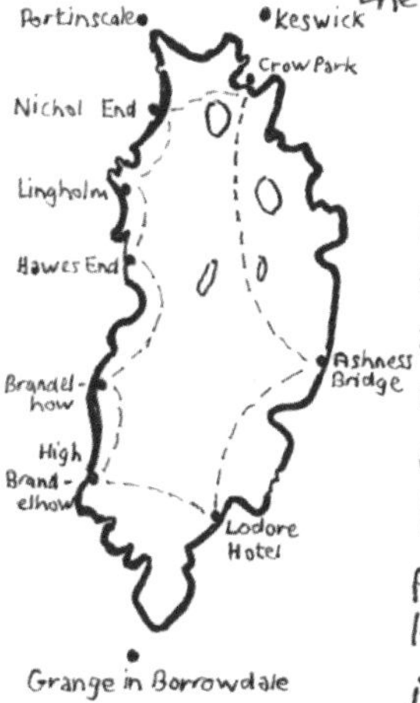

Derwent Water

Derwent Water is the prettiest of the lakes; its broad expanse looked down upon by the celebrities of Skiddaw, Castle Rigg, Castle Crag and Catbells; a truly star studded amphitheatre of stunning fells. Its heavily wooded shores are largely undisturbed, and at its head, in Wainwright's view, the gladed paths and pristine waters around Castle Crag make up the most beautiful square mile in the Lake District. The lake shore art installations, classic views, hollowed trees, boardwalk and perfect picnic places all make for a joyous circumnavigation of the lake. This can be leapfrogged at any moment by jumping on the Keswick Launch at any of its 8 jetties. Charming Keswick is set back from the shore under Latrigg Fell.

Crummock Water

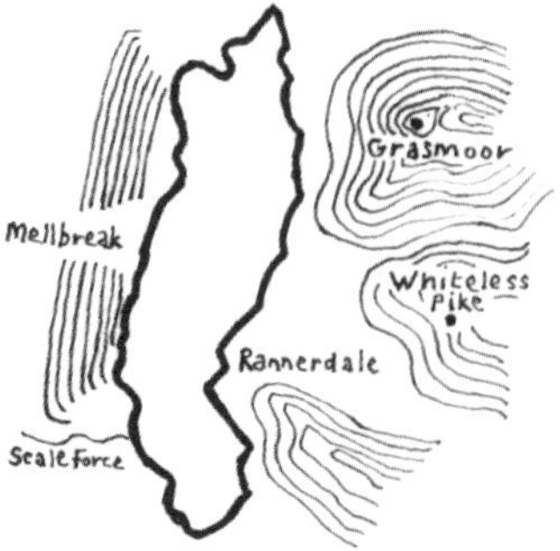

Crummock Water is unspoilt and untroubled by development; along with its neighbour Buttermere it stars in one of the most jaw dropping iconic views in Lakeland, from Haystacks the eye is drawn along the valley floor with a vertiginous corridor of fells diminishing west into infinity. It is 2½ miles long, the origin of the river Cocker and has the majesty of Mellbreak running along its whole western flank. The name originates from the Celtic word for crooked, 'Crumbaco'. It is host to the highest waterfall in the Lakes, Scale Force, and to the most spectacular annual bluebell display at Rannerdale.

Ennerdale Water

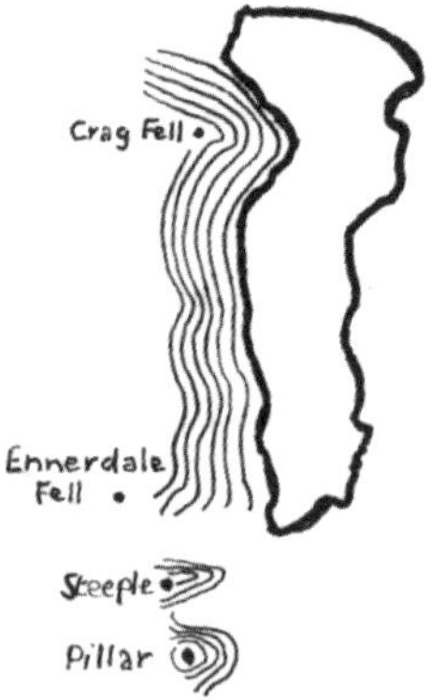

Ennerdale Water is the most westerly and the most peaceful of the lakes, being the only one without a road on its shore. Since 1902 it has fed the west of Cumbria with fresh water, and from the 1930's the valley has been blighted with impenetrable plantations. The formation of Wild Ennerdale (consisting of United Utilities, Forestry England, Natural England and the National Trust) in 2003 kickstarted the rewilding of the valley; plantation fences have been removed, native broad leaf trees are taking hold, sheep numbers have been reduced and from 2022 Ennerdale Water will stop being used as a reservoir. This initiative will rejuvenate the ecology and biodiversity of the valley and river Ehen, safeguarding it for generations, the routes to Steeple and Pillar permanently protected.

Esthwaite Water

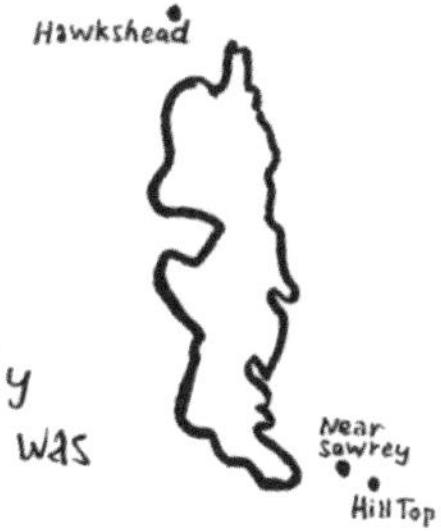

Esthwaite Water is a peaceful haven in a gentle setting between Windermere and Coniston. It made a huge impression on the young Wordsworth who played there endlessly in his time off from Hawkshead school; likewise on Beatrix Potter whose imagination was set free on its serene shores. Esthwaite Water features in both of their works.

Buttermere

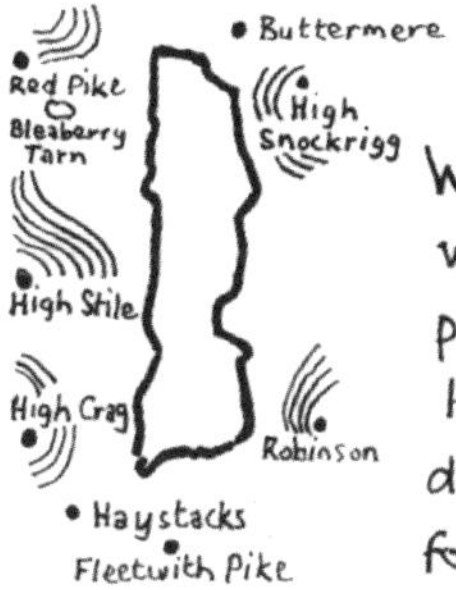

Whichever way you approach Buttermere, by foot, bicycle or car; along the valley floor, winding down Honister Pass or over the crest of a fell.... it is simply spectacular. Its picturesque shores are surrounded by a stadium of fells including Wainwright's favourite, Haystacks, where his ashes are scattered. In the 1890's plans and housing plots were drawn up to populate the shoreline with grand villas; the threat of this accelerated the formation of the National Trust, who thankfully saved this precious landscape for the benefit of us all.

Loweswater

One of the most beautiful ways to enter the Lake District is from Cockermouth, rolling along Lorton Vale until Loweswater causes you to pause. It makes for a delightful short walk especially as its paths are accessible to many as part of the 'Miles without Stiles' initiative; the beautiful cascade of Holme Force is ample reward for the walker.

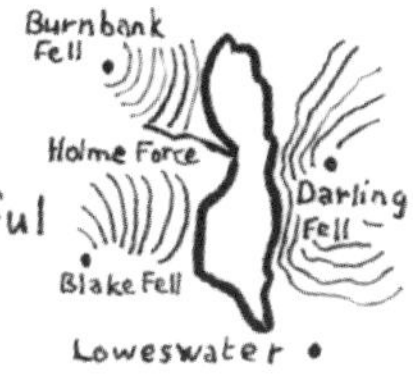

Grasmere

Wordsworth immortalised Grasmere as "the loveliest spot man hath ever found". It is the cultural and geographic epicentre of the Lake District; the home of Wordsworth and the fulcrum from which all the lakes radiate.

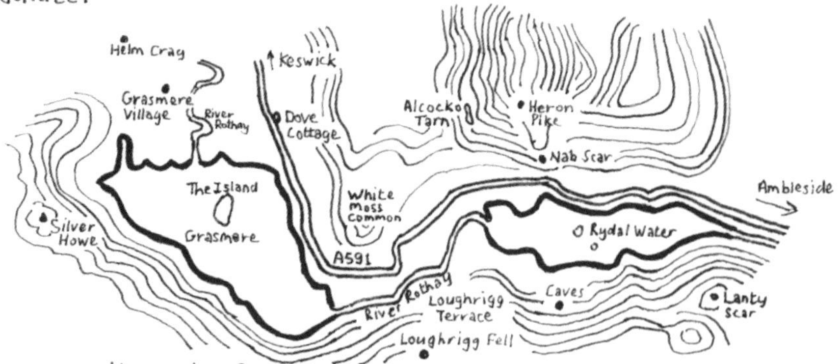

The river Rothay runs through Grasmere and Rydal Water onto Windermere; the valley floor is cradled by the Helvellyn massif to the East and caressed by the gentler fells of Helm Crag, Silver Howe and Loughrigg fell around the other points of the compass. The village and Dove Cottage are now perennial worldwide attractions; the village hosting a constant stream of events, the annual highlight since 1868 being Grasmere Sports. Grasmere water is at arms length from the village and retains its peaceful essence, the path along Loughrigg terrace to Rydal Water being a gem. The other shores of these waters are blighted by the constant traffic of the Keswick to kendal artery, the A591. The 1893 private sale of Grasmere Island frustrated Cannon Rawnsley as there was no way to buy iconic landmarks on behalf of the nation in order to safeguard them. Two years later he co-founded the National Trust.

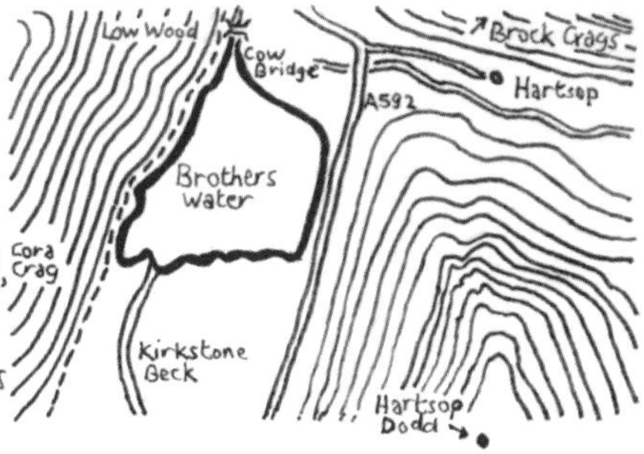

Brotherswater

Brothers Water benefits from being closely surrounded by five steeply raked fells; with the noses of the proper mountain shapes of Hartsop Dodd, Middle Dodd, and High Hartsop Dodd protruding into the valley floor. The wooded water side path is accessible for many as it is a 'Miles without Stiles' standard; it then reverts to a regular path as the delights of Dovedale are revealed. Originally it was known as Broad Water, but changed after the drowning of two brothers in 1785.

Brothers Water, Elter Water and Tarn Hows are left out of many lists of the Lakes in the District. They are included here because simply they are beautiful and popular.

Elter Water

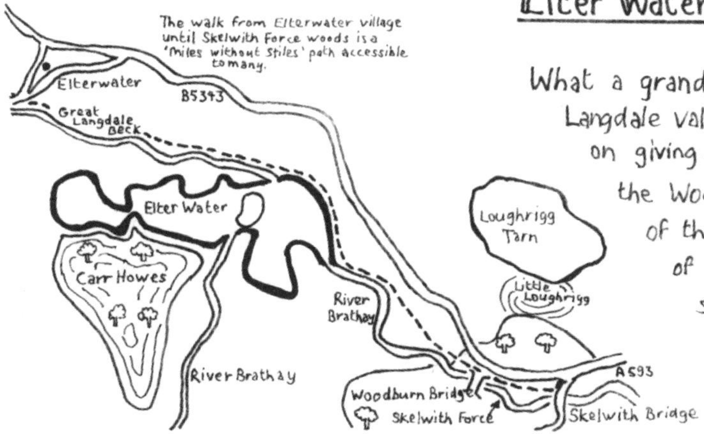

What a grand entrance Elter Water and its village make for the Great Langdale valley. The walk from Skelwith Bridge to the village just keeps on giving... the thunder of Skelwith Force, the charming design of the Woodburn Bridge, the skyline etched with the crenellations of the Langdale Pikes, and the fluctuating fairy land shore line of Elter Water. To top it off is the most idyllic village setting in the Lake District; an intimate triangular village green dominated by a horse chestnut tree encircled by a public bench, populated by a traditional fingerpost sign and lampost, all overlooked by a Cumbrian longhouse pub.

Tarn Hows

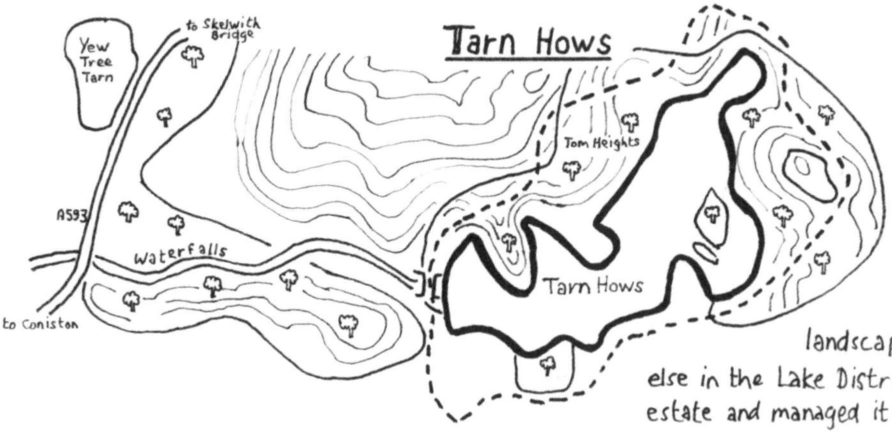

Originally Tarn Hows was three separate tarns; High, Middle and Low. In 1862 James Marshall (M.P. for Leeds) purchased the estate and dammed Low Tarn, creating the Tarn Hows we see today. In addition he planted Larch, Spruce and Pines creating a very pretty landscape more like a Highlands scene than anything else in the Lake District. In 1930 Beatrix Potter purchased the estate and managed it until she passed, bequeathing it all to the National Trust. Set in rolling countryside with the Langdales and Scafell massif decorating the horizon, Tarn Hows hits the bullseye for mass appeal; its 'Miles without Stiles' path can be walked around easily by all ages and abilities in an hour or two.

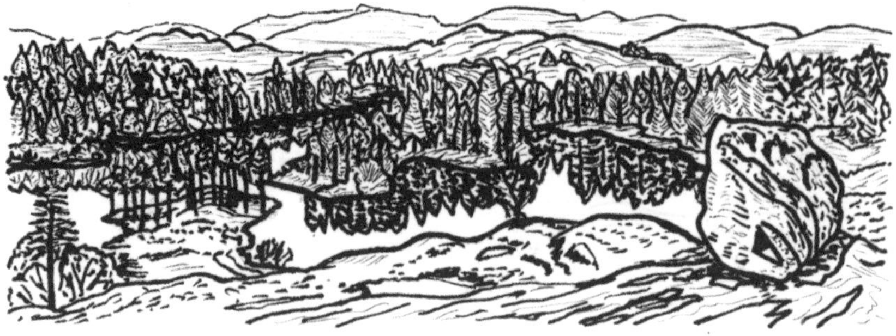

Rocks

"To look at the scenery without trying to understand the rock is like listening to poetry in an unknown language. You hear the beauty but miss the meaning", (Norman Nicholson Cumbrian Poet and writer 1914-87).

Jonathon Otley (1766-1856) a clockmaker and self taught Geologist published the first geological map of the Lake District in 1820; which this simple map here is based upon.

Skiddaw Slates 570 million years old

Borrowdale Volcanic Series 450 million years old

Silurian Sediments or Windermere Supergroup 400 million years old

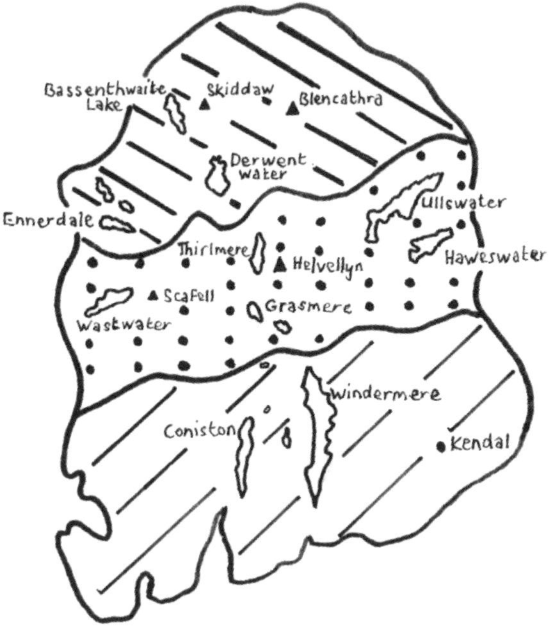

The Skiddaw Slate band is at least 2½ miles deep, its base has never been found; it is characterised by the smooth domes of Skiddaw, Ullock Pike and Great Calva.

The super volcano which erupted around 450 million years ago in the Rosthwaite/Langdale vicinity created the Borrowdale Volcanics, these are incredibly resilient and impermeable rocks. Their angular, hard edges create the drama of Lakeland scenery; this is the bedrock of the Scafells, Great Gable, the Langdales and Helvellyn.

The Silurian Sediments or Windermere Supergroup swathe across the south of the district is a much softer rock than the Borrowdale Volcanics, with a typical land form of rolling hills and gentle slopes, immortalised by the countryside Postman Pat worked his rounds in. John Cunliffe (1933-2020), Postman Pat's creator was inspired by the charm of Longsleddale, north of Kendal where he lived for many years.

Rocks

500 million years ago the Lake District was situated on a fault line deep in the southern hemisphere of the earth. Continents move around the globe at a rate of approximately two inches every year, so a movement of 3000 miles over 100 million years is normal.

300 million years ago Cumbria was a swampy steamy sea, which eventually evaporated into limestone, coal and haematite deposits.

250 million years ago the area was a desert, whose legacy can be seen in the sandstone deposits around Penrith, St. Bees and the Furness Peninsula.

15 million years ago the earth's crust domed up; like a tablecloth being pushed together it formed ridges and wrinkles, Scafell and Great Gable were at the centre of this.

2 million years ago saw the first of four ice ages which have ground and chiselled out the contours of the valleys and mountains. Corries or cirques which are known in Cumbria as 'Coves' which are bowl shaped hollows, and aretes which are sharp ridges such as Striding Edge were formed by the glaciers gnawing right down to the bone of the rock.

10 thousand years ago the glaciers retreated, the district warmed up and vegetation crept in, eventually covering the whole area in dense woodland. The valleys were filled right up to 2000' high with Birch, Hazel, Oak, Lime, Alder, Elm and Pine trees.

Mankind

Eighteen thousand years ago Britain was connected to mainland Europe from the Thames to the Humber by Doggerland; a low lying land bridge where most people lived. Ten thousand years later the North Sea had overwhelmed Doggerland, and Britain was an island. The warming weather led to a slow migration north. Cumbria, cut off by the sea on three sides, and guarded by the Pennines to the east was one of the last places for man to make habitable. On the upper slopes of Pike'o'Stickle, in the Langdale valley, it was found that the rock there could be fashioned fine as flint into axe heads capable of cutting down trees for the first time. This was the stone age; the area became a major axe and arrowhead factory, the porcellanite rock being roughly hewn into shape in the Langdales, then sent to the coastal settlements of Drigg, St. Bees and Walney to be smoothed and sharpened on the local sandstone. Langdale axes have been found all over Britain and Europe, the finest example being on display at the British Museum in London. This was the very beginning of agriculture in Lakeland, clearings and crops, and the concept of 'my land not your land' and defending your ground.

This axe, estimated to be 5-6,000 years old, was found at Ehenside Tarn near Sellafield.

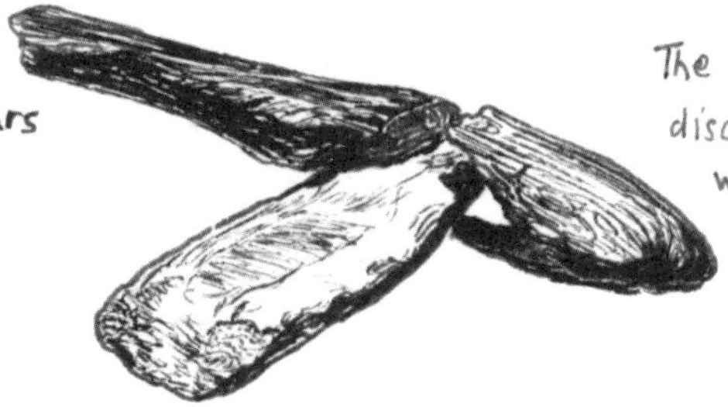

The axe factory was only discovered in 1947 and was of industrial proportions.

Mankind

The New Stone Age (Neolithic) 4,000 - 2,500 BC

Langdale axes were highly prized, one theory is that the wealth generated from trading the axes enabled Cumbrian New Stone Age Man to join in with the building of henges and stone circles. Over 1300 of these were built in Britain around 3,000 BC; it is still unknown what these monuments were for; but it is no coincidence that Castle Rigg Stone Circle near Keswick, Long Meg Stone Circle on the river Eden and Mayburgh Henge at Eamont Bridge all have entrances which align with the rising or setting equinoxal sun.

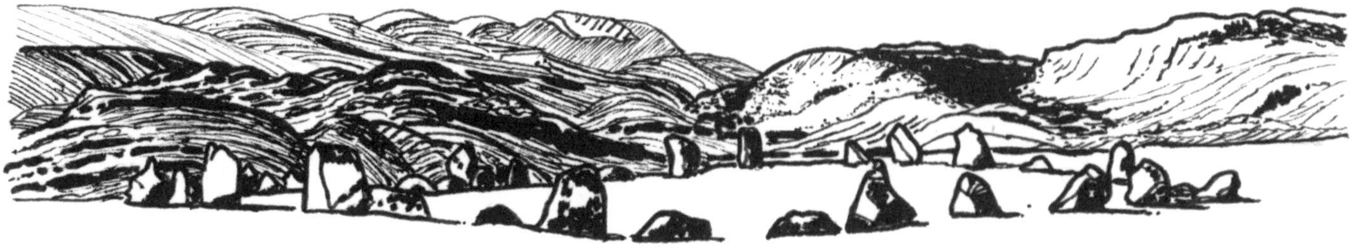

Castlerigg Stone Circle and its forty stones; looking south to St. John's Vale.

Mankind

The Bronze Age 2500BC to 800BC

Bronze (85-95% copper and 5-15% tin) was developed in the Middle East and China around 5,000 BC; it took over 2,000 years to spread to Britain. Gradually the use of bronze tools, utensils and weapons led to better farming with extensive clearances and cereal production on the flatlands around the perimeter of the Lake District. Langdale stone axe production stopped around 1500 BC, Stone Circles and Henges remained in use as bronze cups and artefacts have been found at over sixty sites around the county. The period 1250 BC to 850BC saw the population disperse with a deterioration in the climate; people returned from 800 BC along with the warmer weather.

The Iron Age 800BC to 50BC

Iron overtook bronze with its superior strength and versatility, but because it rusts we are left with little evidence of the age. Britain was divided into tribes; the Celtic Carvetti and Setantii occupying north and south Cumbria; they were later absorbed into the Brigantes who dominated the whole of the north of England. The Iron Age saw stone-based round houses, field systems with dykes and ditches, and the training and riding of horses for the first time. Defendable hill forts were built around the district at Maryport, Silloth, Carrock Fell, Castle Crag, Maiden Hill amongst others. The greatest relic from this period is the two feet long Embleton Sword and Scabbard found in 1854; it is dated by the British Museum at around 50BC. The sword is iron and the scabbard copper alloy decorated with red and yellow enamel.

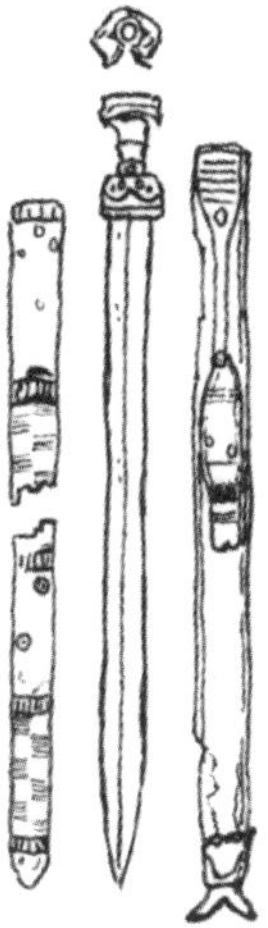

Section 1: Aira Force to Bleaberry Knott

1. Aira Force - Park Brow ♿ 689′
2. Aira Force 540′
3. Aira Force - Aira Beck 590′
4. Green Hill - East of Summit 984′
5. Brackenrigg Inn ♿ 574′
6. Duke of Portland Boathouse ♿ 478′
7. Roadside - Dunmallard ♿ 490′
8. Dunmallard Circular Path 557′
9. Pooley Bridge Pier ♿ 525′
10. Pooley Bridge - Tirril Entrance ♿ 531′
11. Eusmere ♿ 525′
12. Wainwright's Sitting Stone - Ullswater Way 885′
13. Arthur's Pike 1747′
14. Bonscale Pike 1607′
15. Swarth Fell 1639′
16. Loadpot Hill - North West of Summit 2000′
17. The Hause - Howtown 715′
18. Hallin Fell - The Hause ♿ 698′
19. Hallin Fell - South of Summit 1115′
20. Hallin Fell 1271′
21. Hallin Fell - above Swine Slacks 1148′
22. Bridge End - Hallin Fell 457′
23. Bridge End Path - Hallin Fell 590′
24. Hallin Fell - Hause Farm Footpath 721′
25. Beda Fell - Winter Crag 1664′
26. Scalehow Force Path 918′
27. Low Birk Fell 1213′
28. High Dodd - West of Summit 1610′
29. Bleaberry Knott - West of Summit 1508′

This first section of views starts at Park Brow, Aira Force going clockwise around the lake until Bleaberry Knott. The path from Pooley Bridge to Gale Bay is a 'Miles without Stiles' access for many route. A wheelchair logo means the viewing point can be reached by wheelchair and pram users. The heights are in feet only and are approximate; the titles are where the view is from, not its subject. The map opposite shows the location of each wonderful view.

Section 1: Aira Force to Bleaberry Knott

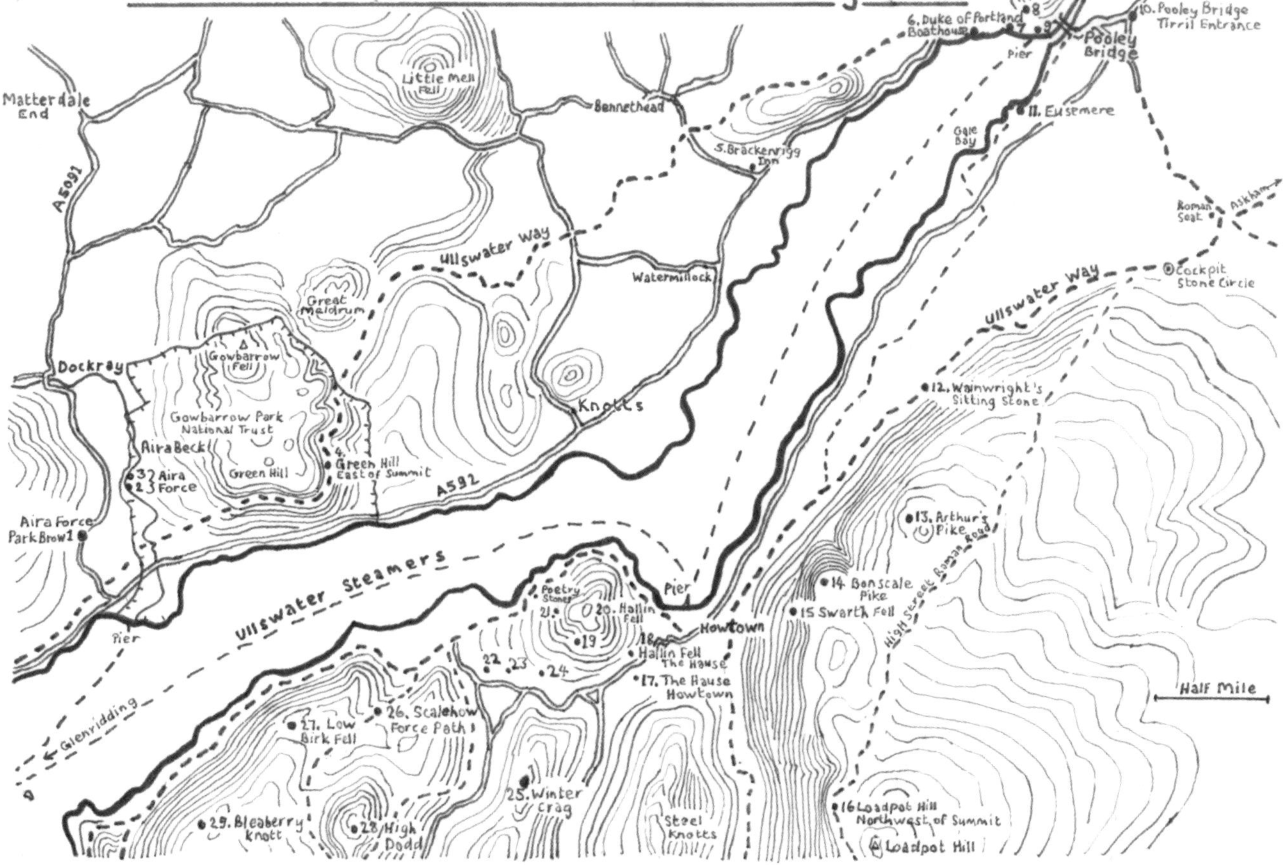

Aira Force - Park Brow

♿ 689′

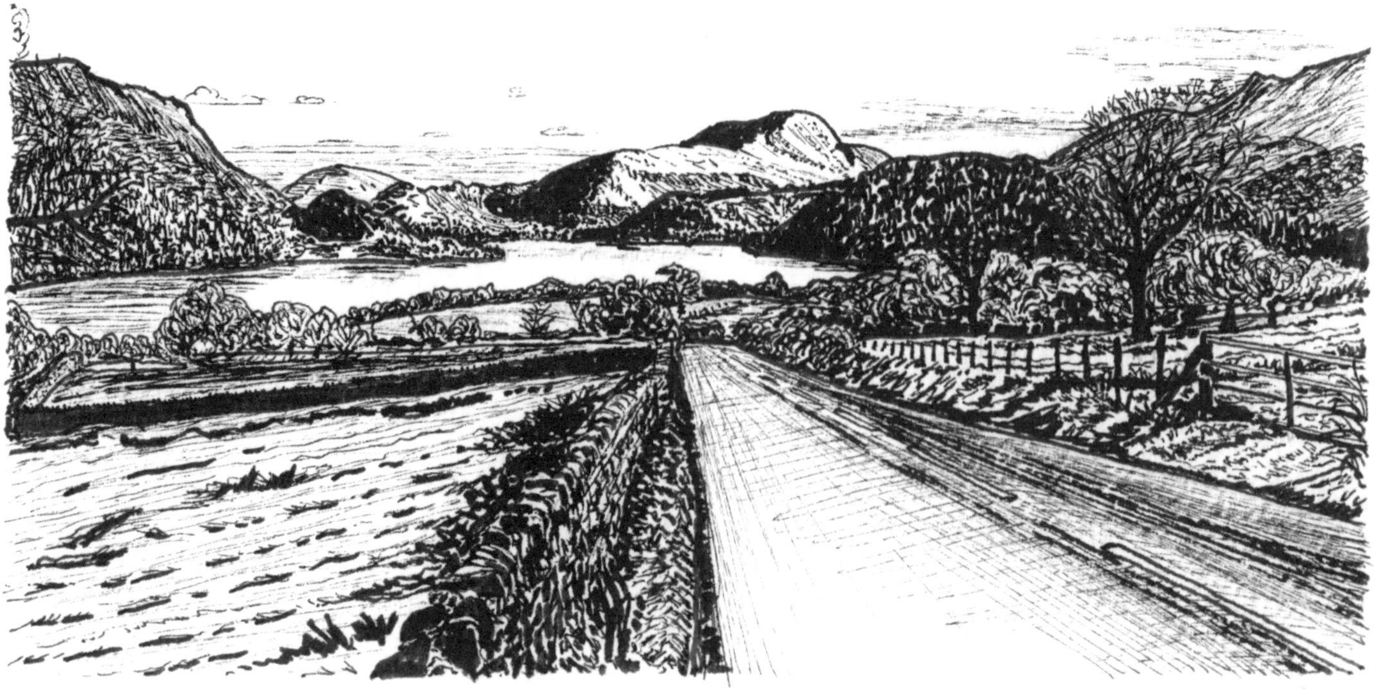

Aira Force

Wordsworth recommended the best way to approach Ullswater "is to go through Matterdale and descend upon Gowbarrow Park; you are at once upon a magnificent view of the two higher reaches of the Lake. Ara-Force thunders down the Ghyll on the left... a powerful brook which dashes through a deep glen, hung on every side with native wood, luxuriant fern, aged hawthorns and hollies decked with honeysuckles".

From medieval times Gowbarrow Park was walled in to create a hunting forest with a bailiff employed to control predators. He was paid 10 groats for a fox, 3 for a pine marten and 2 for a wildcat.
In the 1780's Lyulph's Tower was extended and crenellated – the tower was named after a Saxon owner of the lake, Ulfus, and is one derivation of the name Ullswater.
In 1846 the area was landscaped and an arboretum of over 200 trees were planted.

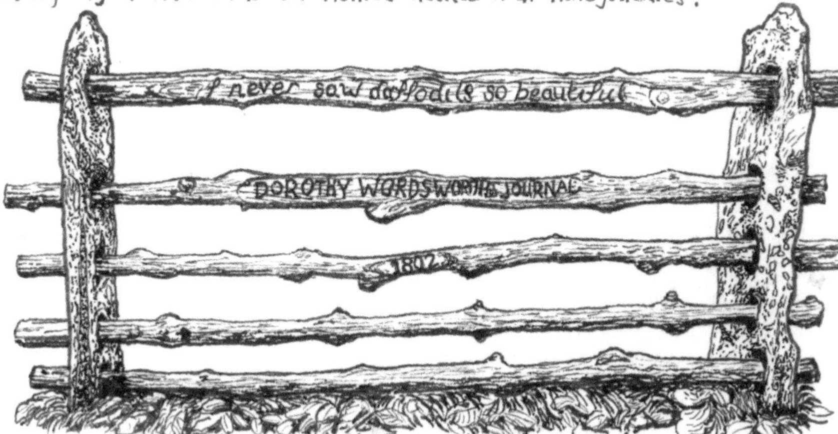

The Dorothy Gate at Aira Force on the Ullswater Way

In 1906 Gowbarrow Park's 750 acres came up for sale; the National Trust furiously fundraised £12,000 to secure it on behalf of the nation.
In the 1930's they built the upper bridge overlooking the falls, and have maintained the site ever since.
In 2015 Aira Force pier opened making the three mile shoreline walk on the Ullswater Way to Glenridding a delightful circular journey when tied in with the Steamers'.

'I wandered lonely as a cloud
That floats on high o'er vales and hills,
When all at once I saw a crowd,
A host of golden daffodils;
Beside the lake, beneath the trees,
Fluttering and dancing in the breeze.

On 15th April 1802 Dorothy and William walked from Pooley Bridge to Gowbarrow Park... Dorothy wrote about their encounter with the daffodils in her journal, "they grew among the mossy stones ... some rested their heads upon these stones as on a pillow for weariness and the rest tossed and reeled and danced". In 1807 William turned these recollections into his world famous poem.

'For oft when on my couch I lie
In vacant or in pensive mood,
They flash upon that inward eye
Which is the bliss of solitude;
And then my heart with pleasure fills,
And dances with the daffodils'.

Aira Force 540'

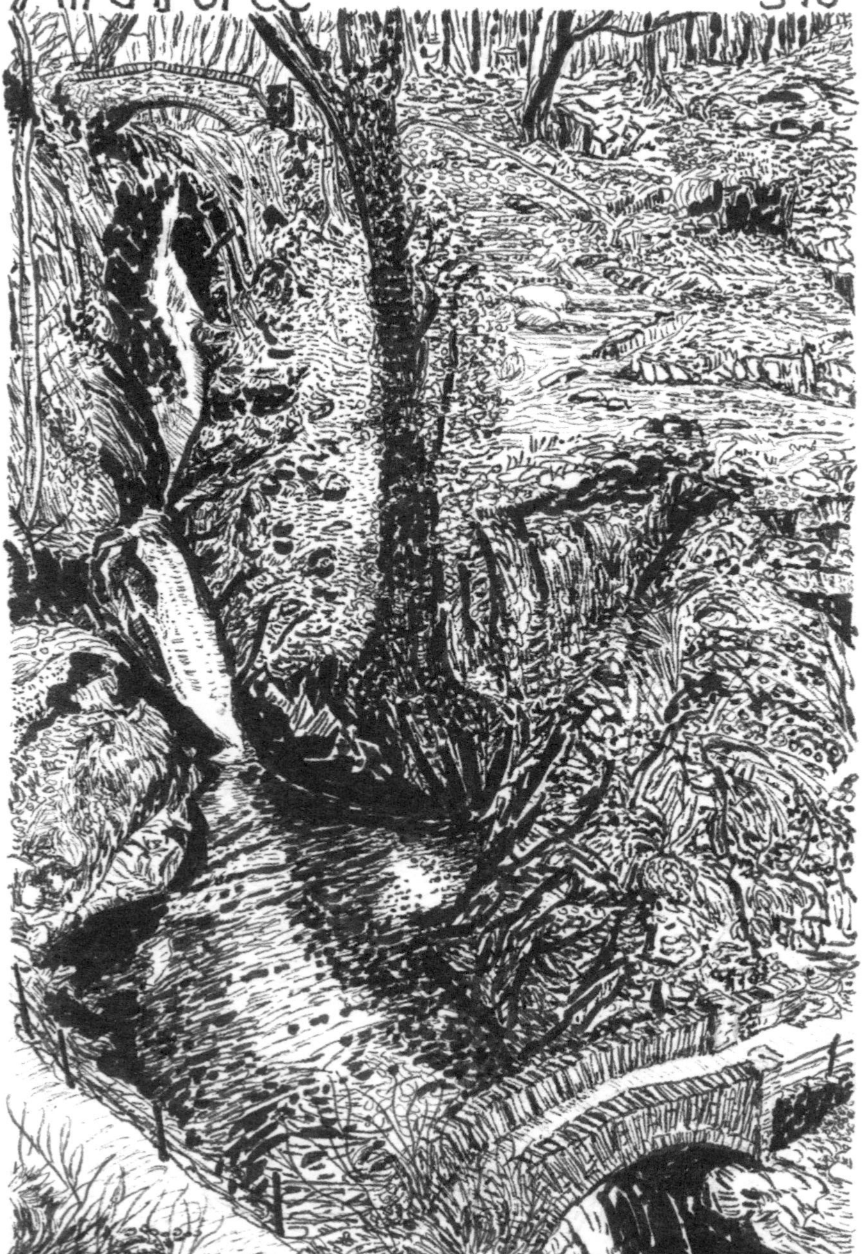

Aira Force - Aira Beck 590′

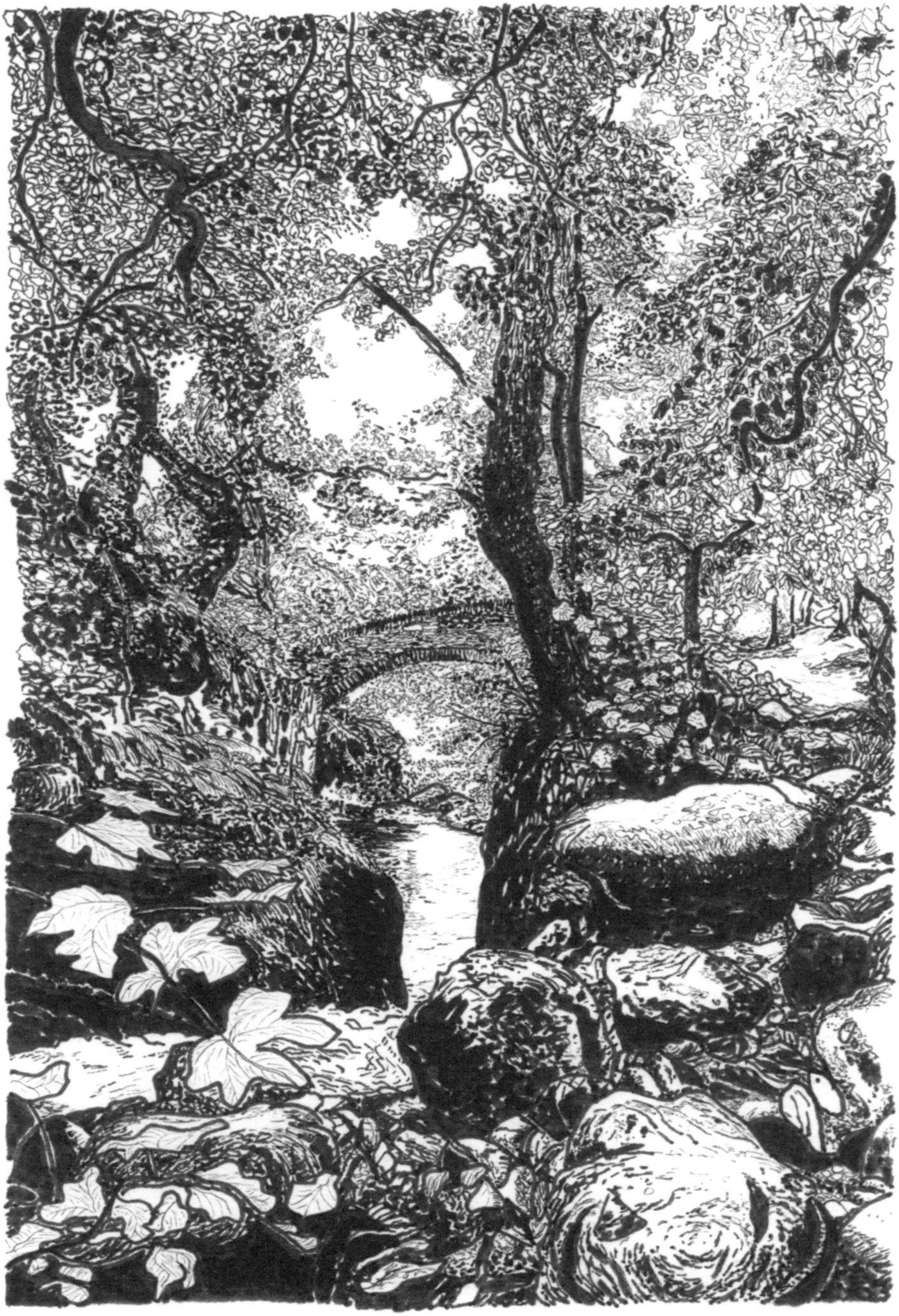

Green Hill - East of Summit

984´

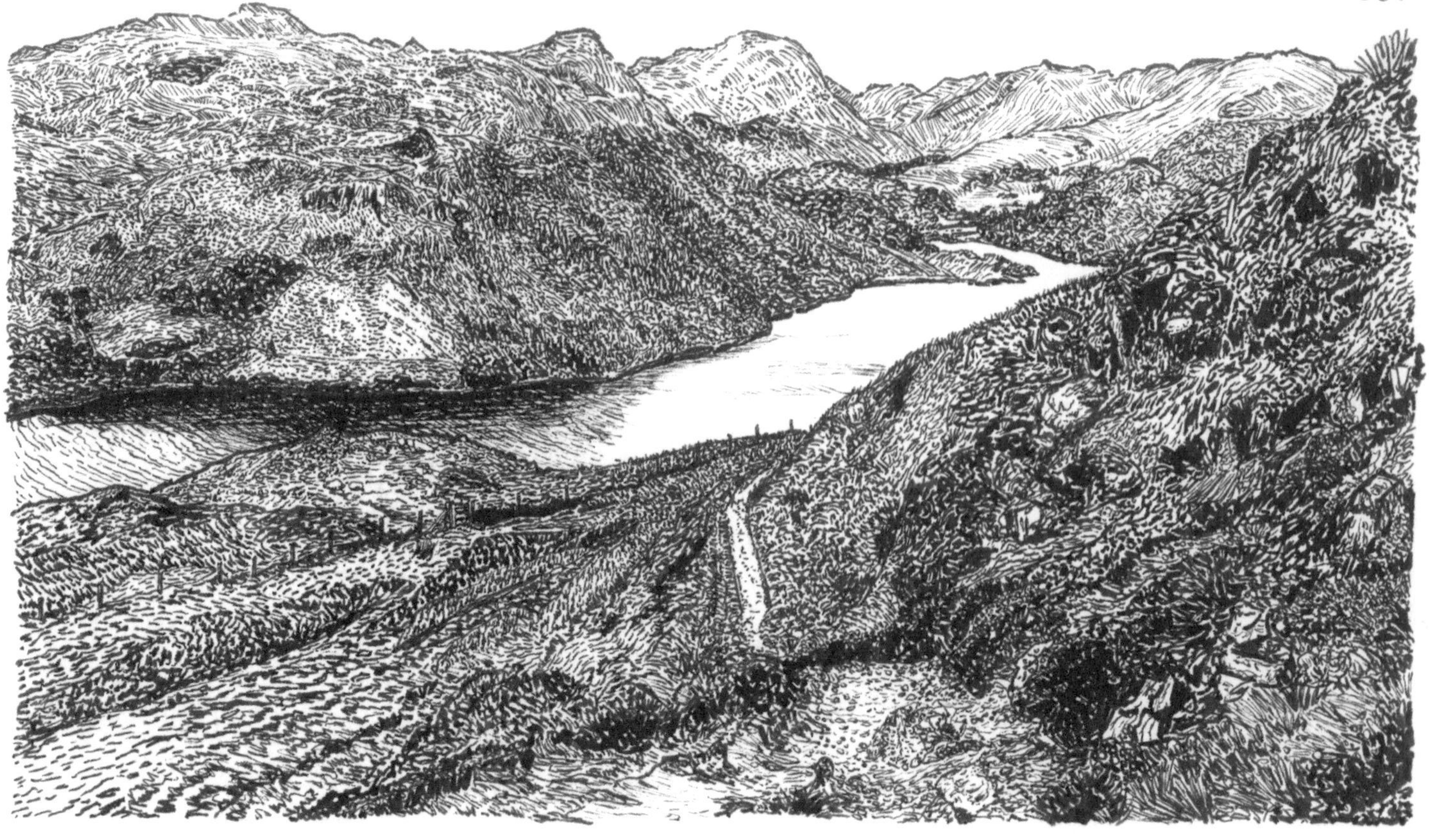

Brackenrigg Inn

♿ 574′

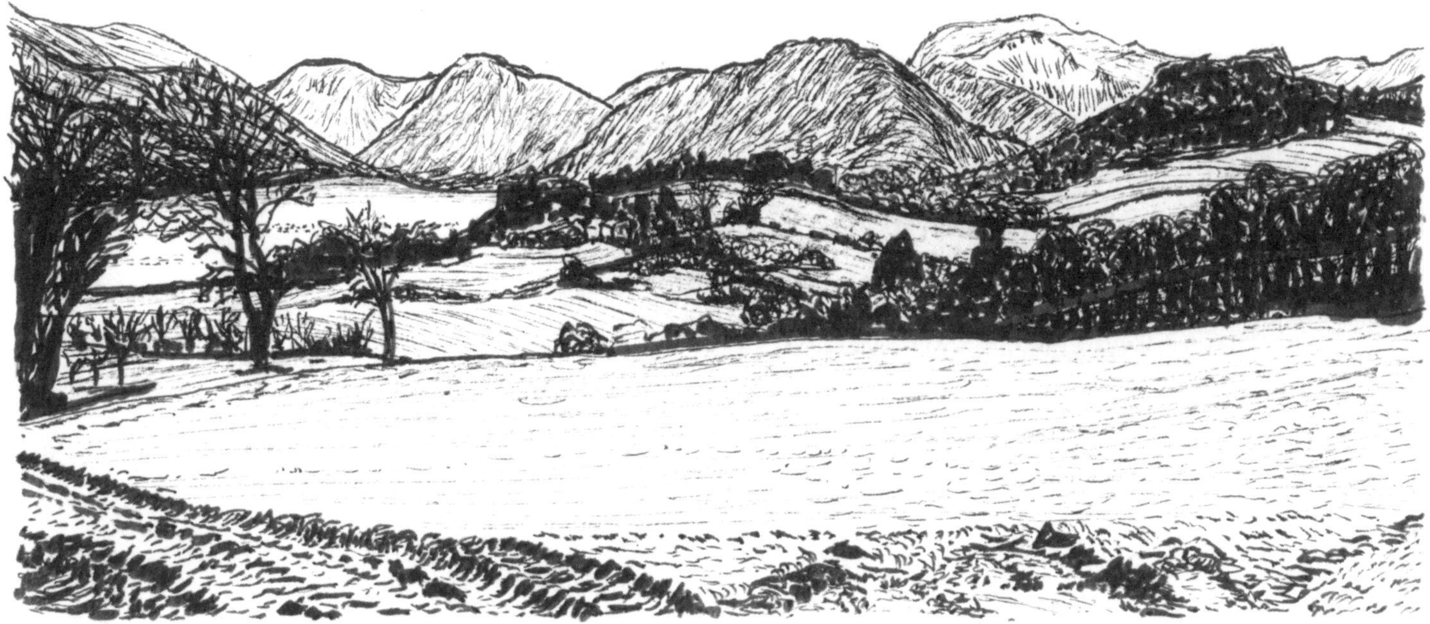

Duke of Portland Boathouse

♿ 478′

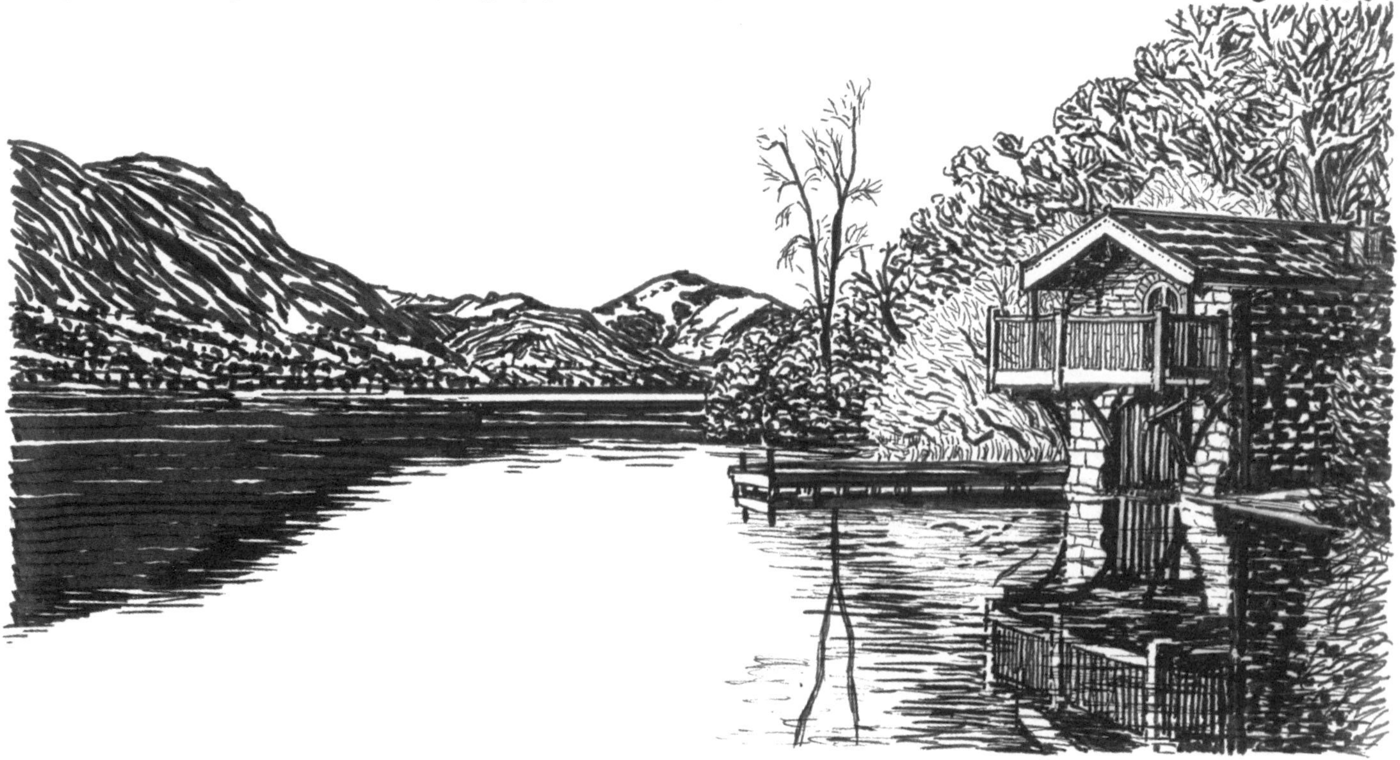

Roadside - Dunmallard

♿ 490′

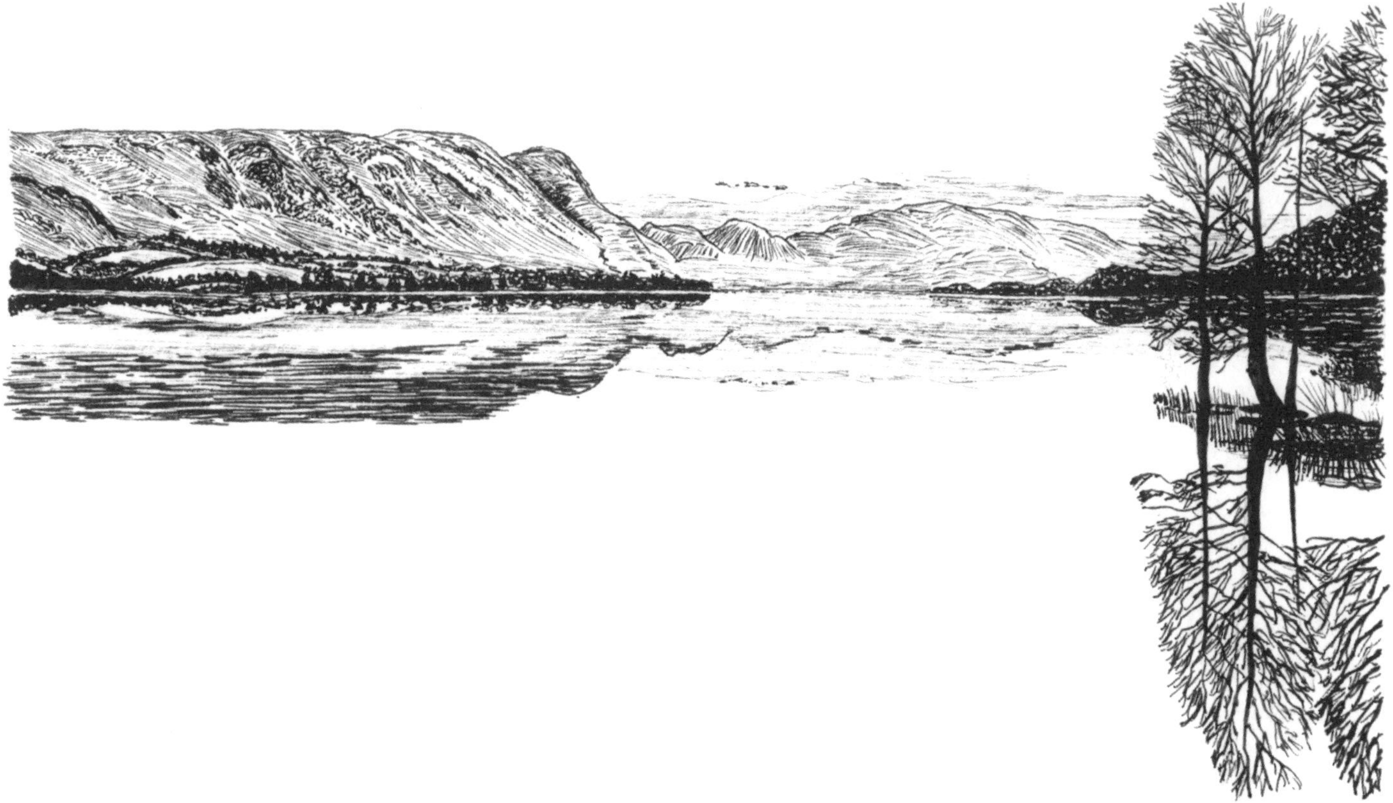

Dunmallard Circular Path

557′

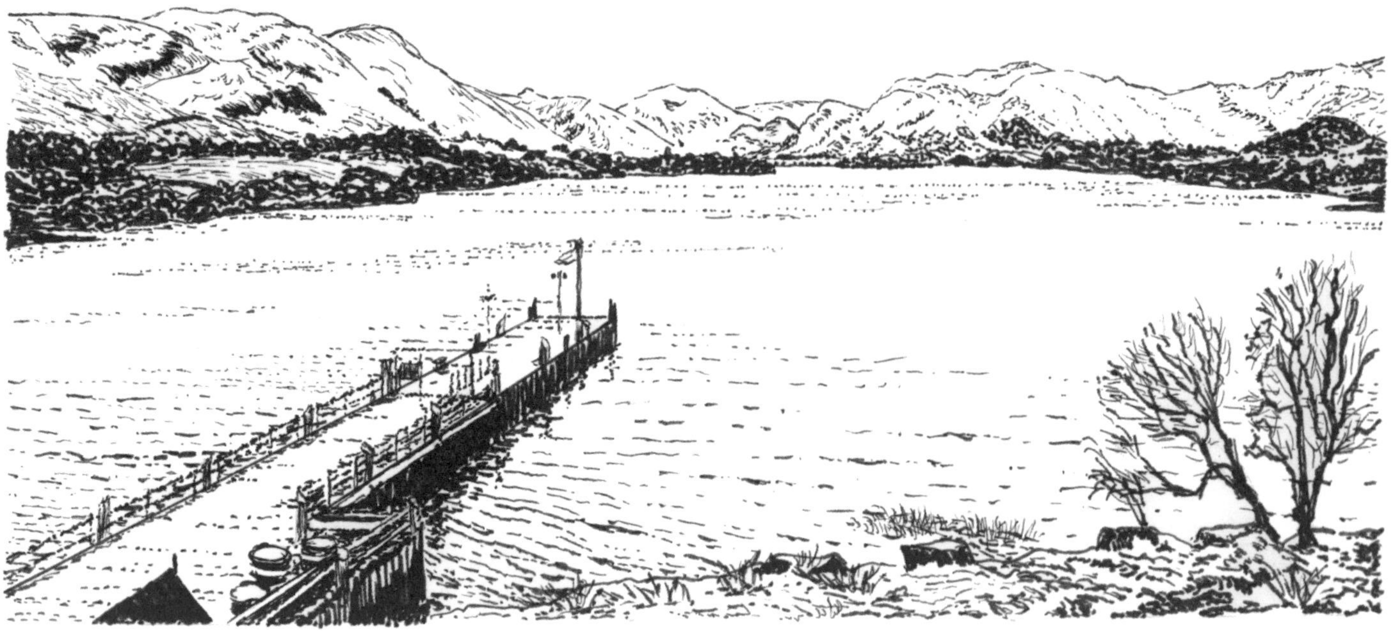

Pooley Bridge Pier

♿ 525′

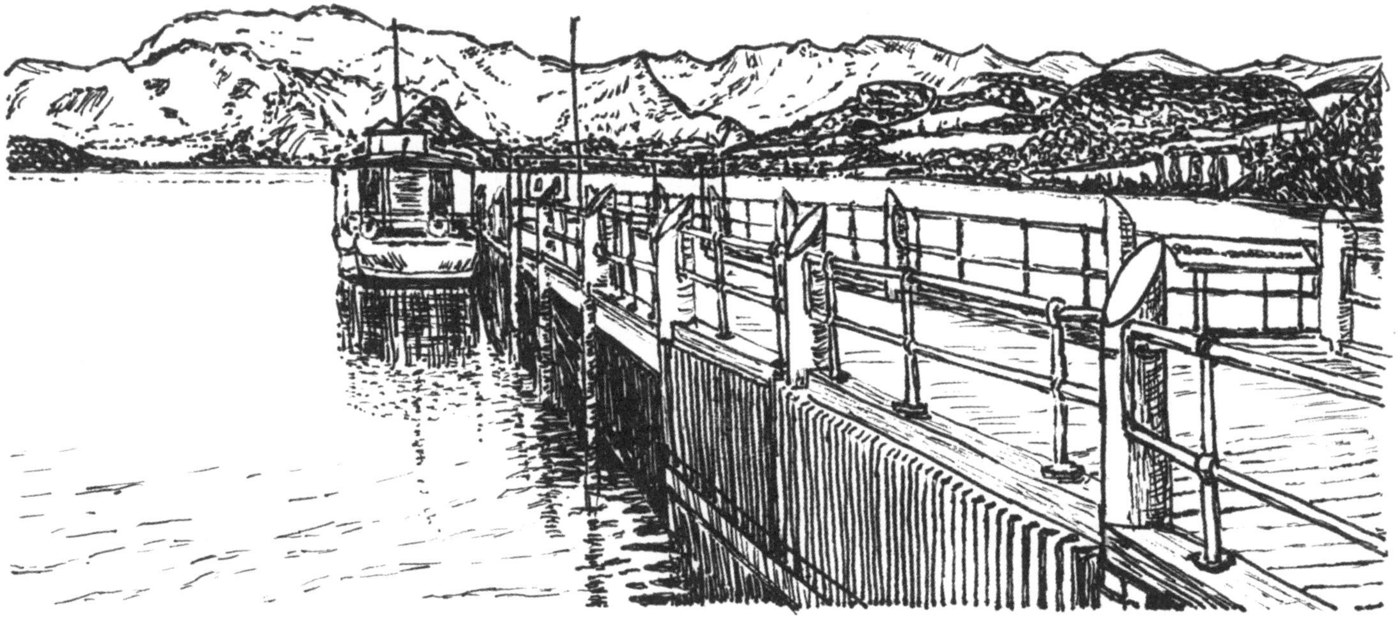

Pooley Bridge

Ullswater is blessed with the thriving settlements of Pooley Bridge at the foot and Glenridding and Patterdale near the head of the lake. The visitor to any of these villages can access the whole valley and its surrounds by foot, bicycle, or Steamer with no need for a car. Pooley Bridge is overlooked by Dunmallard hill which is crowned by the remains of an Iron Age fort from one thousand years before the Romans. The Romans mined for lead around the lake and built clay-banked canals to transport the ore to the river Eamont for smelting. The Eamont was the boundary between the counties of Cumberland and Westmorland; its name derives from the Norman (French) Eau-Mont - water by the hill.

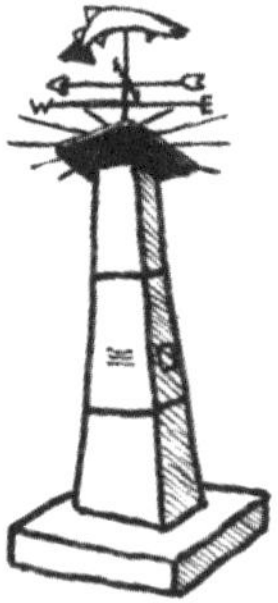

In 1214 King John granted a market Charter to Pooley; a fish trap and stepping stones across the river were used to catch trout, salmon, char and vendace for the weekly market held in front of the Crown Inn. A wooden two arched bridge was built in the 1600's which was then upgraded in 1764 to a three arched stone version (this was destroyed in the floods of 2015). By Wordsworth's time fishermen were using nets across the lake; here is his diary from 9th November 1805:

"In the large bay under Place Fell, three fishermen were dragging a net ... a picturesque group beneath the high and bare crags! ... The Fishermen drew their net ashore, and hundreds of fish were leaping in their prison. They were all skellies ... a sort of fresh water herring, shoals of which may be seen dimpling or rippling the surface of the lake in calm weather. This species is not found in any of the other lakes ... here are no pike, and the char are smaller than those of other lakes ... but the grey trout attains a very large size, sometimes weighing above 20lbs."

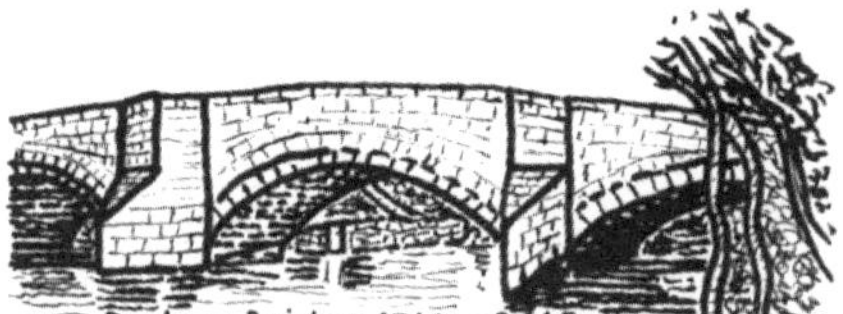

Pooley Bridge 1764 - 2015

The pollution from Greenside lead mine slowly destroyed the fish stocks; by 1860 the cross in the market square was removed. The present fish monument was installed in 2000.

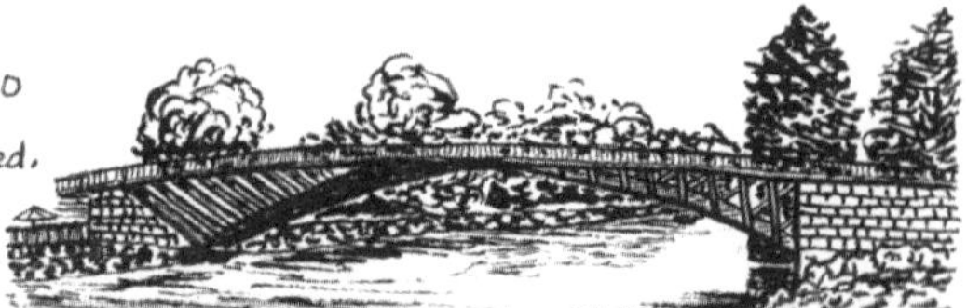

Pooley Bridge 2020

Pooley Bridge

In 1961 Manchester announced plans to turn Ullswater into a reservoir raising the lake by 3 feet; this would destroy delicate shorelines and create an ugly, permanently stained perimeter rim. The Ullswater Preservation Society was re-formed and gathered a 500,000-strong petition against the plan; despite this the Bill sailed through the House of Commons. Norman Lord Birkett's impassioned defence of Ullswater in the House of Lords defeated the Bill and the lake was saved. It was his last act; two days later he died.

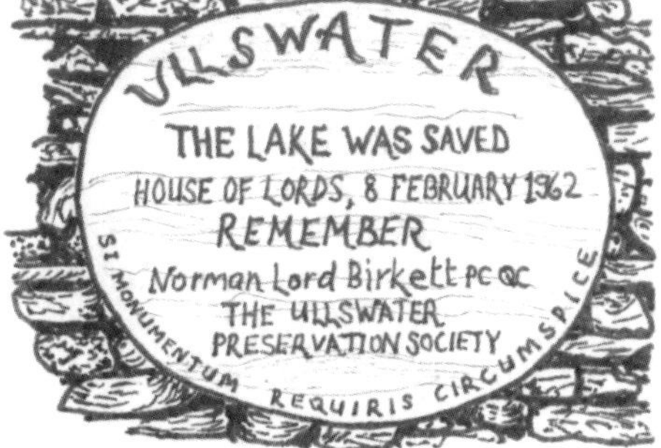

The Birkett Memorial installed in 2017 beside Pooley Bridge Pier

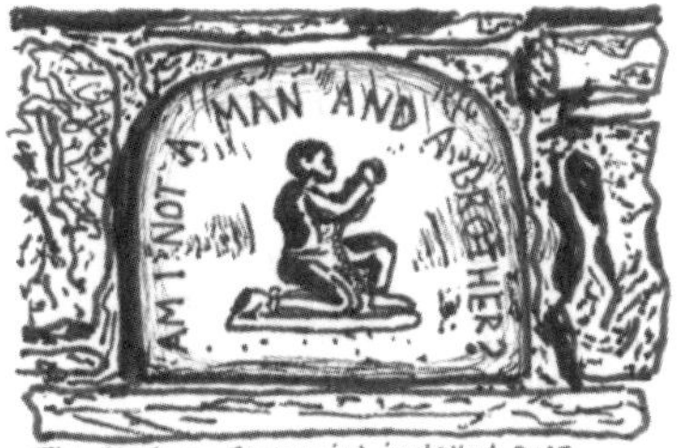

The Clarkson Memorial installed 2017 beside Eusemere boathouse

In 1787 Thomas Clarkson co-founded The Society for the Abolition of the Slave Trade. He lived at Eusemere House from 1797 to 1807 and became great friends of the Wordsworths; he hosted them on 14th April 1802 the night before their encounter with the daffodils at Gowbarrow. Clarkson travelled 35,000 miles on horseback campaigning against slavery; he took shackles, stocks and chains used on the slave boats to educate the public. He narrowly escaped a murder plot on Liverpool Docks in 1789. The kneeling slave motif was the Society's emblem; it was made into medallions which were instrumental in swinging popular opinion against slavery. Slavery was abolished in 1807.

Gale Bay, Pooley Bridge

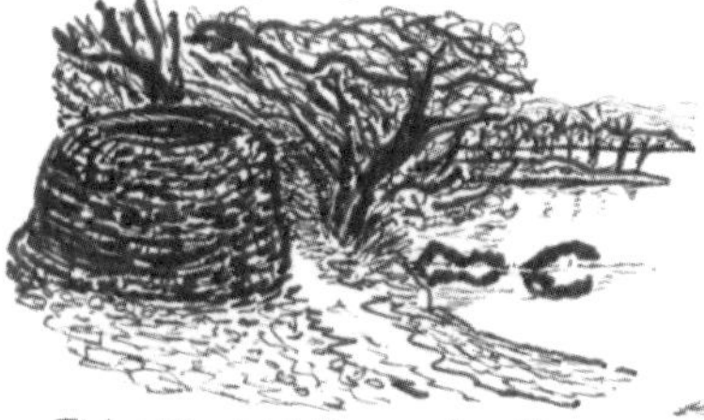

This Water Well-like construction was actually a machine-gun turret built to defend against German Seaplanes landing on the lake in World War Two.

The Cockpit is between 3500 and 5000 years old with features from the early and late Bronze Age. It is a 90 feet diameter penannular bank of stones surrounding a centre of beautiful green turf. Close your eyes, absorb the exuberant soundtrack of the skylarks and visualise those who have been here before us.

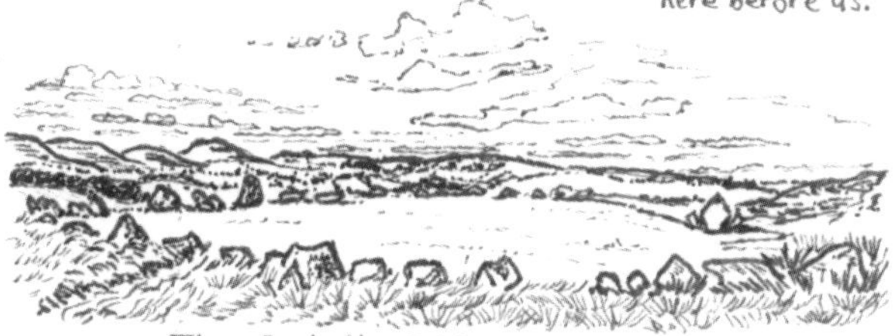

The Cockpit, Askham Common

Pooley Bridge - Tirril Entrance

581′

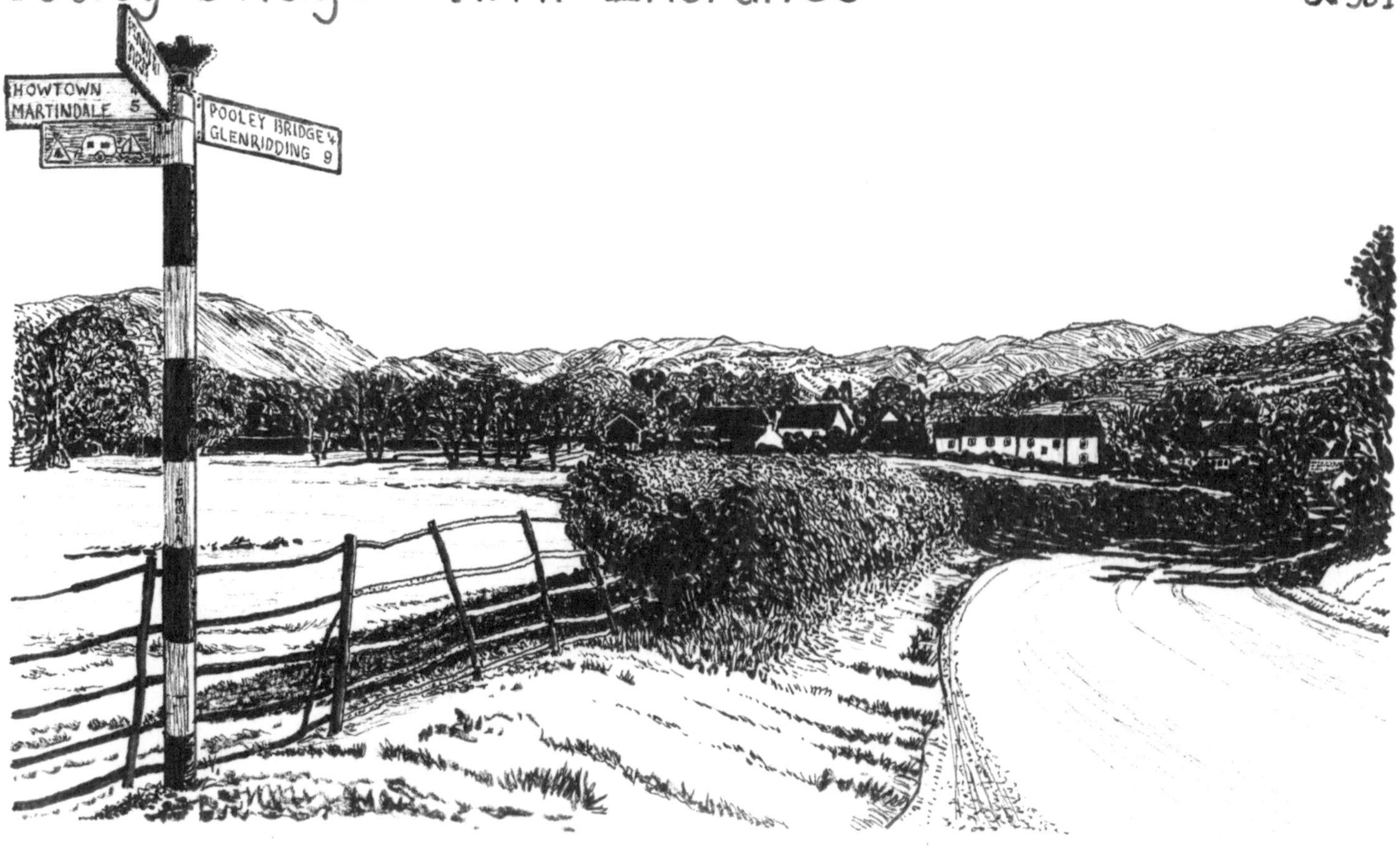

Eusemere ♿ 525'

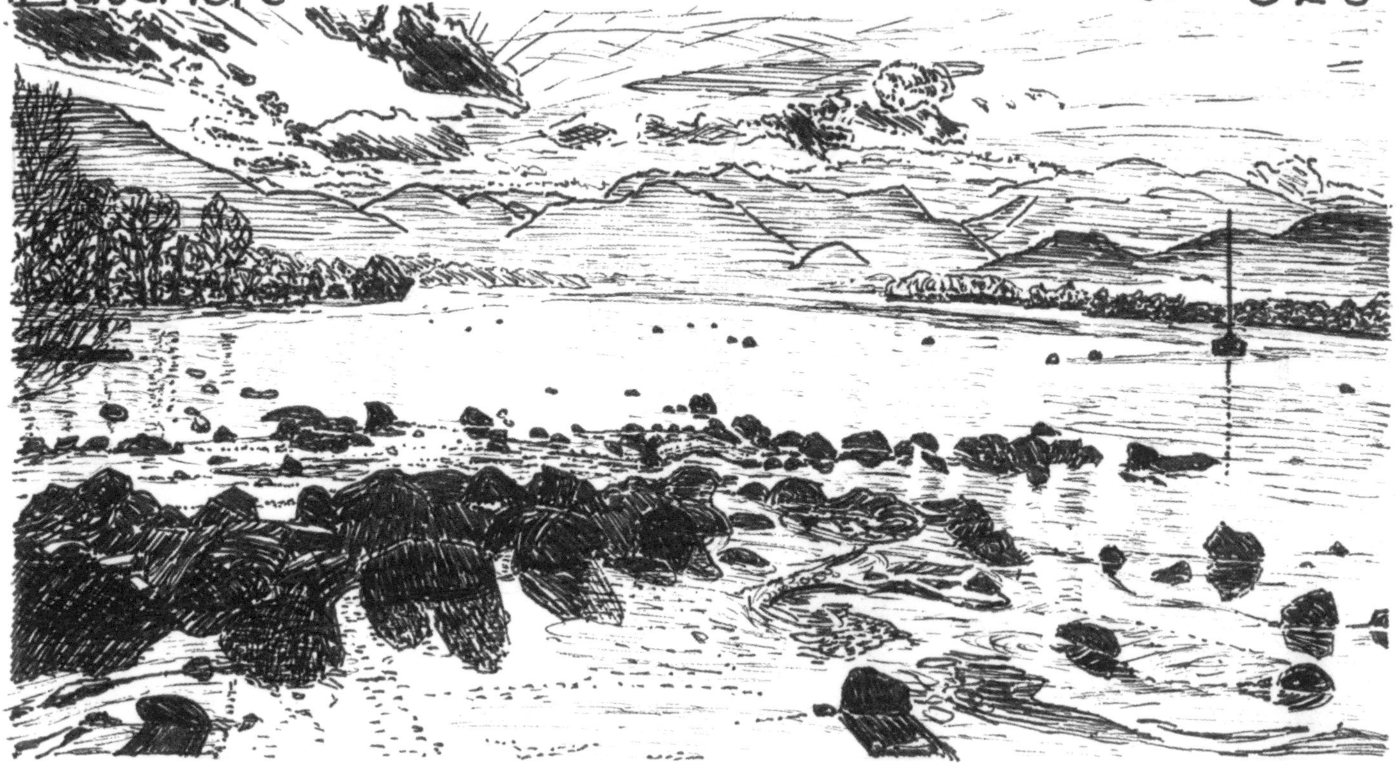

Wainwright's Sitting Stone - Ullswater Way

885'

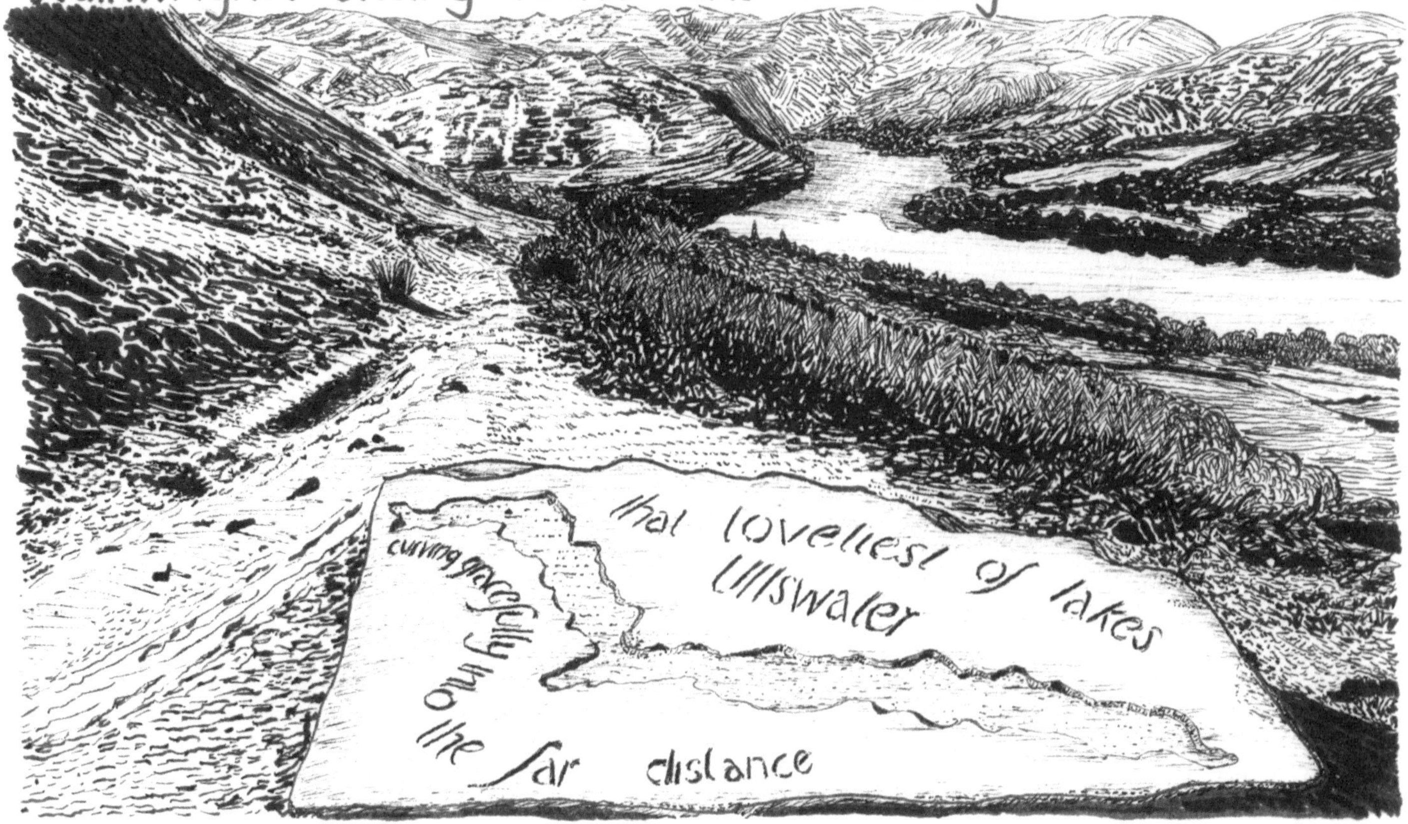

Arthur's Pike

1747′

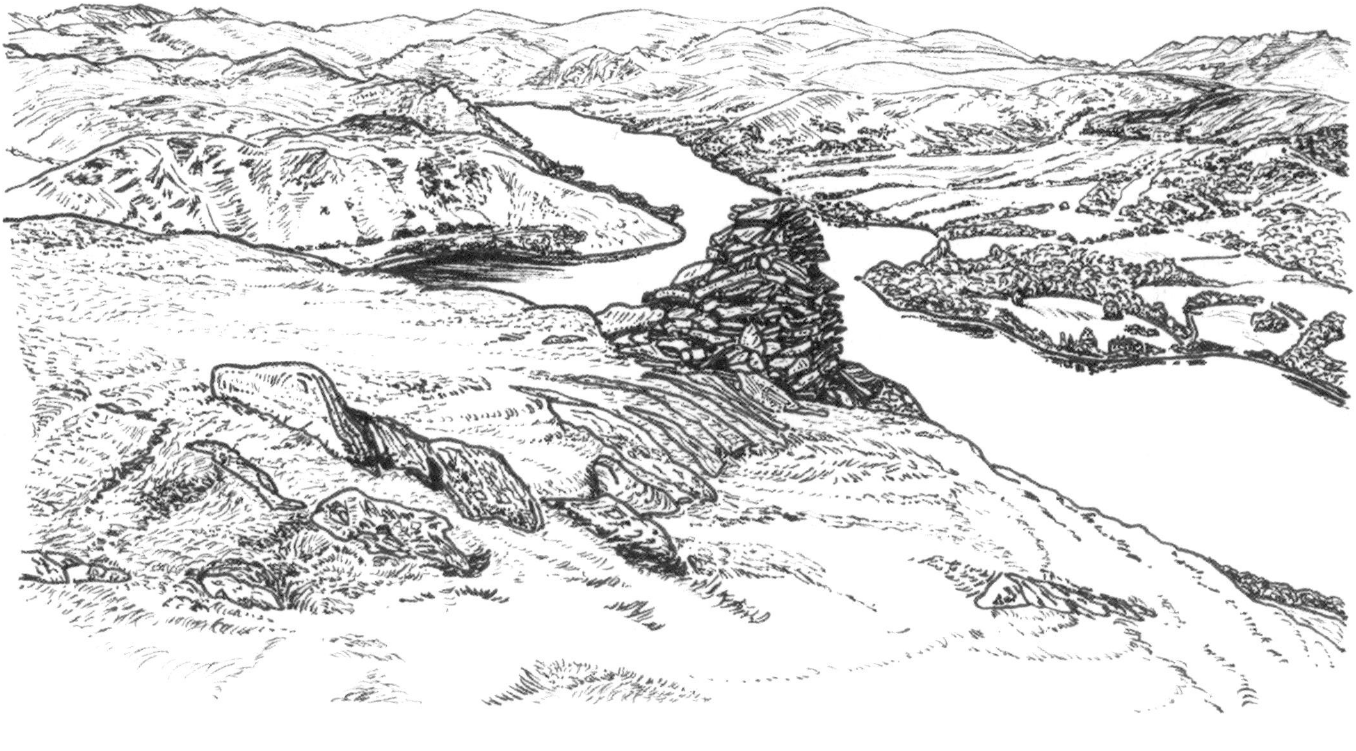

Bonscale Pike

1607′

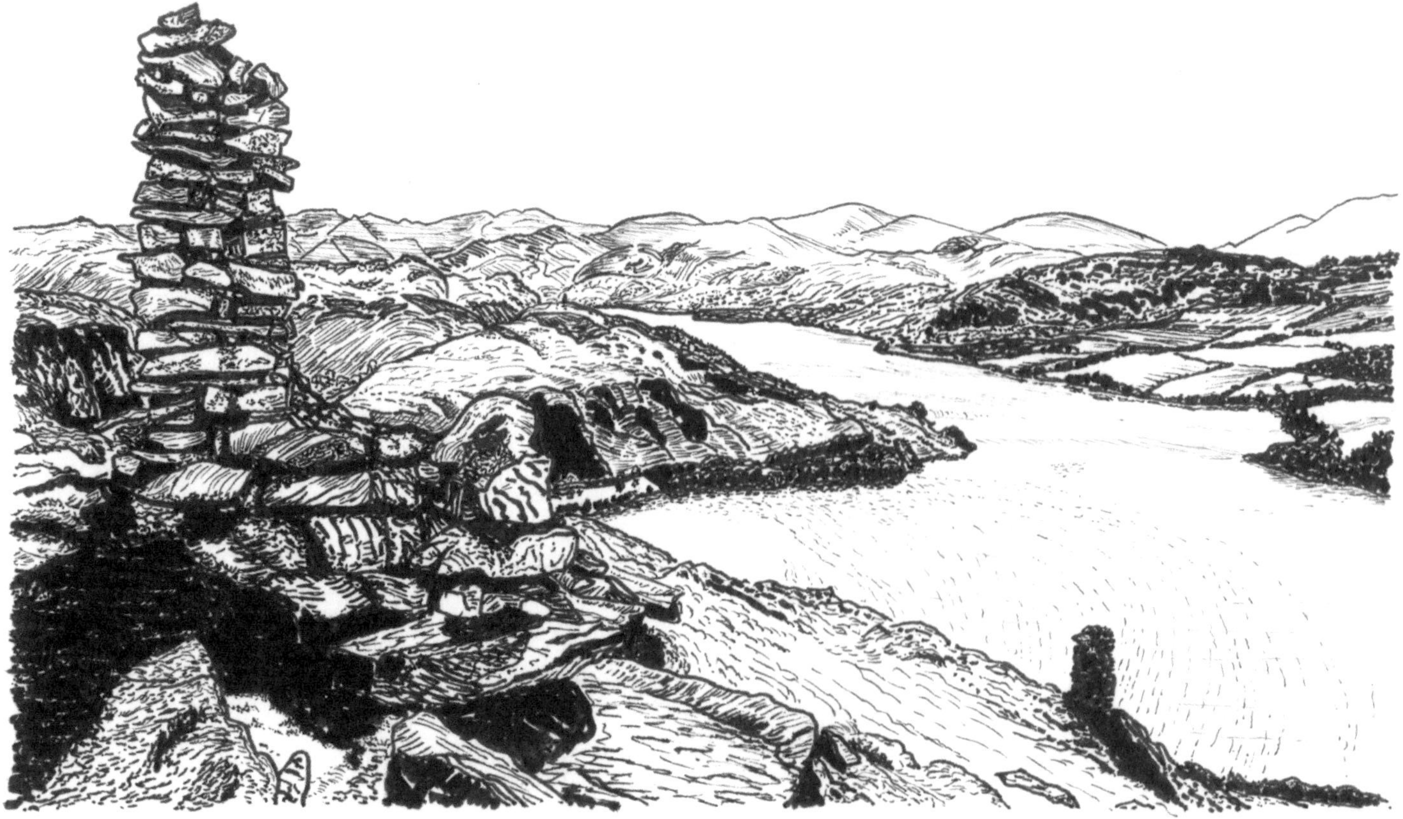

Swarth Fell

1639'

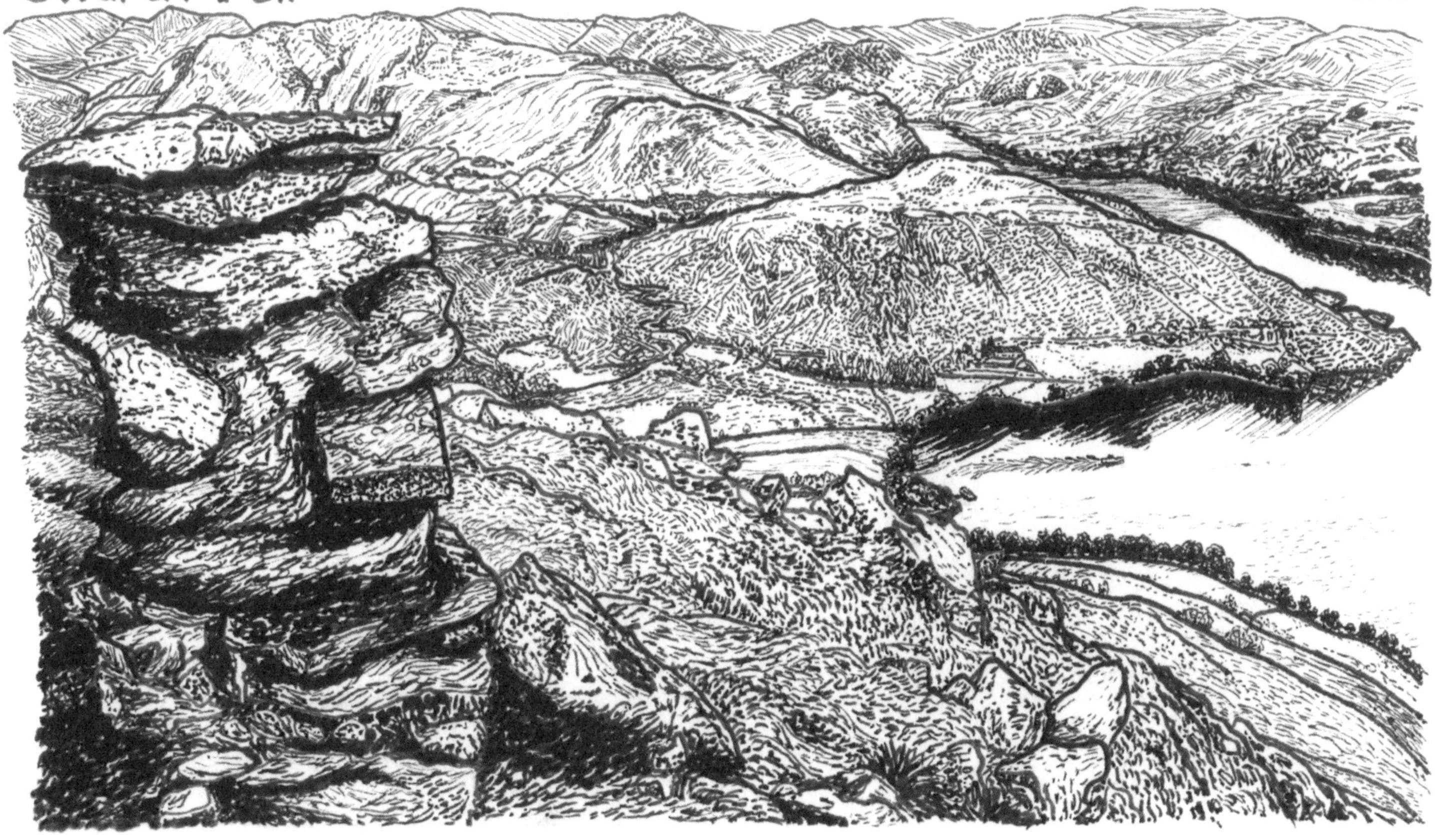

Loadpot Hill - north west of summit 2000'

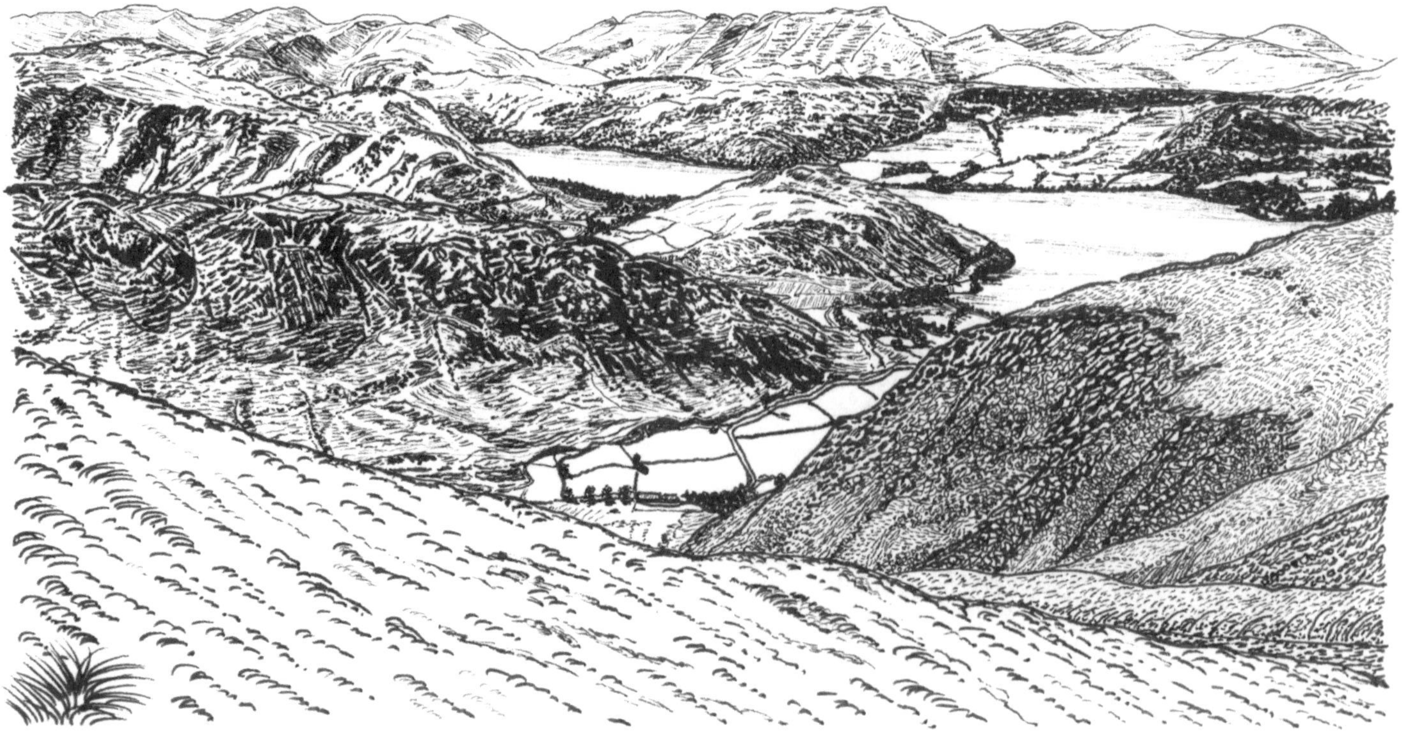

The Hause ~ Howtown 715'

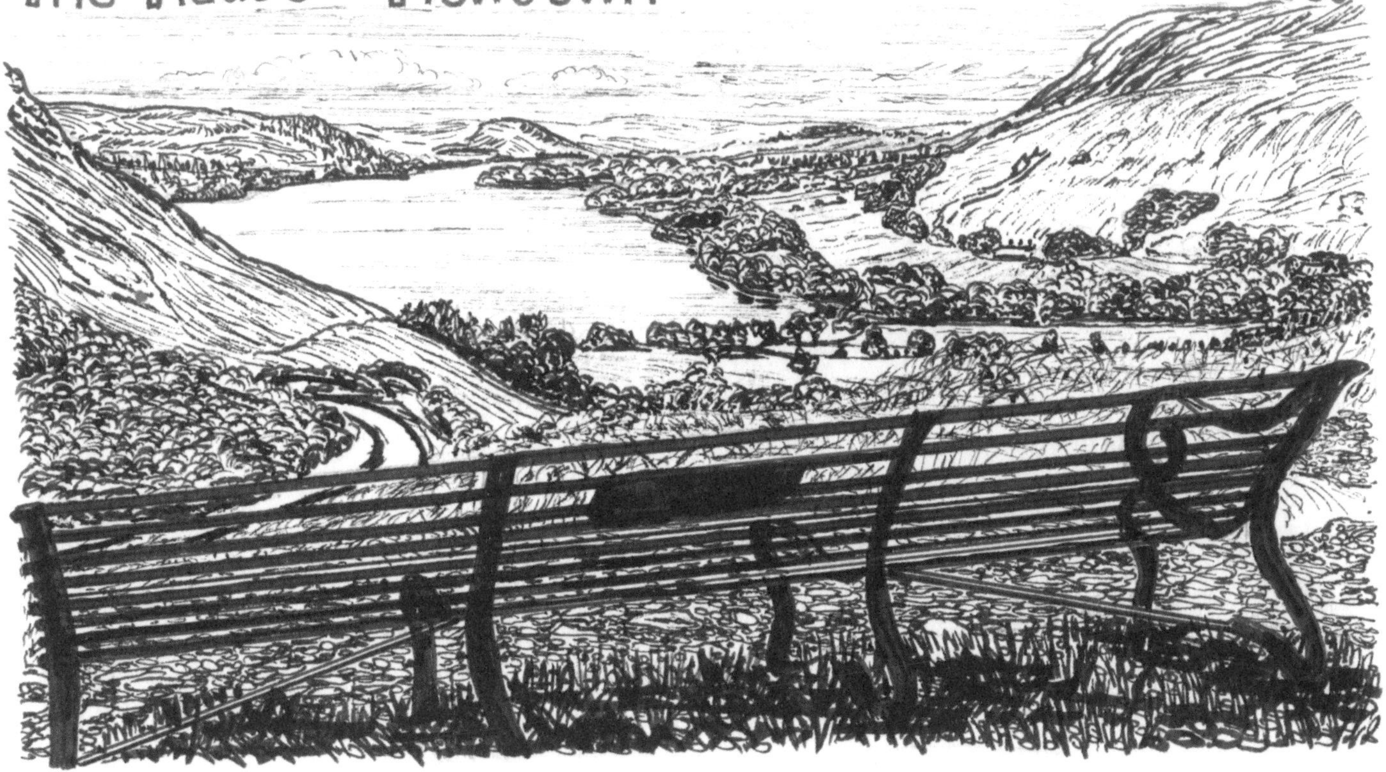

Hallin Fell and Howtown

Hallin Fell is the axis, the fulcrum around which Ullswater's magnificence radiates; it is the junction of the middle and lower reach. Plucky Hallin fell stands proud, indomitable; formed from resisting the force of four glaciers. The views from it and of it from all angles in this the prettiest square mile of Ullswater are tremendous..... it never disappoints. It is rightly crowned not by a mere cairn, but by a finely crafted obelisk standing stoutly twelve feet tall.

Many visitors are perplexed on arrival at Howtown: how-is-this-a-town? There is a hotel and a handful of homes, the Steamers' pier, that's it. The name derives from the Howe family who owned much of the area once upon a time. On the crest of the wonderful windy Hause is St. Peter's church, built in 1882 because St. Martin's church half a mile away had fallen into disrepair. Before 1859 the normal route to Glenridding and Patterdale was via Howtown and Sandwick. Travellers could overnight just over the Hause at the Star Inn (now named Cotehow) and either take a rowboat or walk via Boredale Hause to Patterdale and Glenridding. The start of the Steamers' service bypassed the need for this route.

Joseph Walker (1780-1820) lived at Waternook, Howtown, in 1817 he published 'The Shepherds Guide', cataloging the sheep markings of each farm in the district, so that sheep who wandered into the wrong valley could be claimed by the right farmer in the Spring meetings. The Guide was regularly updated and is still used throughout the district to this day.

IN MEMORY OF
NORMAN WILLIAM BIRKETT
BARON of ULVERSTON
HE LOVED ULLSWATER
HE STROVE TO MAINTAIN ITS BEAUTY FOR ALL TO ENJOY

The Kailpot Crag Memorial to Norman Lord Birkett can only be seen from the water. Since 1963 Ullswater Yacht Club have hosted a two day, weekend race every July in his honour. It is a spectacular sight with 230 monohulls dancing across the diamond speckled waves.

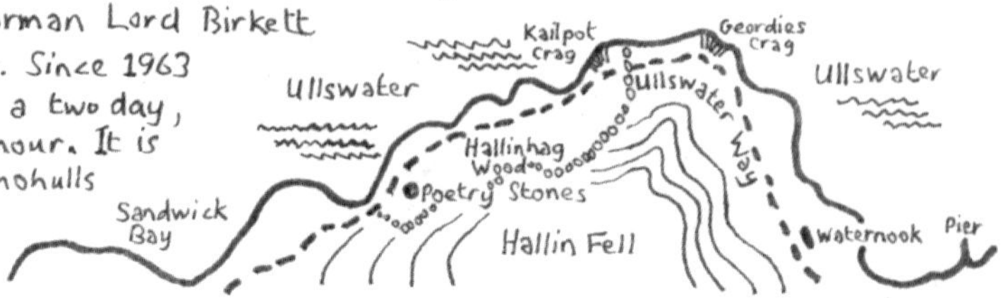

Hallin Fell ~ The Hause

♿ 698′

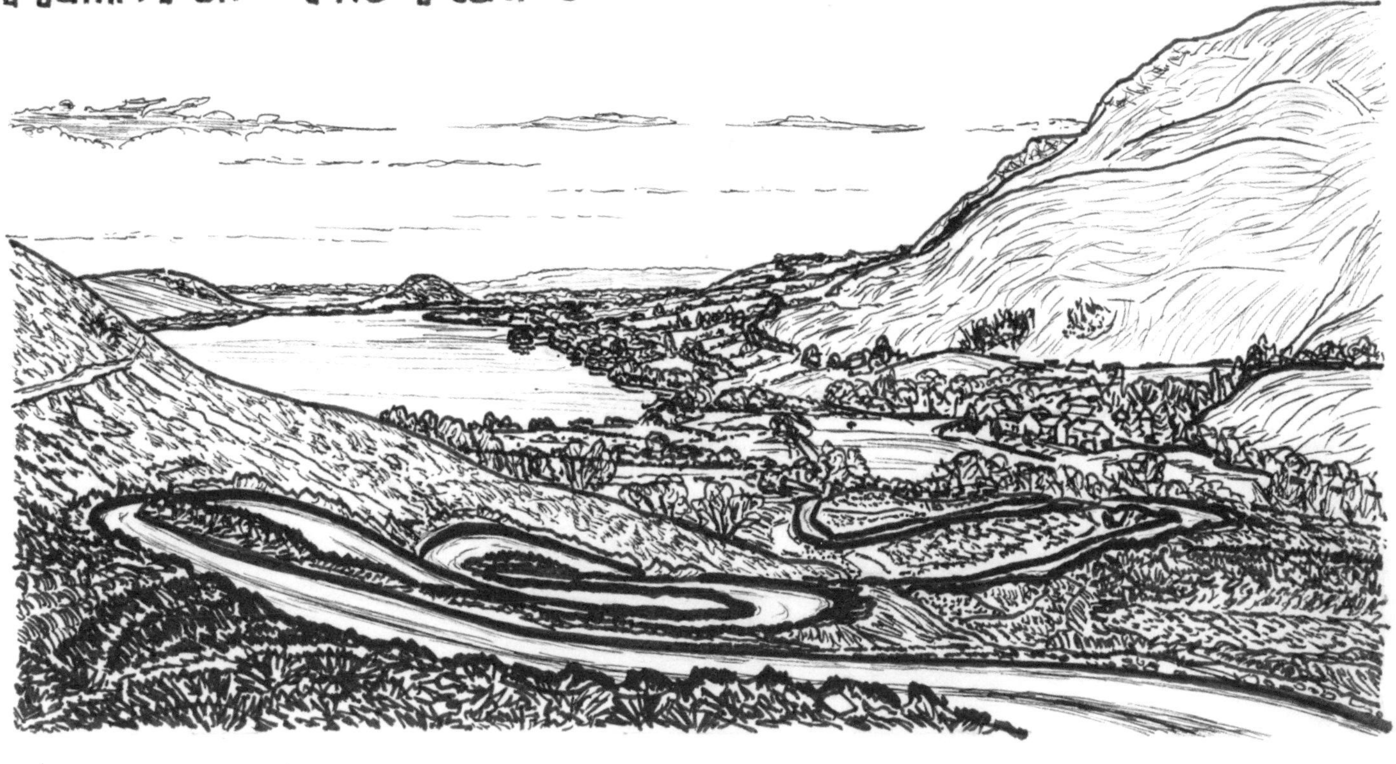

Hallin Fell - south of summit

1115′

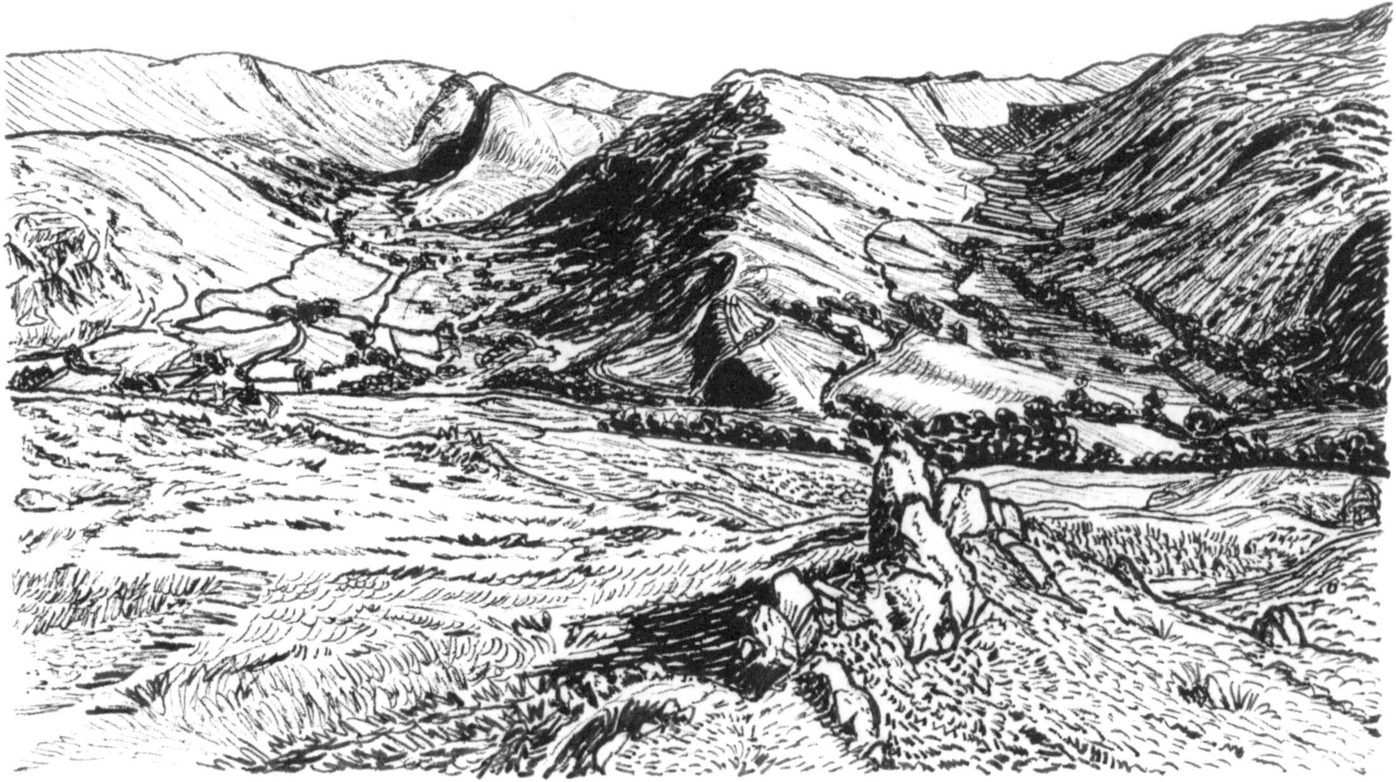

Hallin Fell

1271′

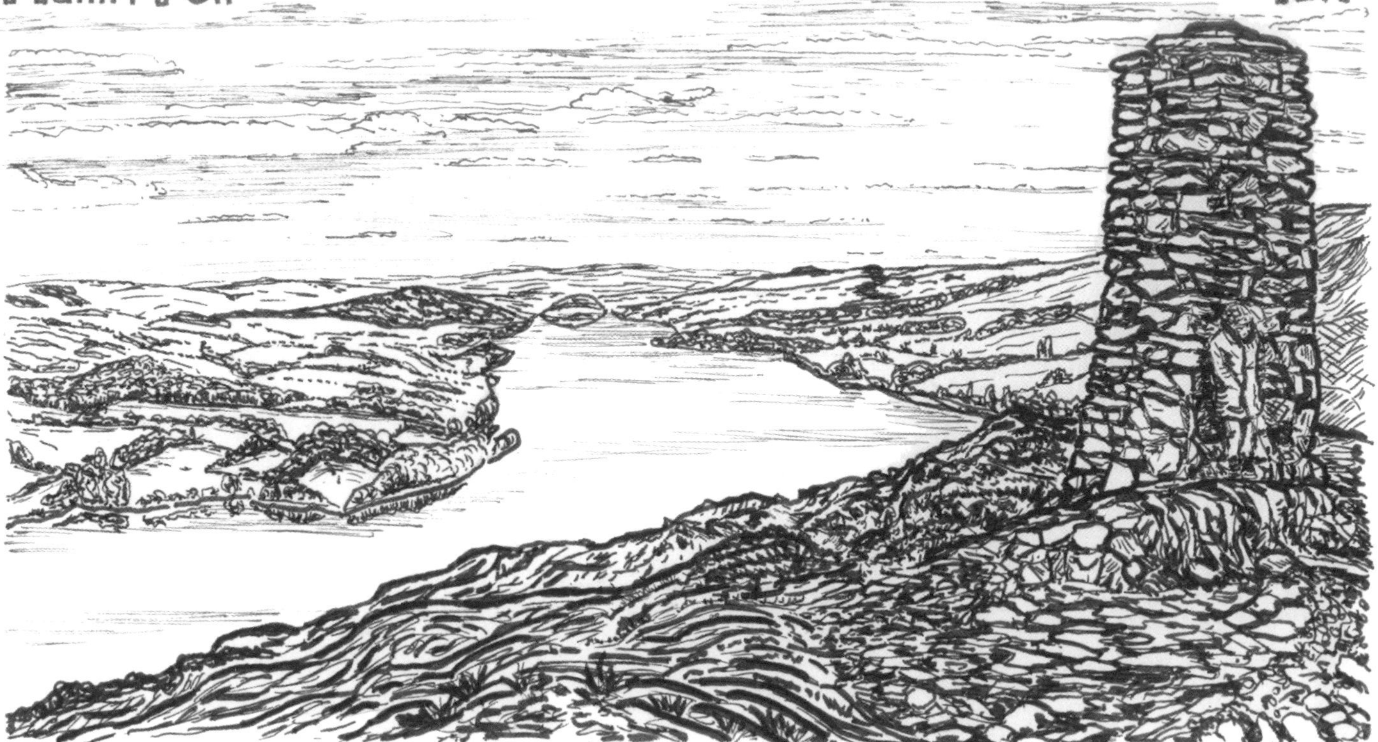

Hallin Fell - above Swine Slacks

1148′

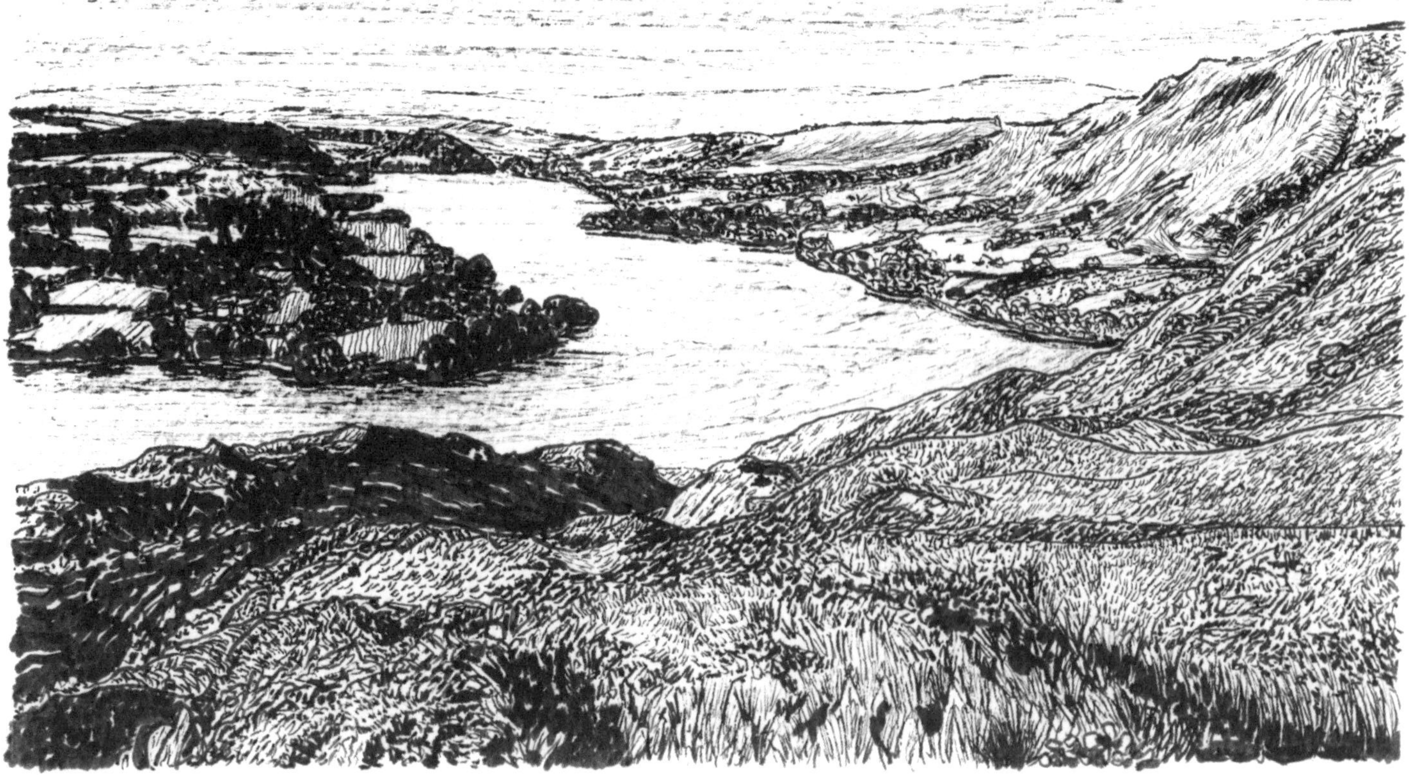

The Poetry Stones - Hallinhag Wood

'Martindale is an experience in solitude but never loneliness" - Kathleen Raine (1908-2003). Kathleen Raine moved to the Vicarage in the early 1940's from London with her children to avoid the war. She regarded Martindale as an idyllic world apart, writing some of her best poetry there. Her first book "Stone and Flower" was illustrated by artist Barbara Hepworth and received critical acclaim, it was published in 1943.

The walker must pay attention to find the stones; there is a small sign at the southern or Patterdale end of Hallinhag Wood which directs you above the Ullswater Way path.

Kathleen Raine was awarded the Queens Gold Medal for Poetry and was honoured in France and the USA also.

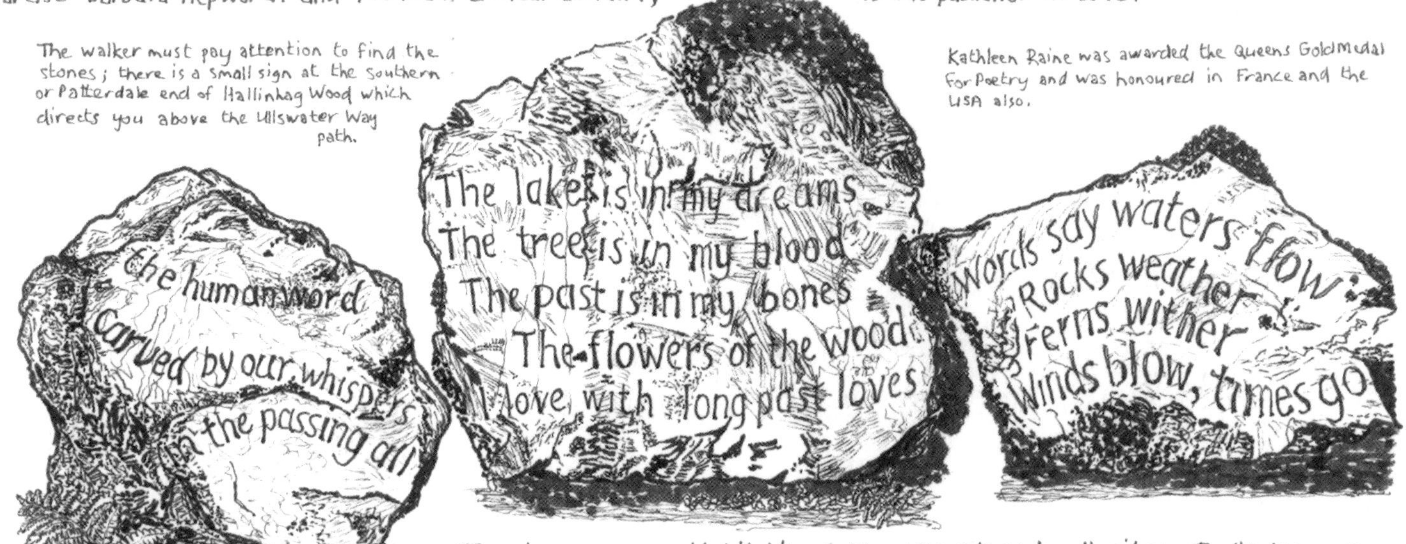

The stones are a highlight of the Ullswater Way Heritage Trail; they were carved in situ by Pip Hall in 2017. The central stone above is from the poem 'On Leaving Ullswater'; the two outer stones have lines from 'Night in Martindale'.

Bridge End - Hallin Fell

457′

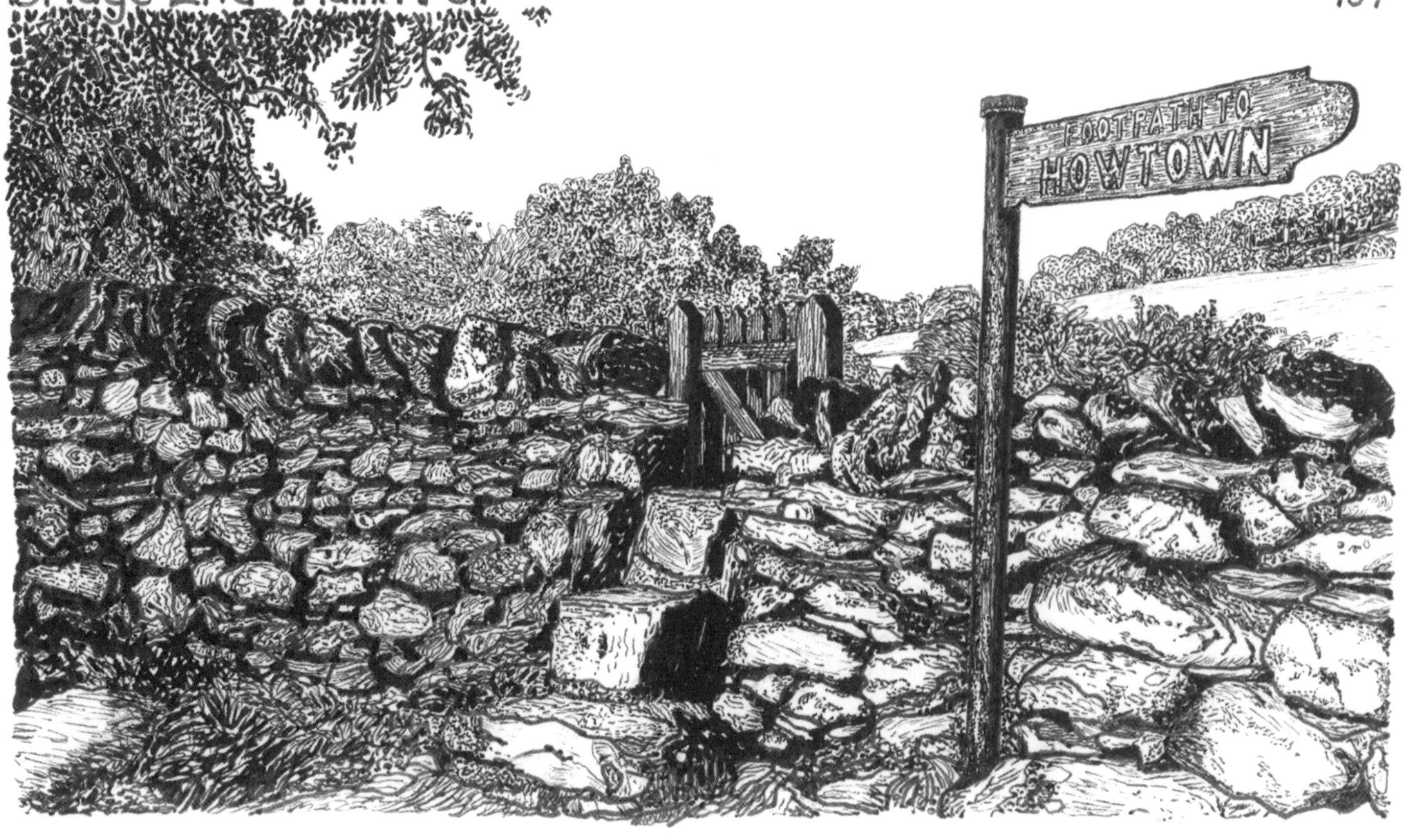

Bridge End Path - Hallin Fell

590′

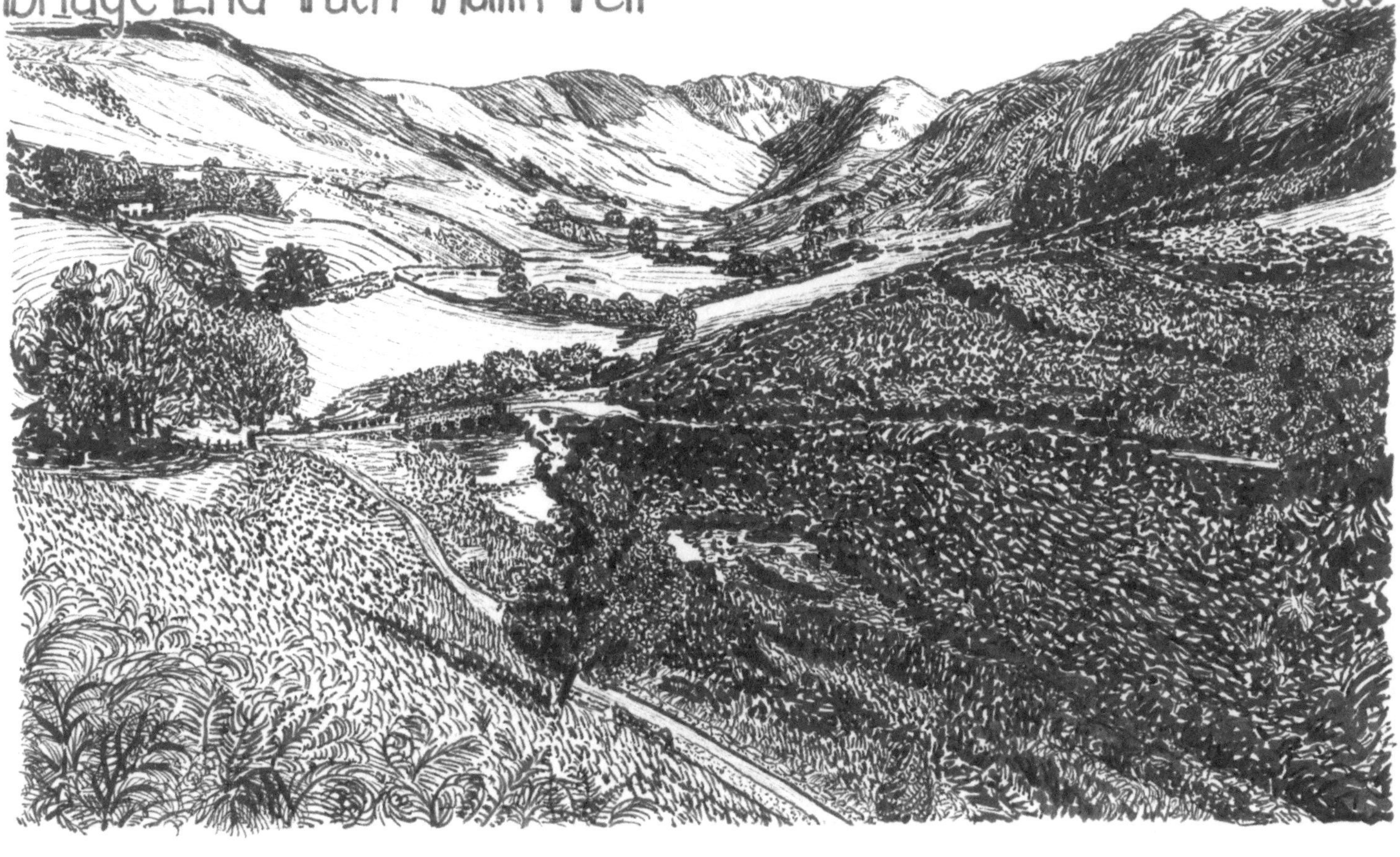

Hallin Fell ~ Hause Farm Footpath

721′

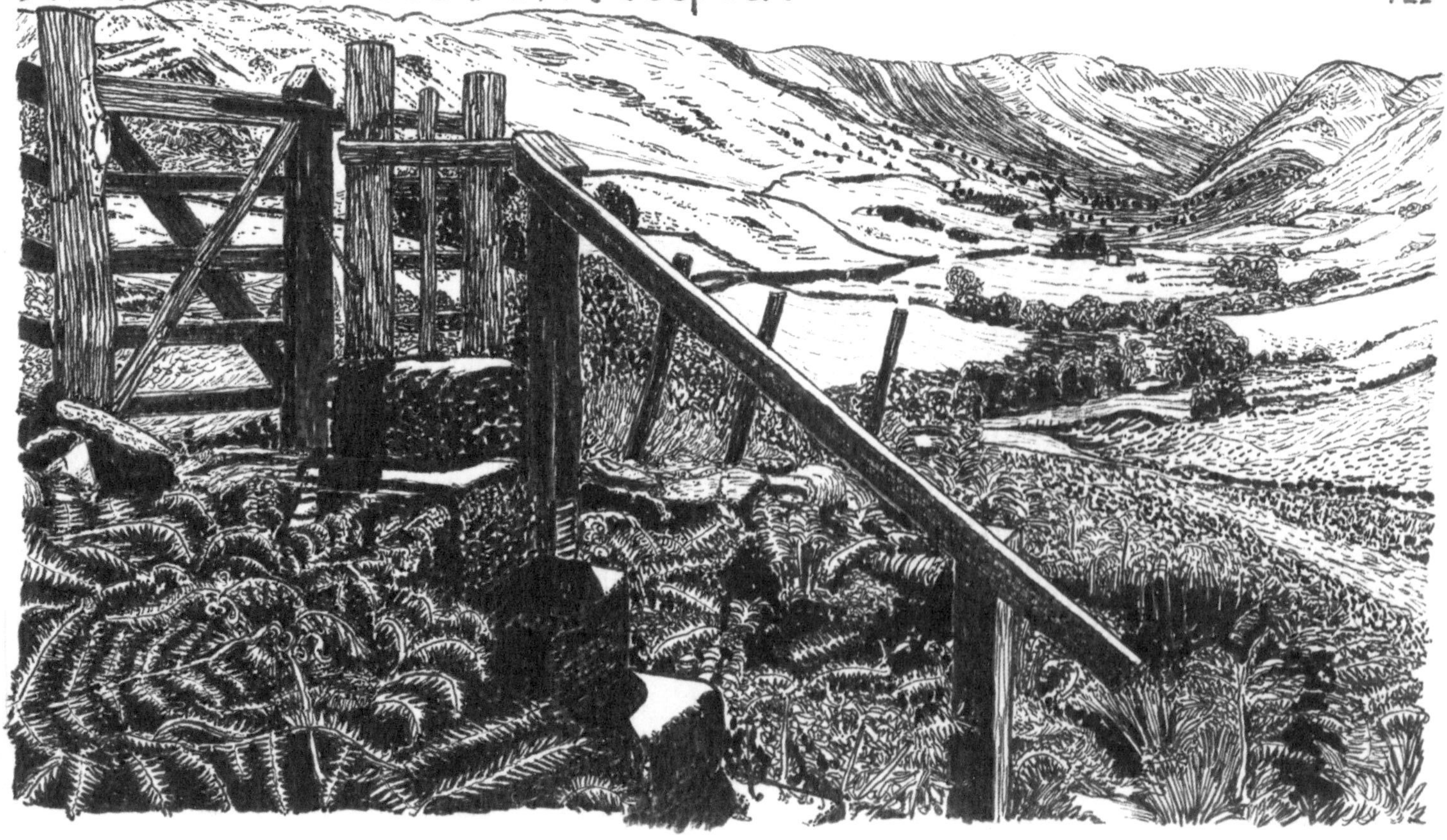

St. Martin's and its dale

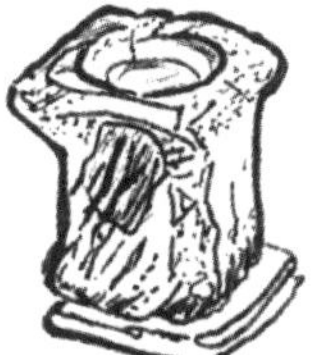
The Roman Font

The earliest reference to St. Martin's Church is from 1220; it may have been a place of worship from 700 AD as the Yew tree in the churchyard is confirmed as being at least 1300 years old. It is a beautiful, simple building, presenting today as it did in the 1600's. The pulpit dates from 1634 and the earthen floor was flagged in 1714. The font is believed to be a Roman Wayside Shrine brought down from High Street in the 1500's; the striations on its side are from tools and swords being sharpened. The churchyard has only eleven gravestones but 722 burials are recorded here, a sure sign of rural poverty in the valley. In the corner an ethereal scene is set by the Yew tree creeping around and above a solitary tomb.

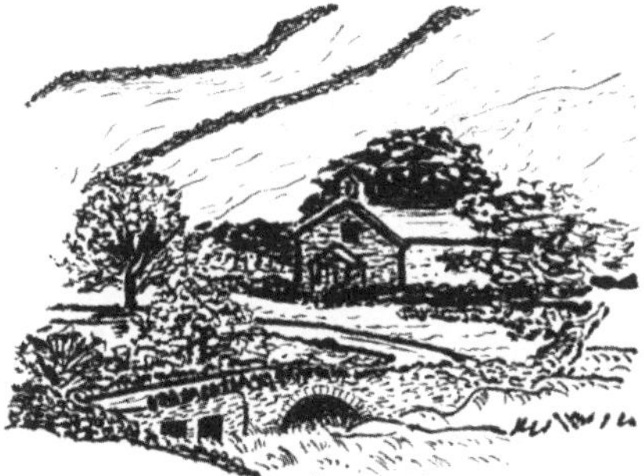
St. Martin's Church

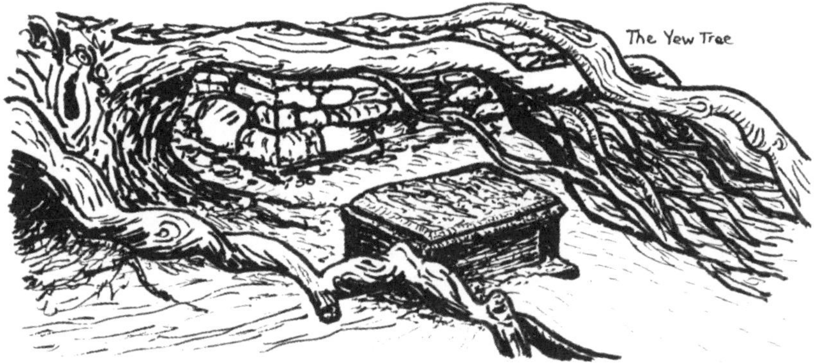
The Yew Tree

The Bungalow, Martindale

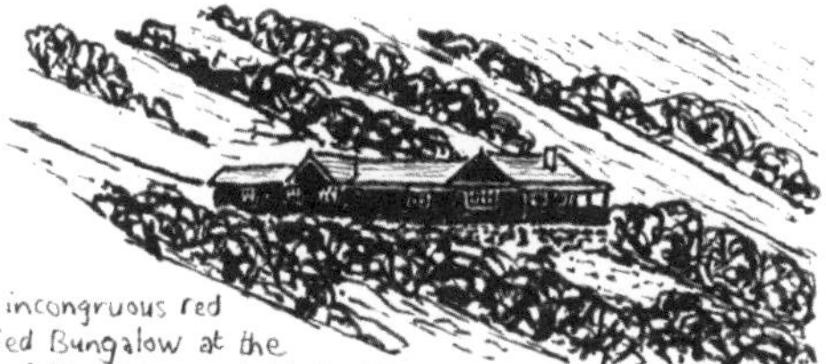

The incongruous red roofed Bungalow at the foot of The Nab was built in 1910 as a hunting lodge by the Lowther Estate. It was used as a base for shooting the wild red deer herd, the only truly wild herd in England with a blood line back to 1100. Kaiser Wilhelm II the Emperor of Germany visited in 1910.
The area is now managed by the Dalemain Estate; walking access to the Nab is restricted from September to Februery when culling takes place. Visitors are advised to call ahead to ensure their safety.

Beda Fell ~ Winter Crag 1664'

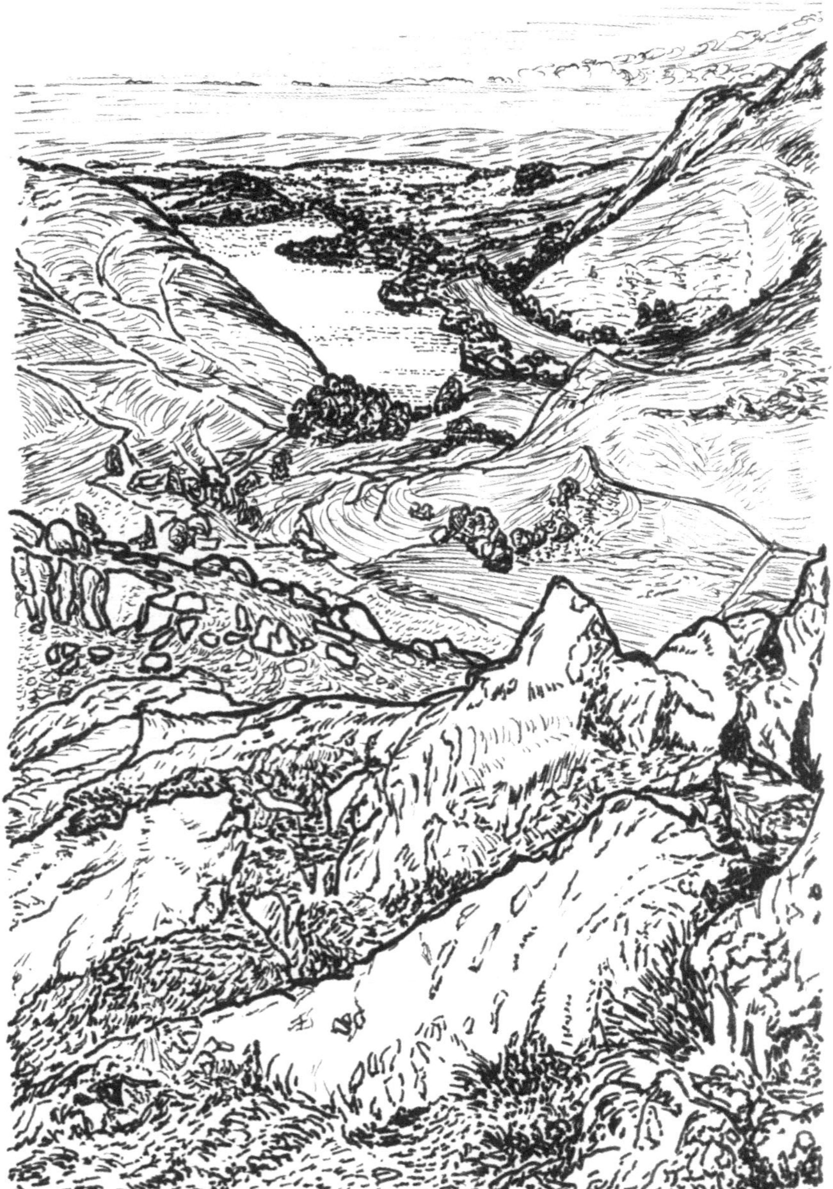

Scalehow Force Path

918'

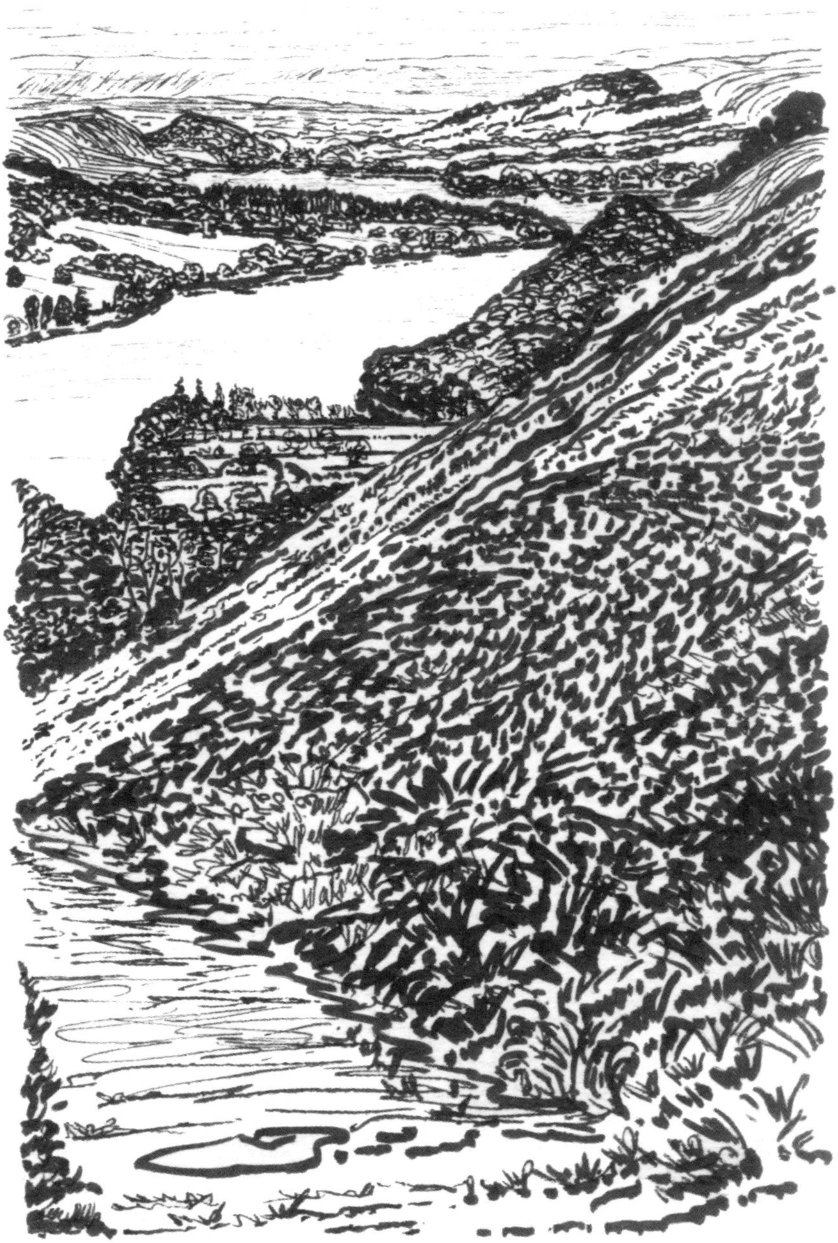

Low Birk Fell

1215′

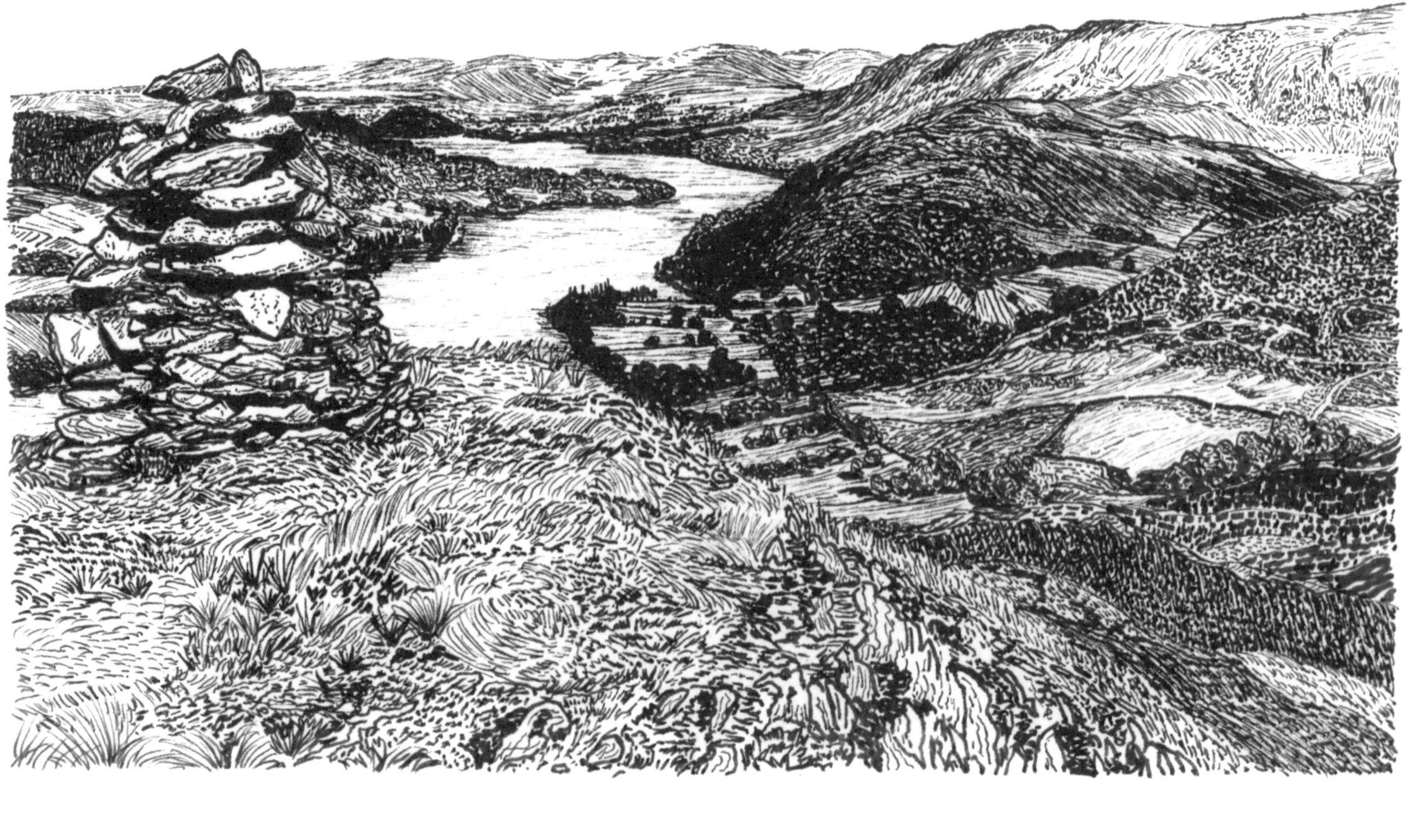

High Dodd - West of Summit

1610′

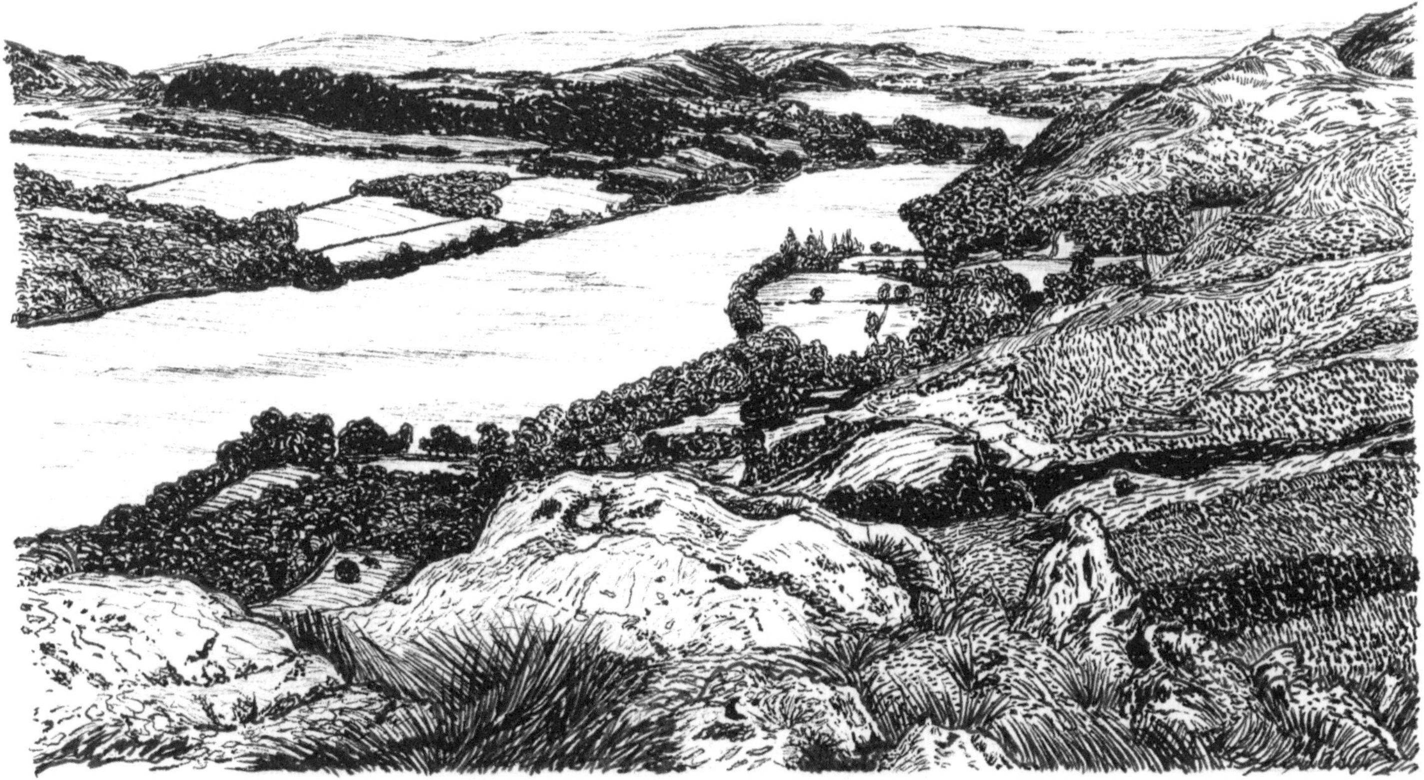

Sandwick from Ullswater Steamers'

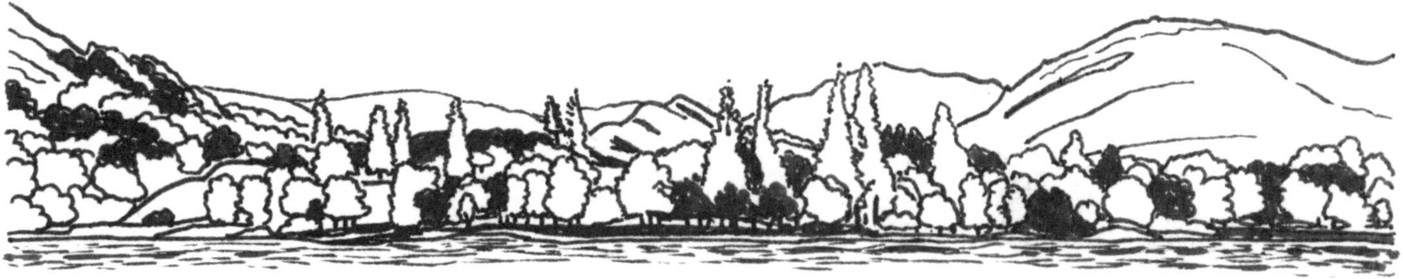

Ullswater Steamers' Fleet

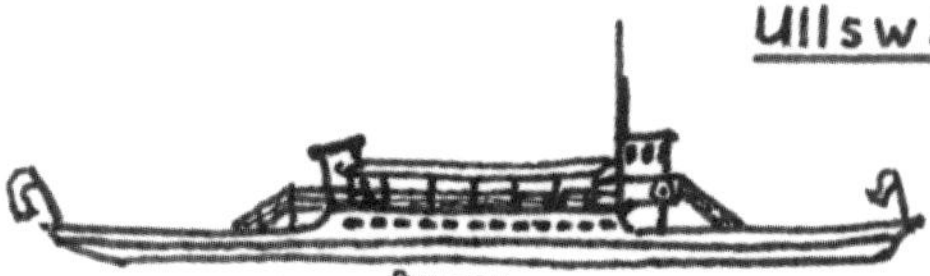

Raven
Built: 1889 Length: 120 Feet Capacity: 250

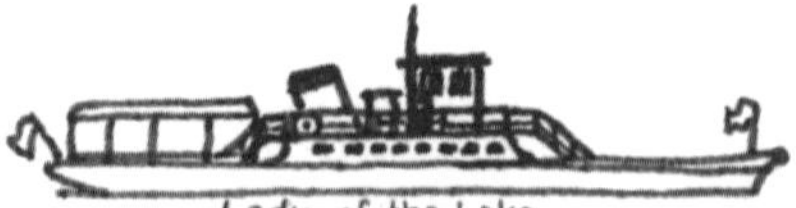

Lady of the Lake
Built: 1877 Length: 100 feet Capacity: 200

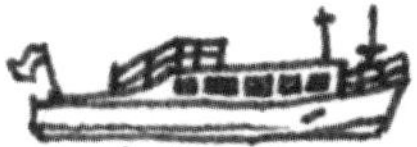

Lady Dorothy
Built: 1967 Length: 50 Feet
Capacity: 63

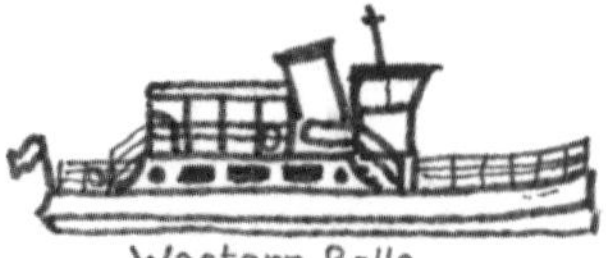

Western Belle
Built: 1935 Length: 75 Feet
Capacity: 160

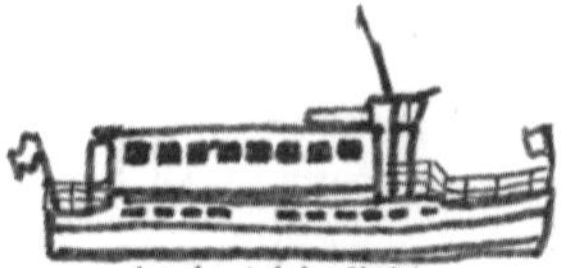

Lady Wakefield
Built: 1949 Length: 67 Feet
Capacity: 150

Bleaberry Knott - West of Summit

1508′

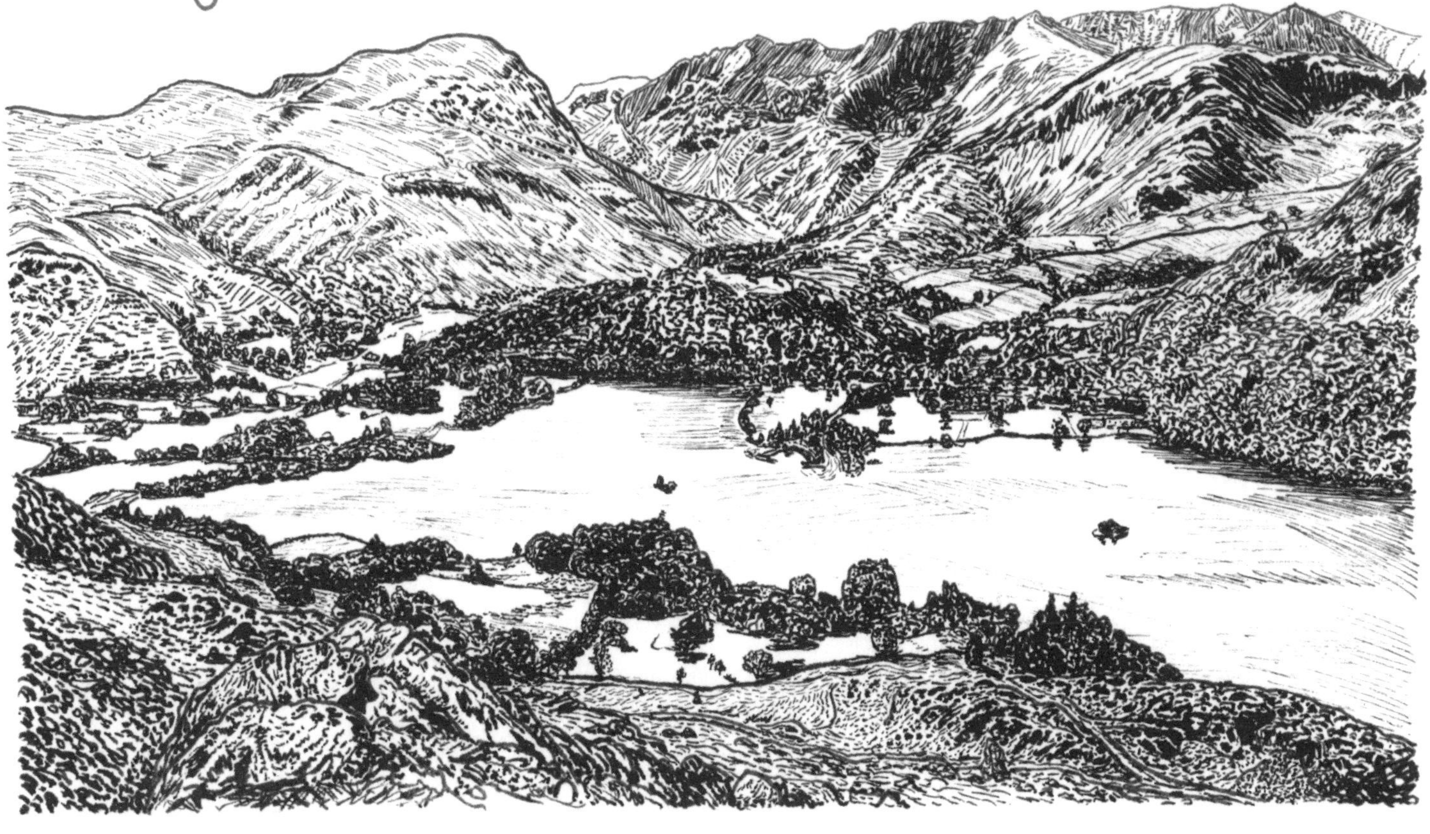

Mankind

The Romans AD43-410

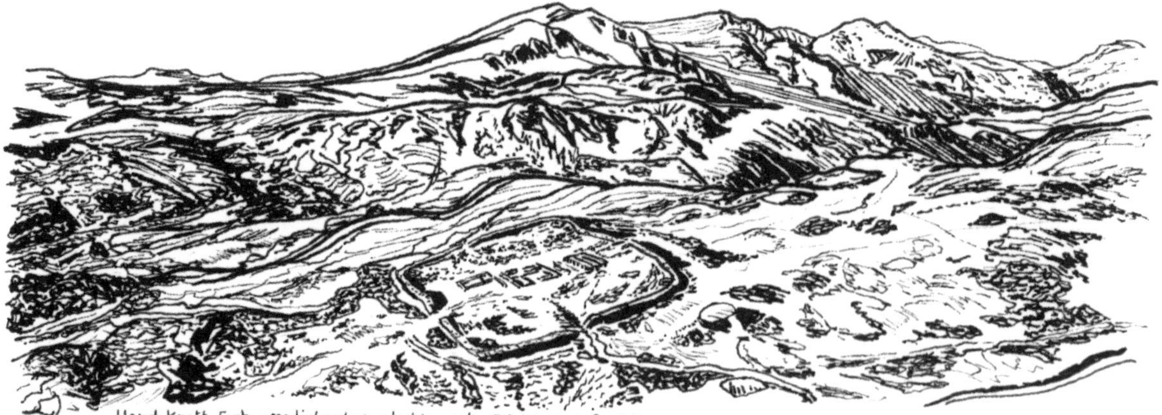

Hard Knott Fort - Mediobogdum - looking onto Eskdale and Scafell

The Romans invaded the South East of England in AD43 with an armada of 50,000 soldiers; it took them forty years more to overcome the north and extend well into Scotland. Treaties and agreements were made with the various tribes including the Brigantes who controlled Cumbria and the North. Forts were positioned to divide the tribes and to protect major routes. The impressive Hard Knott Fort was built under Emperor Hadrian from AD117-138 to protect the inland from the rebellious seafaring west coast communities. From AD192 Roman soldiers were allowed to marry locals; two centuries of relative stability ensued. In the early 400's the Romans left Britain as its empire contracted.

Mankind

The Kingdom of Rheged 410 - 875 AD

King Coel Hen (AD350 - 420 of 'Old King Cole' nursery rhyme fame) was the first King of Rheged. The Kingdom roughly covered Cumbria and Lancashire. These were the times of the warrior kings, defending or advancing their territory depending on the success of their horse riding and fighting skills. Much of the history of this age is a mixture of mythology and fact as there is little written or physical record.

The legend of King Arthur was borne out of these times as the Celtic west (Rheged, Wales, Devon and Cornwall) fought off the Anglo-Saxons from Germany, who controlled the South and East of England. Noone knows if King Arthur truly existed or if he is an amalgam of Celtic battle folklore as the first written records of him appeared 400 years after his death. However, his story is deeply embedded in Cumbria: his father's Pendragon Castle at Mallerstang; Lancelot's duelling ground at Arthur's Round Table at Eamont Bridge; Arthur's mansion is mentioned being in Carlisle according to a Henry I Charter, and his final fatal battle took place at Camlann near Birdoswald.

The Irton Cross from the early 800's AD It is 10 feet tall

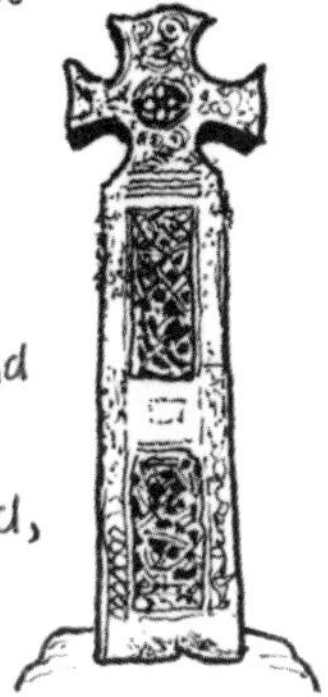

Some religious records survive from this time; in the early 600's King Aethelfrith established abbeys across his kingdom including those at Furness and Shap. It was at this time when the name 'Westmoringaland' was christened (land of the western border of the Anglian empire). There are a number of stone crosses which have survived from the 700 and 800's AD; these were not gravestones but monuments to the Saints; the best examples are at Irton, Bewcastle, Gosforth, Dacre and Kendal. King Dunmail was the last King of Rheged, he died in 945AD fighting off Scottish King Malcolm and Anglo Saxon King Edmund; on Dunmail Raise near Grasmere a large stone mound marks the site of his death.

Mankind

The Viking Age 875-1066AD

The word 'Viking' simply means plunderer; they came from East and West in their swift longboats and easily took advantage of the undefended monasteries and communities. The God-fearing Christians at the time believed the Saints would protect them and their churches from attack. The absence of help from the Saints was seen as an expression of the wrath of God against a sinful people.

Britain was split into six tribes with the Vikings in control across the north of England. They were excellent farmers; forests and bracken were cleared, stone walls built and boulder strewn fields made good for crops and cattle. The landscape which Wordsworth sought to protect in the 1800's as "unsullied by man" had in fact already been shaped by farming for a thousand years and mining for several centuries.

On July 12th 927AD the five Kings of Britain; Athelstan - King of the Anglo-Saxons, Constantine II - King of Scotland, Owain - King of Strathclyde and Cumberland, Hywel Dda - King of Wales and Ealdred son of Eadulf - King of Northumbria met and made a treaty at Eamont Bridge. This date is now seen as the foundation of the Kingdom of England, with the River Eamont being the northern border.

In the Norman Conquest of 1066 William the Conqueror took control of most of England. He commissioned a survey of all his land and buildings; this, the Domesday Book was completed in 1086. Most of Cumbria was excluded from the Domesday Book as William didn't win control of the county from the Scots until 1092.

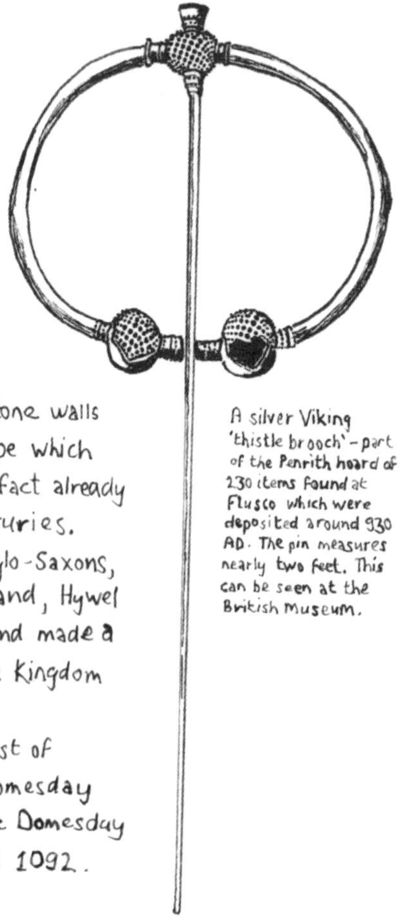

A silver Viking 'thistle brooch' - part of the Penrith hoard of 230 items found at Flusco which were deposited around 930 AD. The pin measures nearly two feet. This can be seen at the British Museum.

Mankind

Medieval Times 1100-1600

From 1100 to 1350 the population of England grew, the economy prospered, castles and abbeys were built e.g. Carlisle Castle, Priories at Cartmel and Shap. Norman churches were established around the perimeter of the Lake District; corpse roads came into use, where the dead of a small parish would be taken, usually by donkey to the mother church to be buried eg. if you died in Coniston you would be buried in Ulverston; likewise if you died in Mardale then Shap would be your resting place. The late 1100's saw the drawing of the Lancashire, Cumberland and Westmorland borders which remained in place until Cumbria was founded in 1974.

In the early 1200's King John granted market charters to Cockermouth, Keswick and Pooley Bridge. Despite the increasing power and wealth in England, the Scots fiercely protected their independence with the inspired leadership of Wallace and Robert the Bruce. The Black Death 1348-50 killed two million people in England, nearly half the population, bringing the period of prosperity to an end. However this did nothing to dampen the emnity between the Scots and the English; for several centuries Cumbria and Northumbria were near lawless buffer zones between the two countries. A cycle of raid, defence and counter raid persisted spawning the phrase the 'Reiver Raiders', about those who survived and fought - the grievers. The Reiver Raids only dissipated after 1603 when the Crowns of England and Scotland were united under James I.

Dacre Castle circa. 1350
Built to protect the Dacre family from Scottish raiders

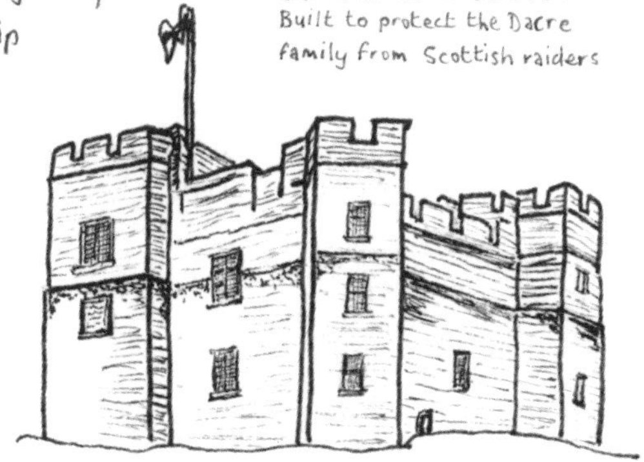

Section 2: Place Fell to Patterdale

30. Place Fell - west of summit 2065′
31. Silver Crag - upper path 689′
32. Artist's Seat - Ullswater Way & 672′
33. Side Farm Camping Field & 656′
34. Boredale Hause - Angle Tarn path 1246′
35. Angle Tarn - north west approach 1672′
36. Angle Tarn - east shore 1639′
37. Brock Crags 1846′
38. Rest Dodd - north of summit 2000′
39. The Nab 1803′
40. Gray Crag - north of summit 1902′
41. Hartsop Dodd - north of summit 1967′
42. Caudale Moor summit - west cairn 2459′
43. Red Screes - Trig Point 2539′
44. The Kirk Stone 1449′
45. Red Pit Car Park - Kirkstone Pass & 1439′
46. Dovedale 724′
47. Priest's Hole - Dove Crag 2262′
48. Dove Crag - east of summit 2495′
49. Patterdale & 485′
50. Arnison Crag - north of Oxford Crag 787′
51. Arnison Crag - north west of summit 1344′
52. St. Sunday Crag - north ridge 2571′
53. Deepdale Hause 2426′
54. Patterdale to Glenridding Path & 482′

Scene taken from 'Ullswater with Goldrigg Bridge'
by John Glover (1767-1849)

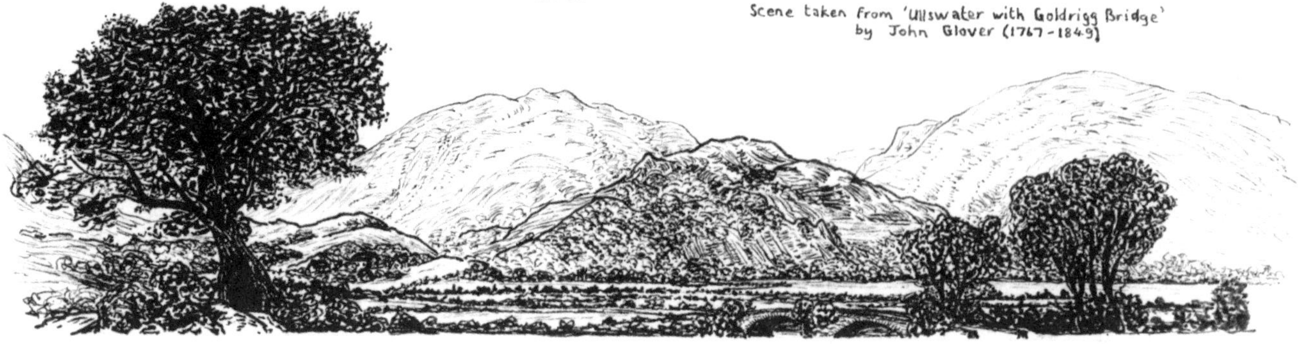

Section 2: Place Fell to Patterdale

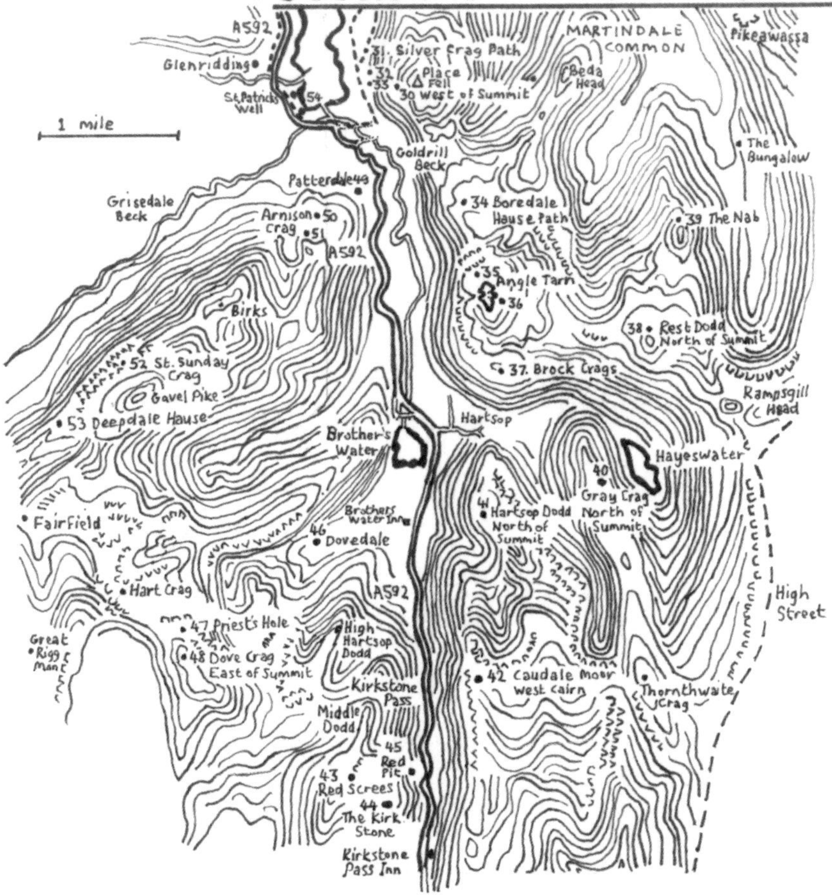

North to south Section 2 explores the wonderful corridor of wilderness west of High Street and east of the A592 and the Kirkstone Pass. It then turns back north on the west flank of the pass taking in the delights of Dovedale, St. Sunday Crag and Patterdale. Throughout these high lands there are glimpses of the southern reaches of Ullswater; Brotherswater from many aspects, and a visit to the magical Angle Tarn. The steeply creased valley sides mean that only **three** of the views here are easily accessible to wheelchair users. Views 32 and 33, The Artist's Seat and Side Farm can only be reached with off-road wheelchairs or prams.

Place Fell - west of summit

2065'

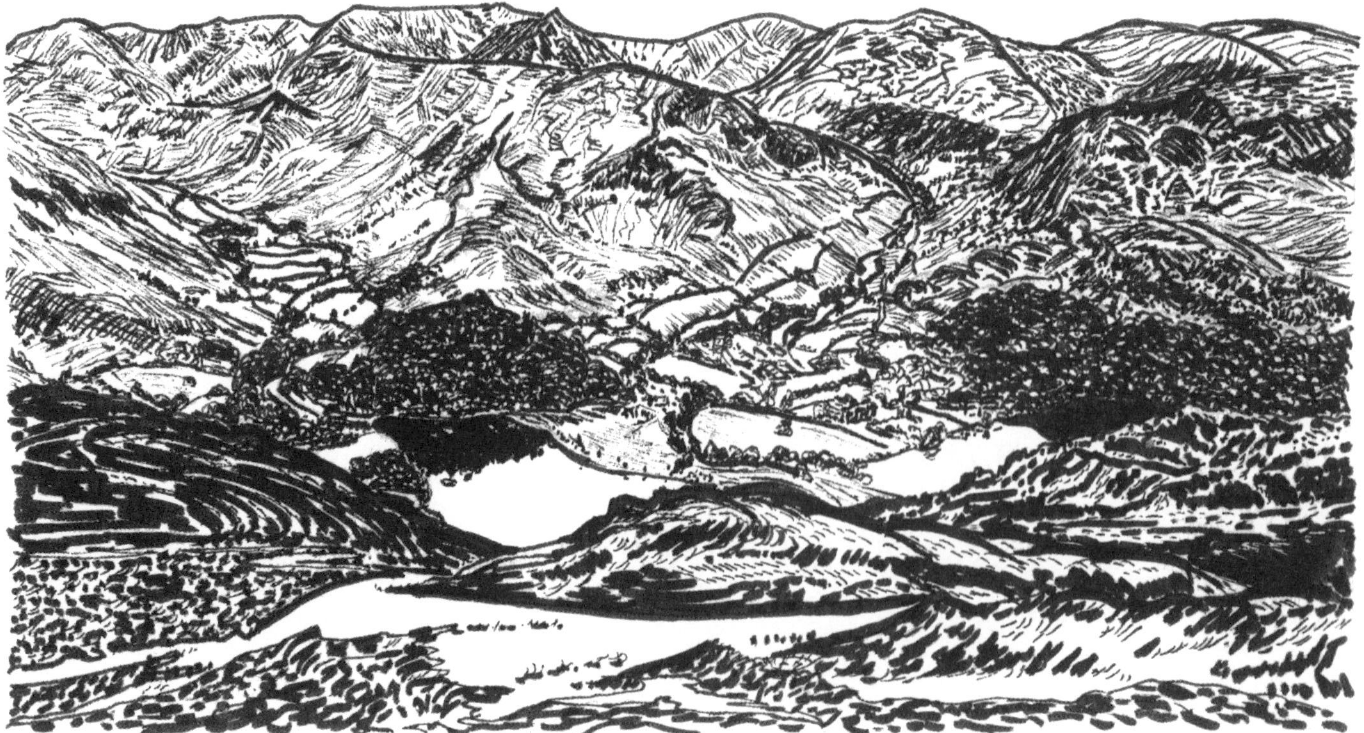

Silver Crag

689′

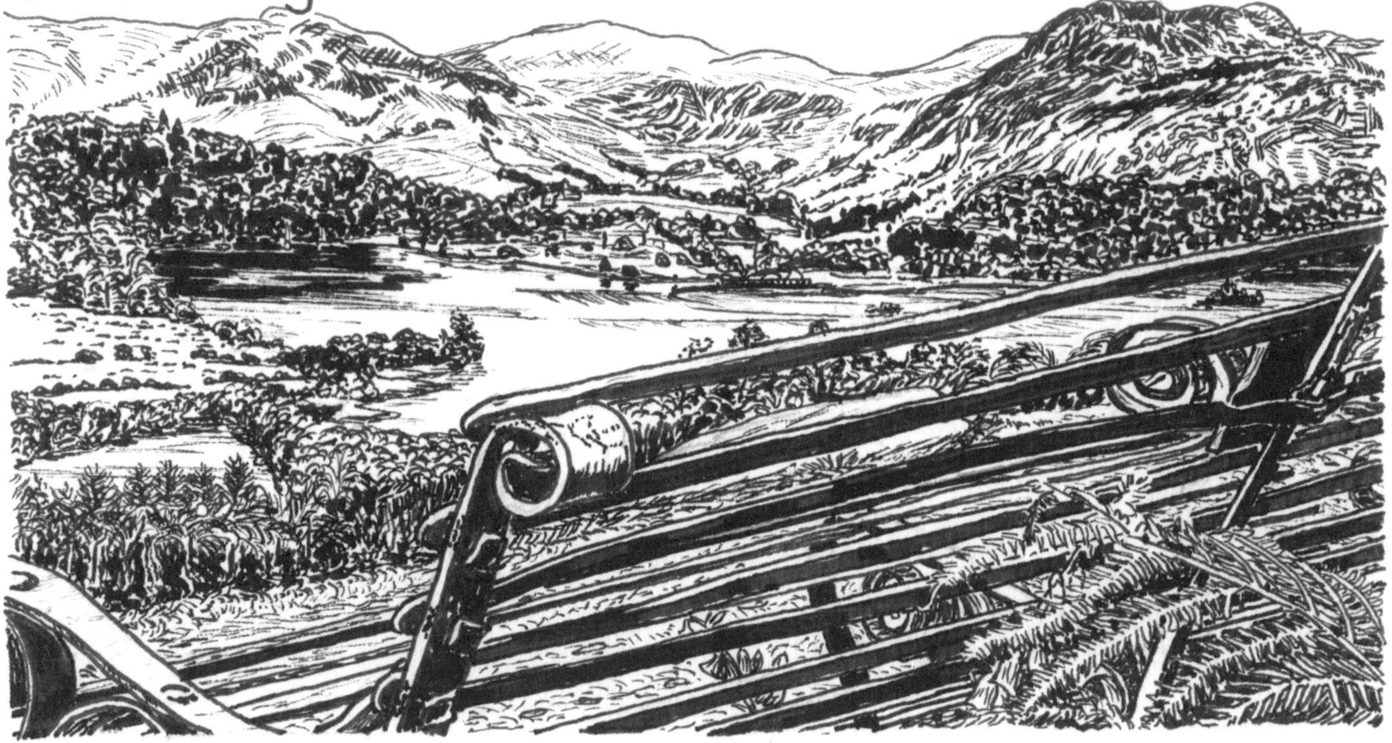

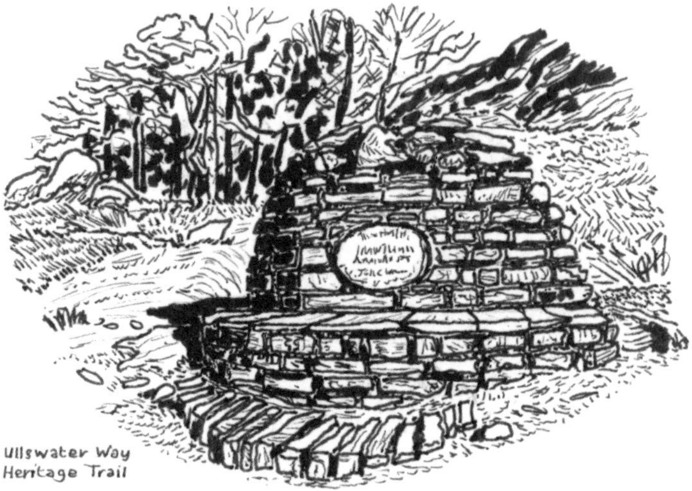

Ullswater Way Heritage Trail

The Artists' Seat celebrates three artists who lived or visited here. John Glover (1767-1849) lived up the hill from the Seat in Blowick before moving to Australia in 1831, founding the Landscape Movement there. Ann Macbeth (1875-1948) lived in Hartsop and Patterdale; she was an acclaimed embroiderer and designer, an associate of Rennie Mackintosh and an active suffragette. J.M.W Turner (1775-1851) was the greatest English landscape painter. He visited Ullswater in 1797, returning to the lakes in 1801 and 1809.

A sense of Place........

In my life, until making this book Place Fell was somewhere to be walked around, along the ever changing movie set of the shoreline; around the back via Boredale or Bannerdale; or over the top vectoring in on the summit via the most direct route. The circle was always completed with a satisfying and stimulating Steamers' trip back to the origin of the day. The book then gave me a reason to pause, to explore and savour; what a joyful, liberating, rewarding time was had when the plan was simply to amble around the faerie land like plateau. The summits of the supporting cast of Birk and Sleet Fell, High Dodd and The Knight were visited; followed by tracking back along the peerless, precipitous, deer dotted west ridge with virtually the whole lake laid out sharply below.

Three artists

J.M.W Turner
Ann Macbeth
&
John Glover

Were inspired by this landscape

Artists' Seat ~ Ullswater Way

672′

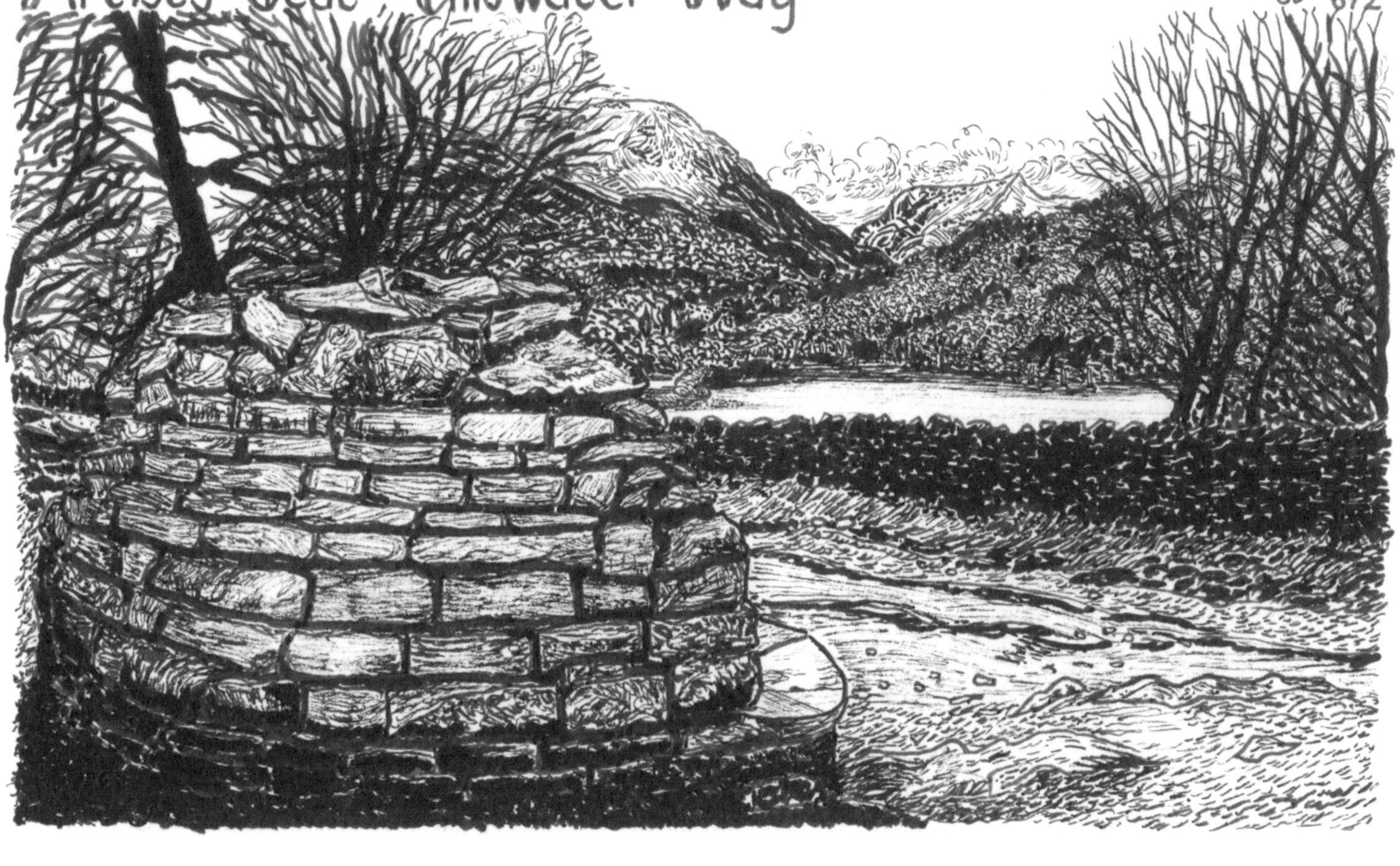

Side Farm Camping Field

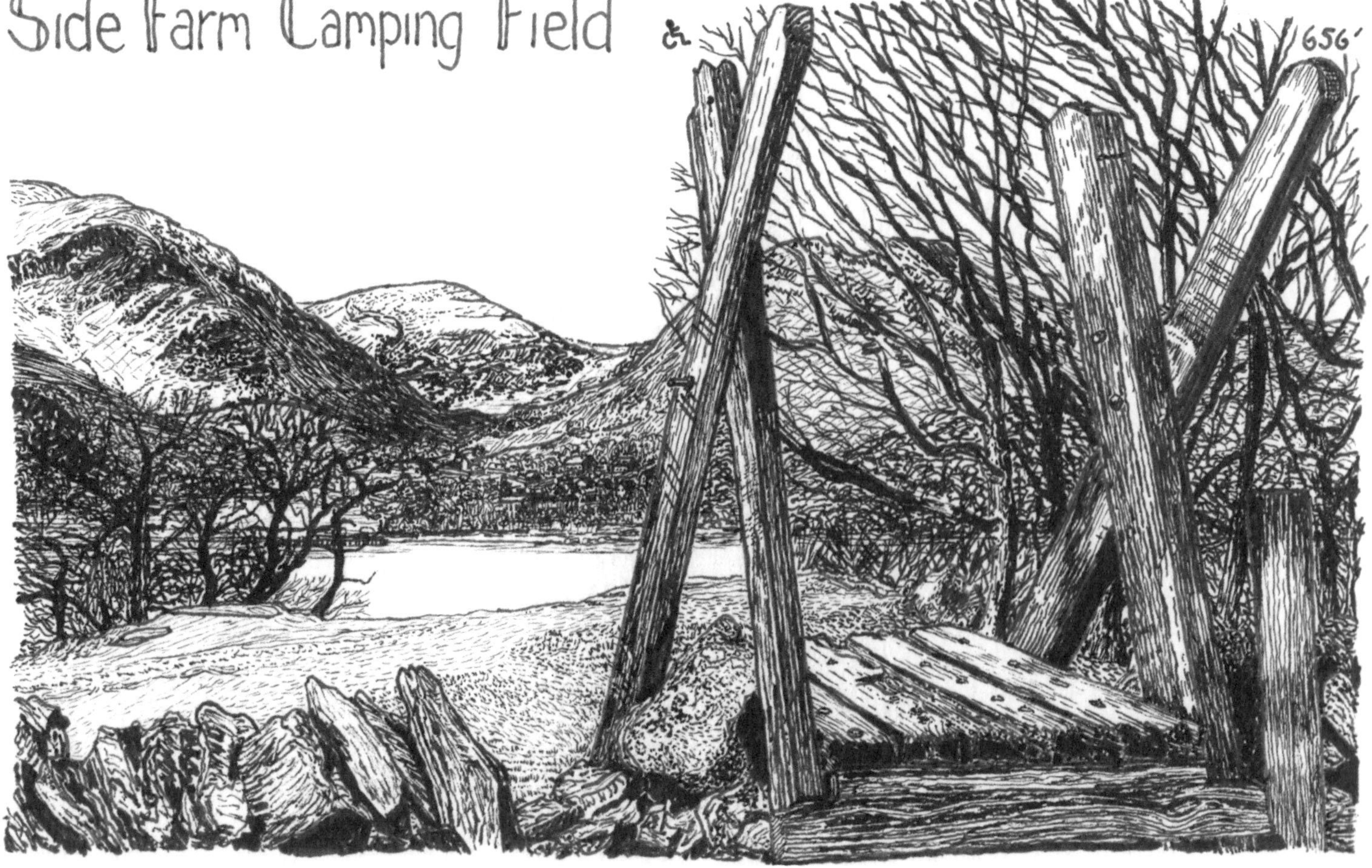

Boredale Hause ~ Angletarn Path

1246'

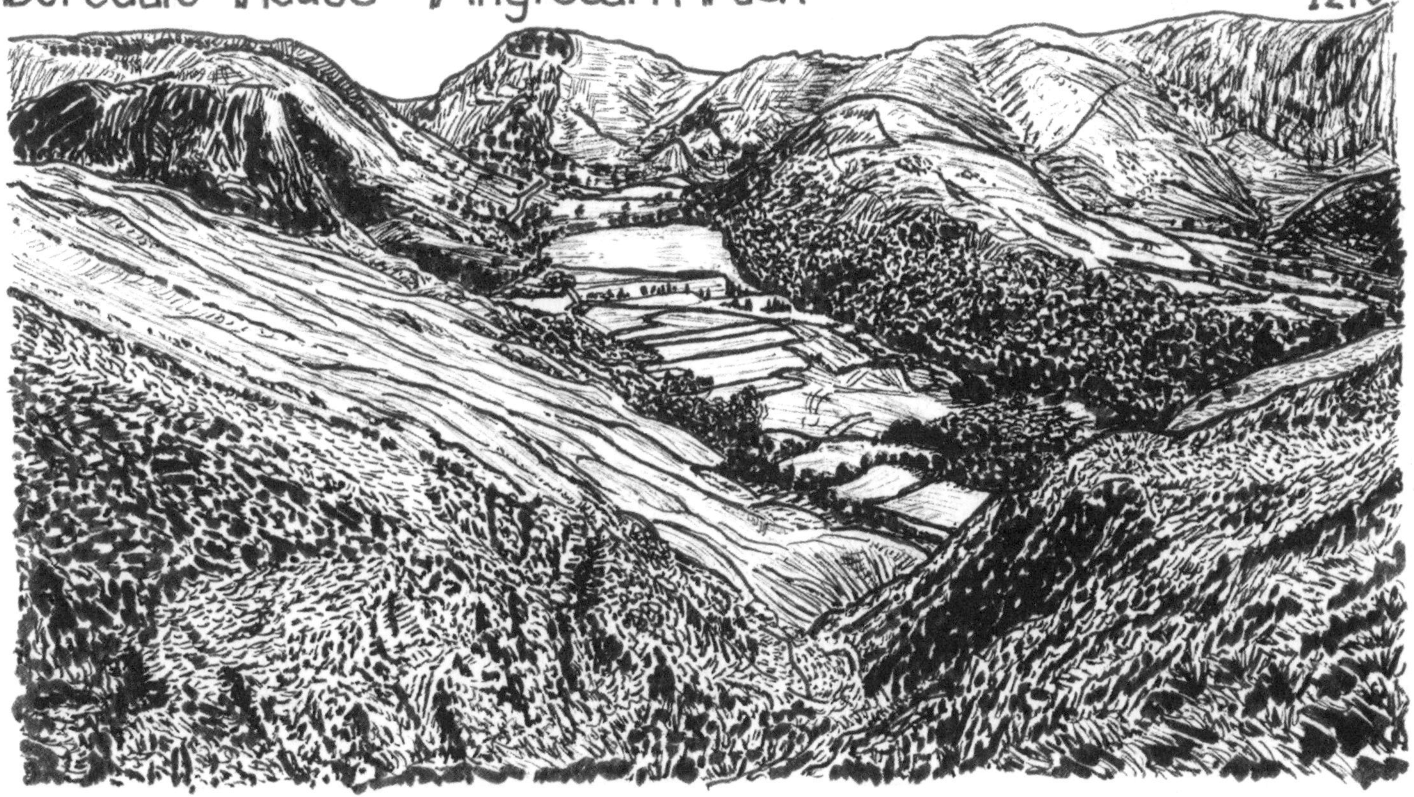

Angletarn ~ North West approach

1672'

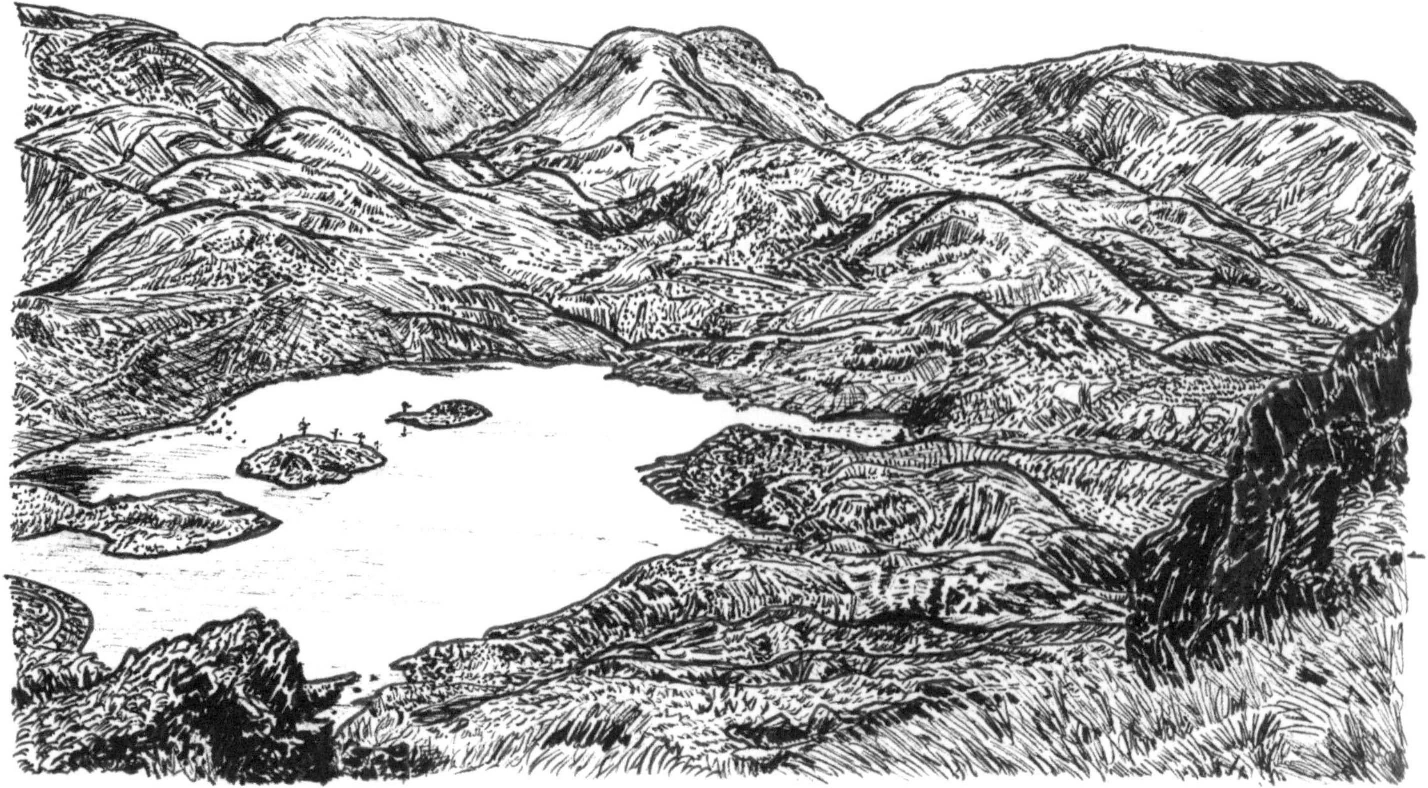

Angletarn~East Shore

1639′

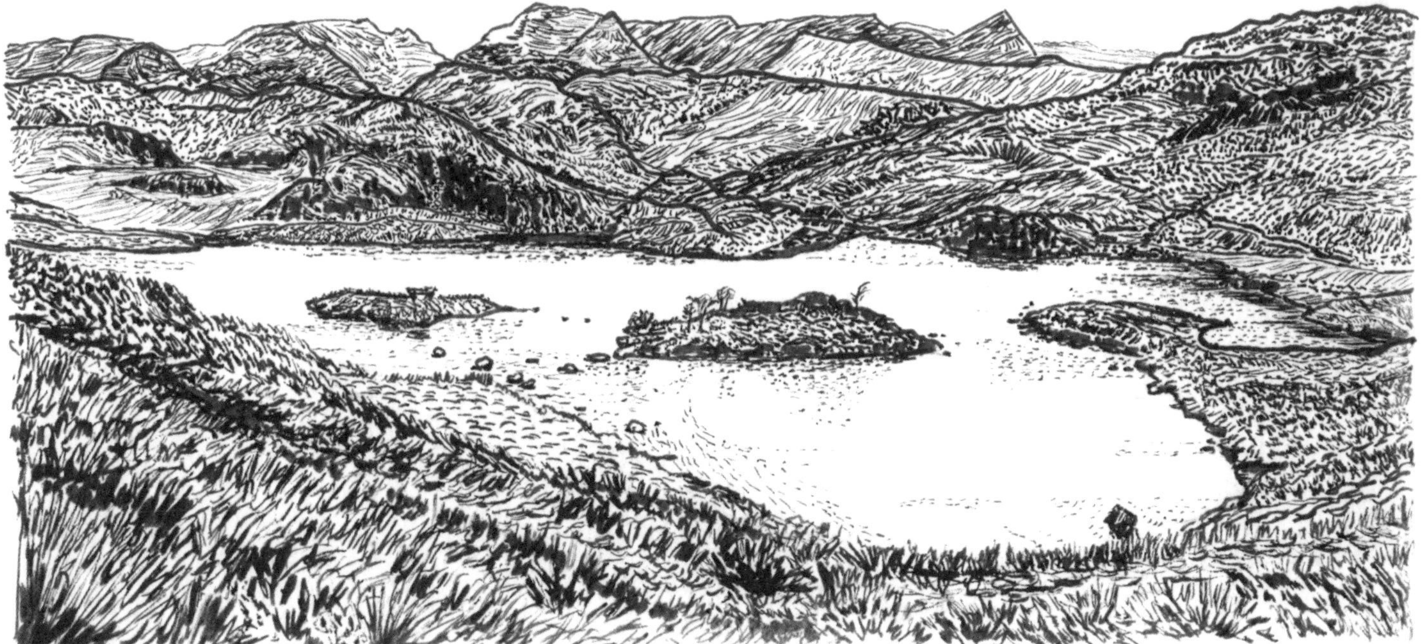

Angle Tarn

Angle Tarn is truly a gem, having a wow factor from all aspects. It is no ordinary tarn; the word tarn derives from the Norse for teardrop, tjorn, this being the classic shape of a tarn.

It is a tarn blessed with an intricate, treeless shoreline and two islets; its indented sheltered setting making it a favourite for wild camping and swimming.

Standing beside the tarn you are completely surrounded by the Helvellyn Massif to the west and south, the High Street range to the East, and immediately supervised by the Angletarn Pikes to the north.

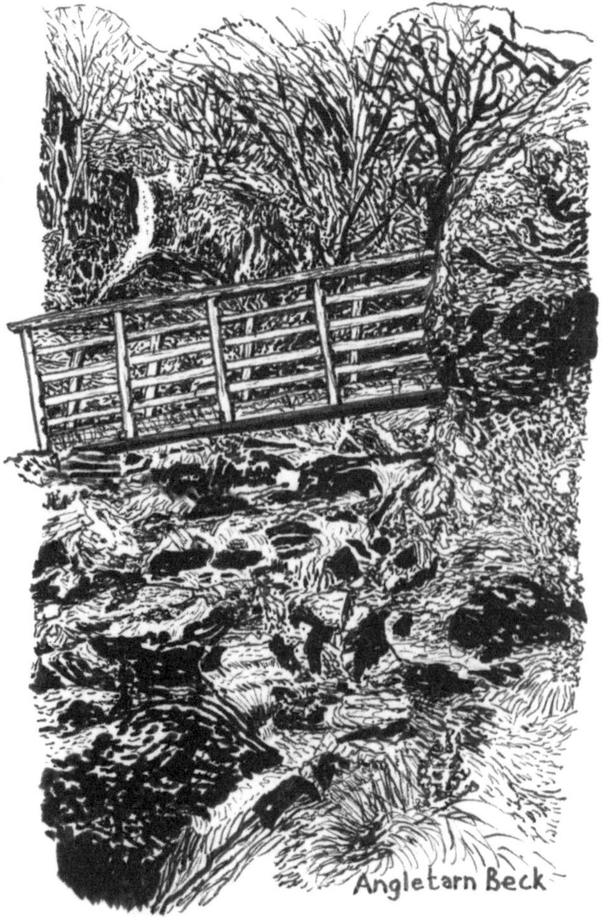

Angletarn Beck

Tarns in the Lakes

"the eyes of the mountains" William Heaton Cooper called them in his 1960 illustrated guide to 87 tarns. The number of tarns in the lakes is a matter of dispute and definition. From 1951-59 Colin Dodgson and Tim Tyson swam without the benefit of swimwear in 463 tarns and 144 small pools; they defined a tarn as any patch of water you could submerge in and swim a stroke or two. Dodgson said of their quest, "it's a good thing in life to have something to strive for".

In 1995 John and Anne Nuttall documented 335 tarns in their two volume guide to small mountain lakes.

Brock Crags

1846'

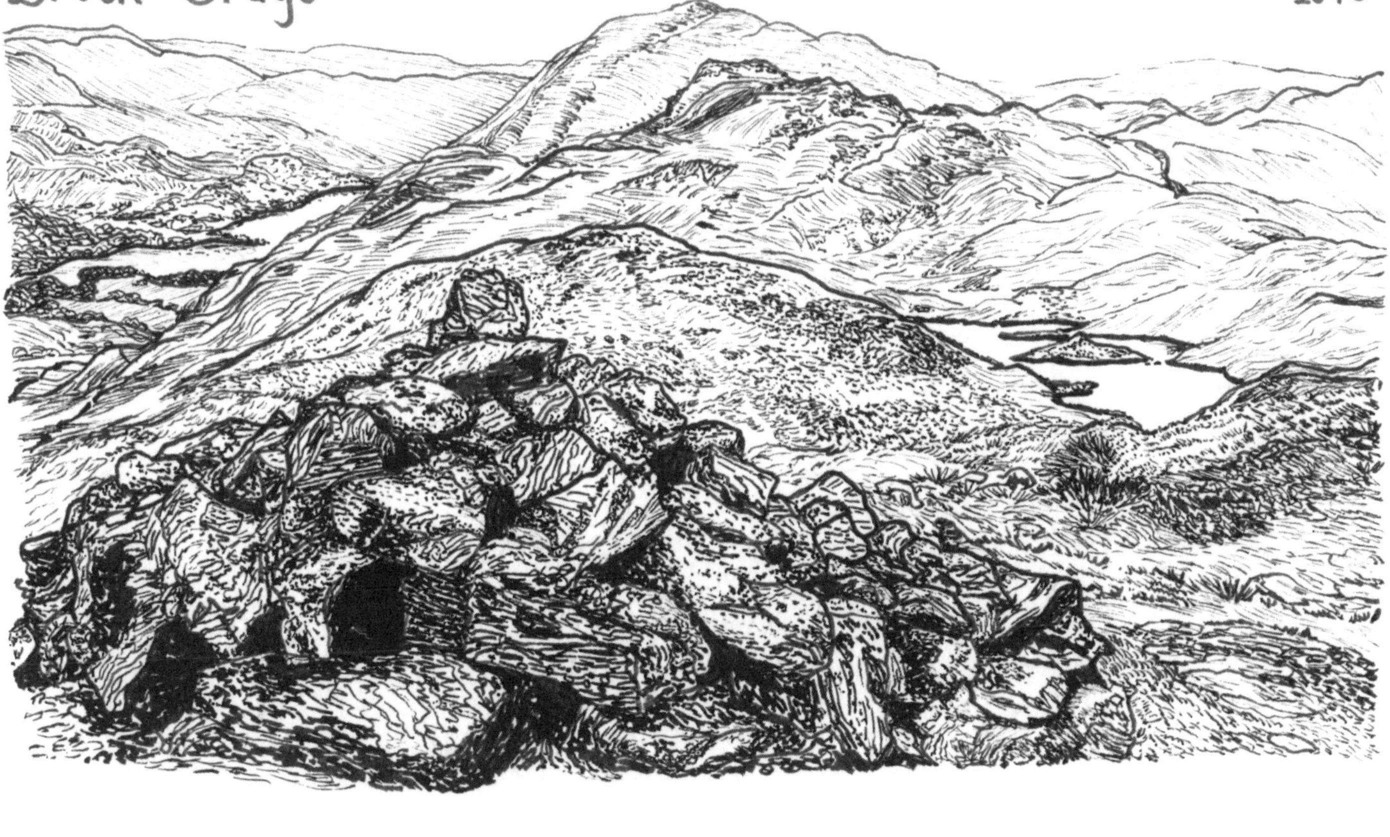

Rest Dodd - North of Summit

2000′

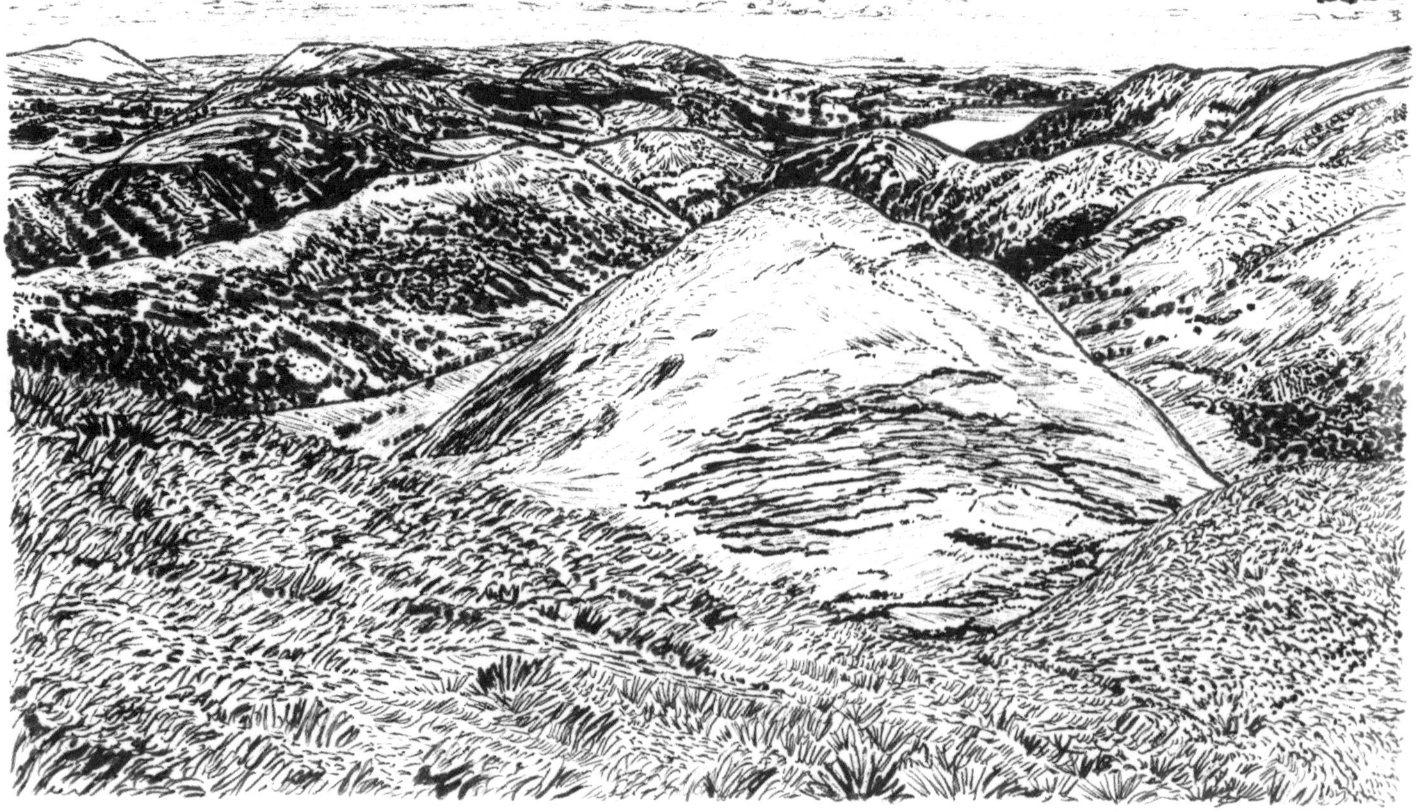

The Nab

1803′

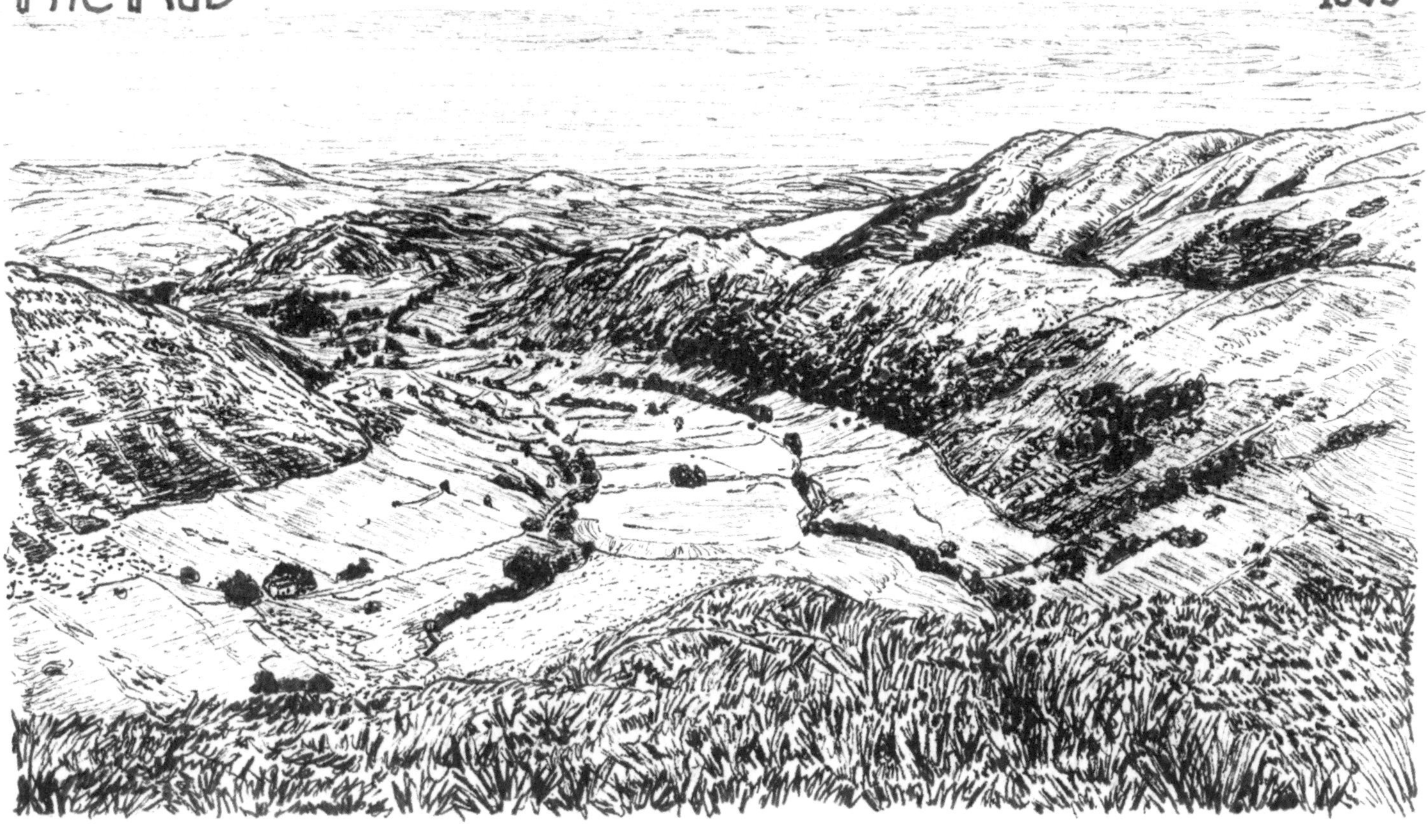

Gray Crag - North of Summit

1902'

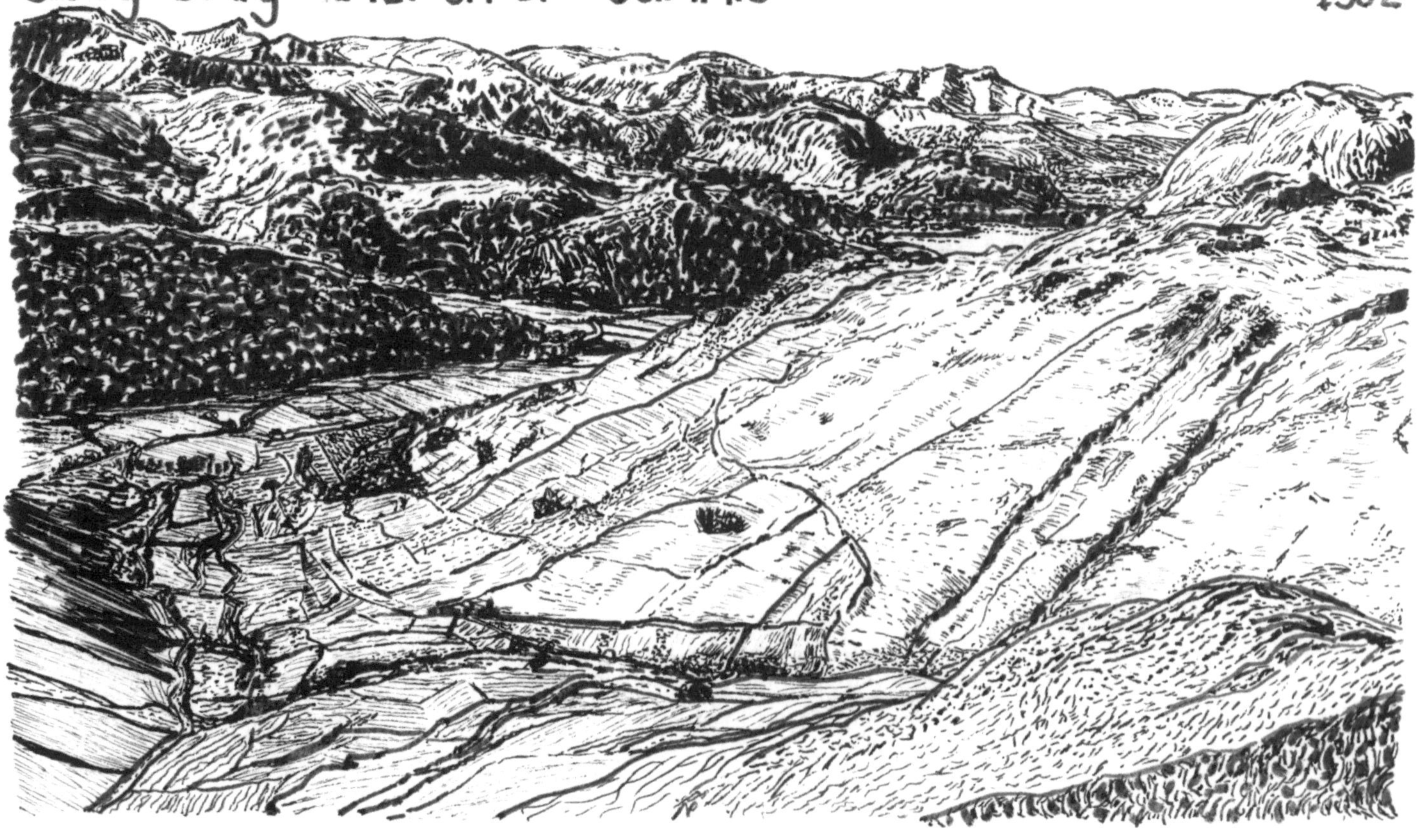

Hartsop Dodd - North of Summit

1967'

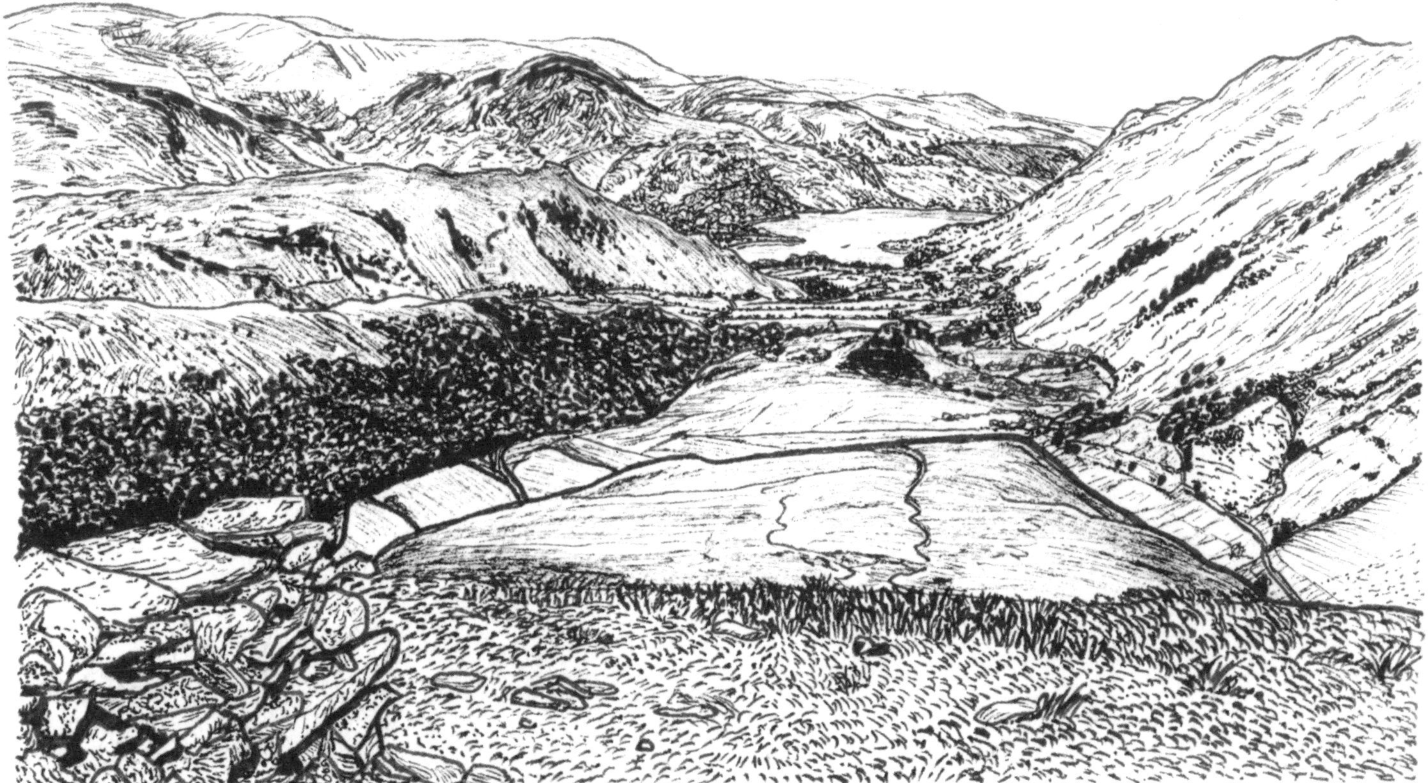

Caudale Moor Summit - West Cairn

2459'

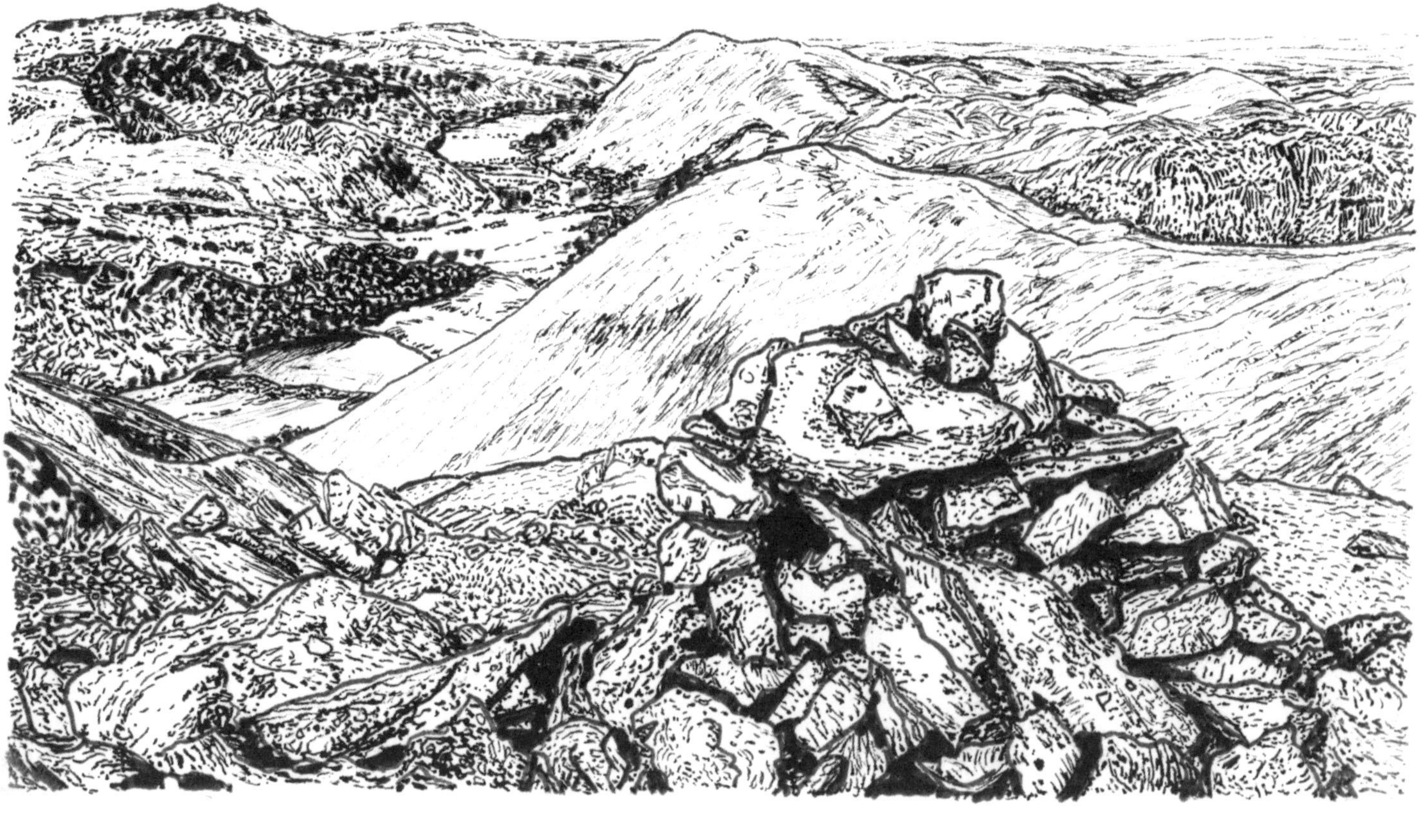

Red Screes - Trig Point

2539′

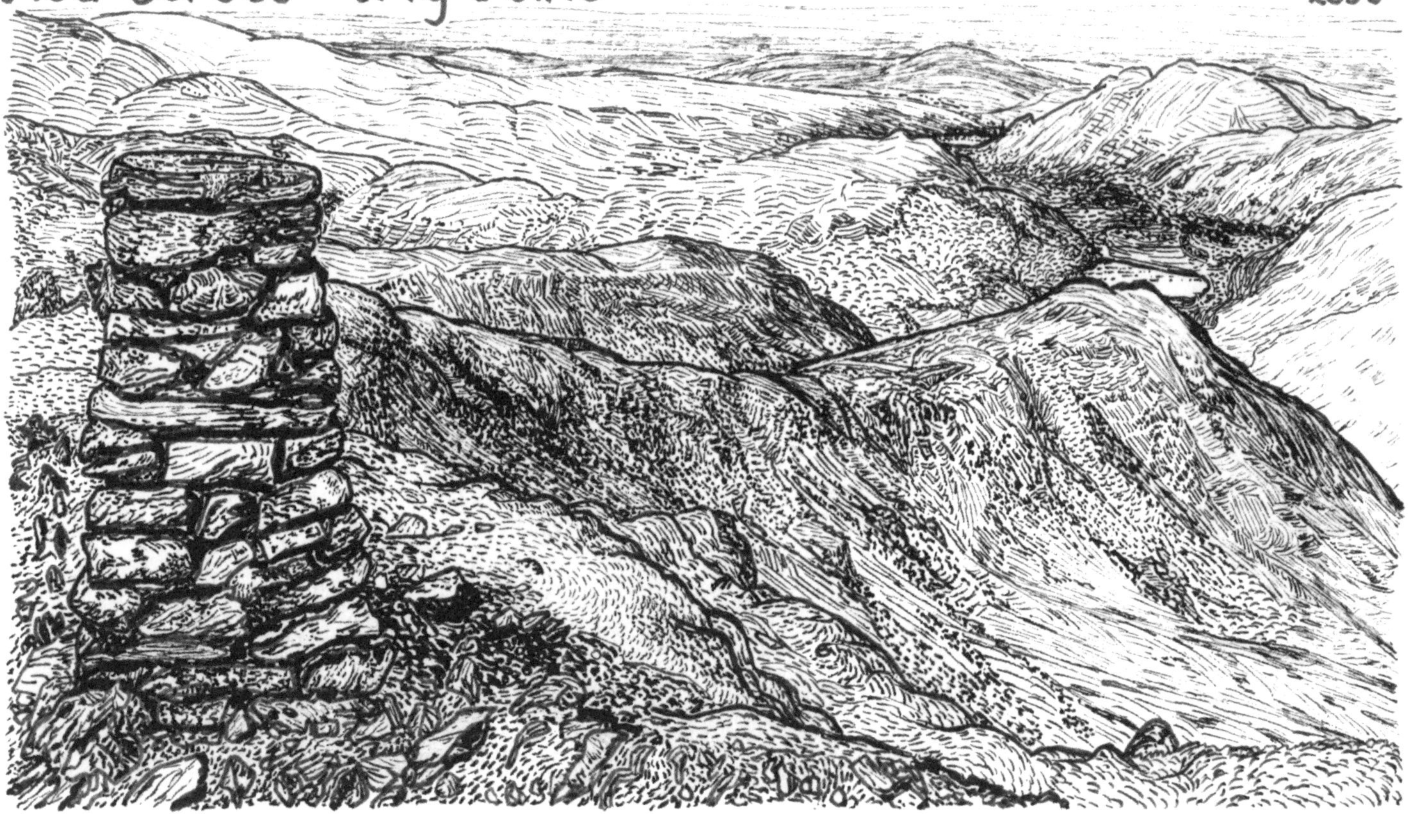

The Kirk-Stone

1449′

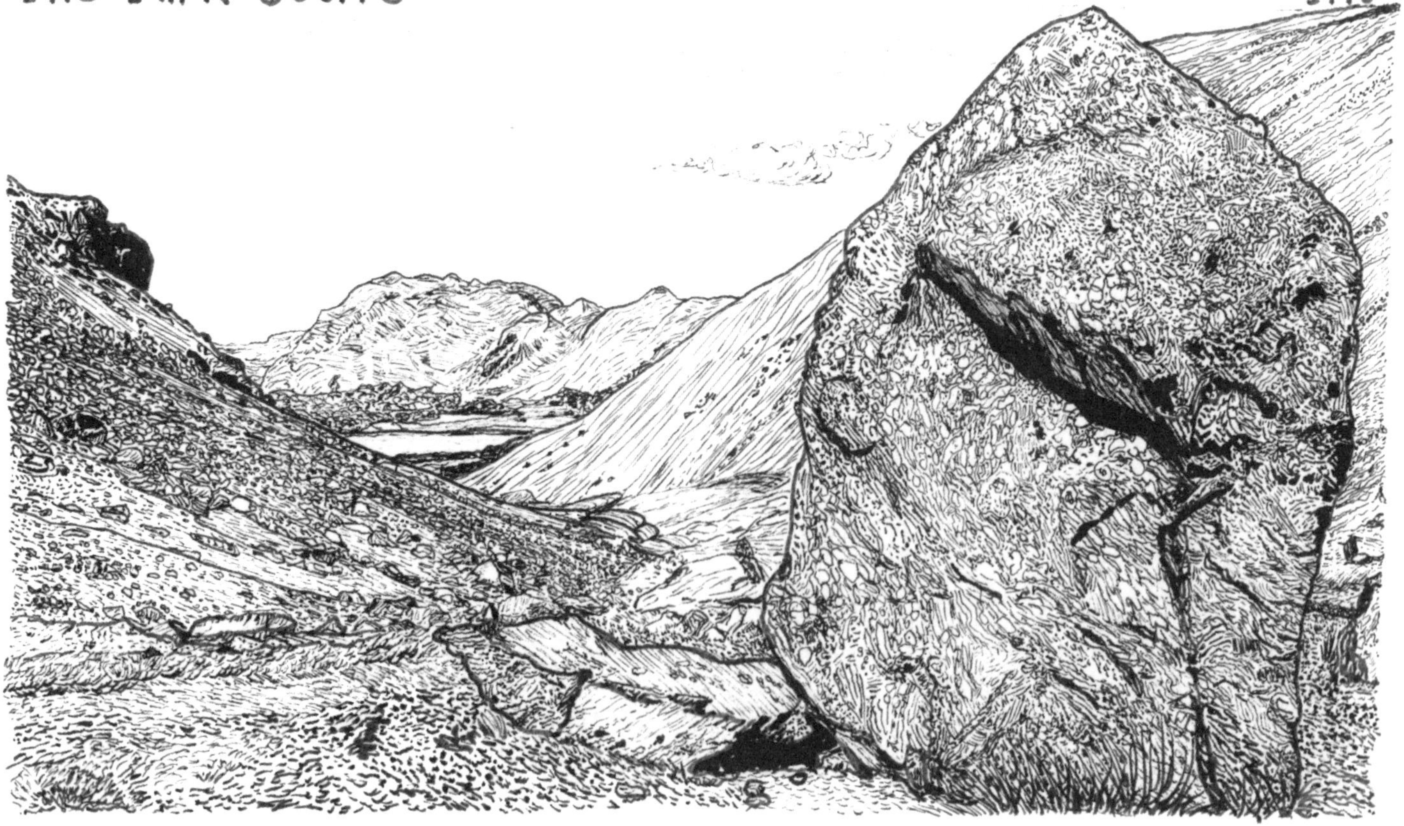

Kirkstone Pass

The Kirk (norse meaning: church) Stone which the pass is named after can be seen a few hundred yards from the summit on the north side. It is an ancient trading and packhorse route, the threshold separating Ullswater and Windermere. An historic source of raw materials, notably green slate, arrow and axe heads; the last slate was mined here in 2012.

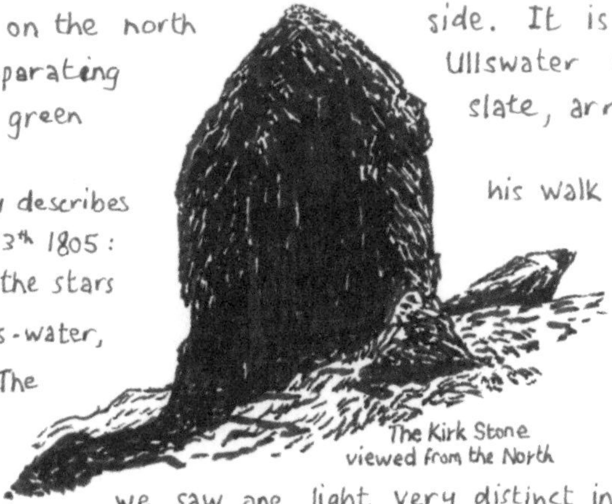

The Kirk Stone viewed from the North

Wordsworth beautifully describes his walk with Dorothy over the pass from Patterdale to Grasmere on November 13th 1805: "a fine evening; the seven stars close to the mountain-top; all the stars seemed brighter than usual. The steeps were reflected in Brothers-water, and, above the lake, appeared like enormous black perpendicular walls. The Kirkstone torrents had been swoln by the rains, and now filled the mountain pass with their roaring, which added to the solemnity of our walk. Behind us, when we had climbed to a very great height, we saw one light very distinct in the vale, like a large red star – a solitary one in the gloomy region. The cheerfulness of the scene was in the sky above us. Reached home a little before midnight." Here are a few lines from the third verse of Wordsworth's 'The Pass of Kirkstone':

"List to those shriller notes! – that march
Perchance was on the blast,
When through this Height's inverted arch,
Rome's earliest legion passed!
– They saw, adventurously impelled,
And older eyes than theirs beheld,
This block – and yon, whose Church-like frame
Gives to the savage Pass its name,
Aspiring Road! That lov'st to hide
Thy daring in a vapoury bourn,
Not seldom may the hour return
When thou shalt be my guide:"

Red Pit Car Park - Kirkstone Pass

& 1439'

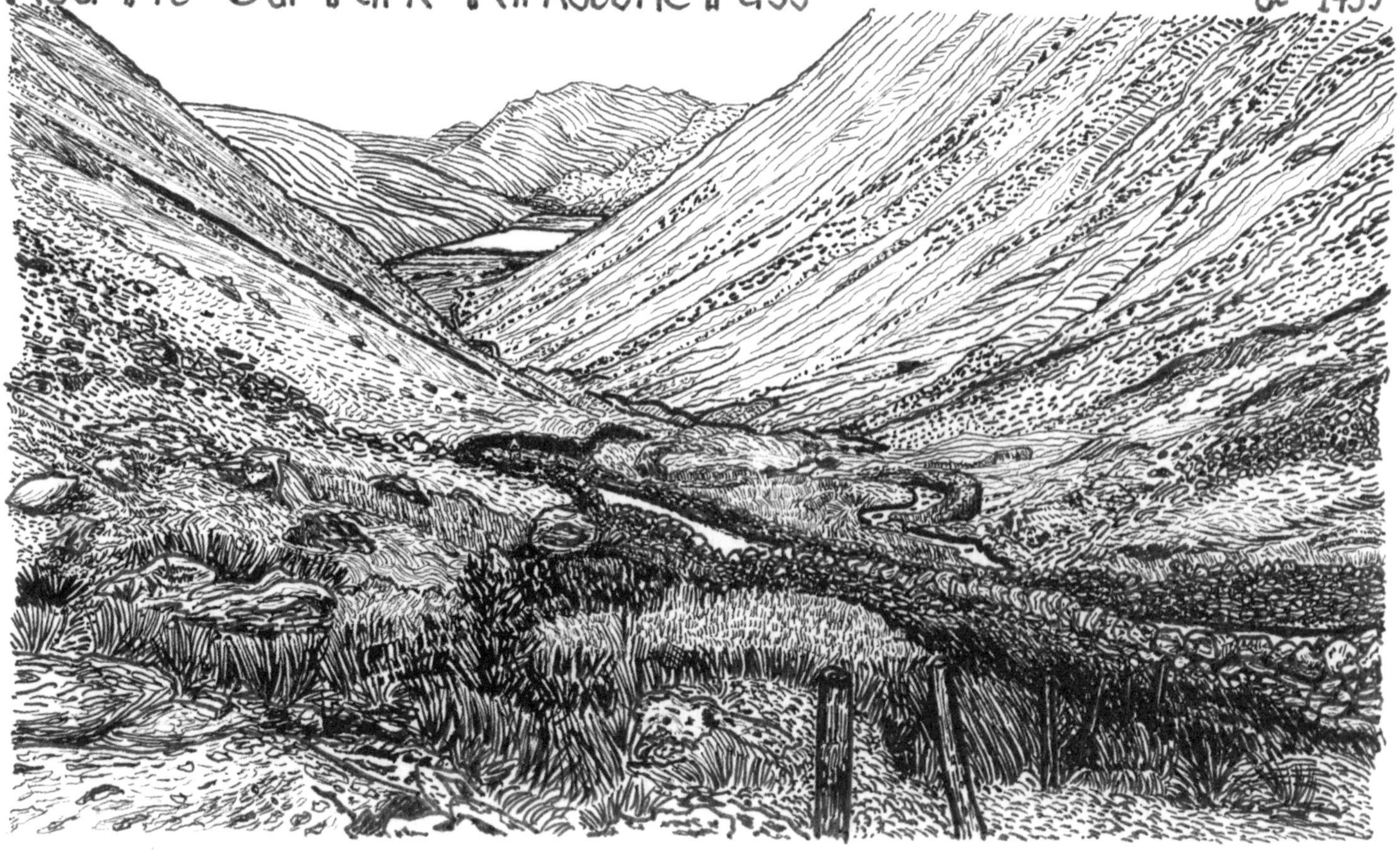

Kirkstone Pass

Kirkstone Pass delivers dramatic scenery, whether seen on foot, cycle or car.

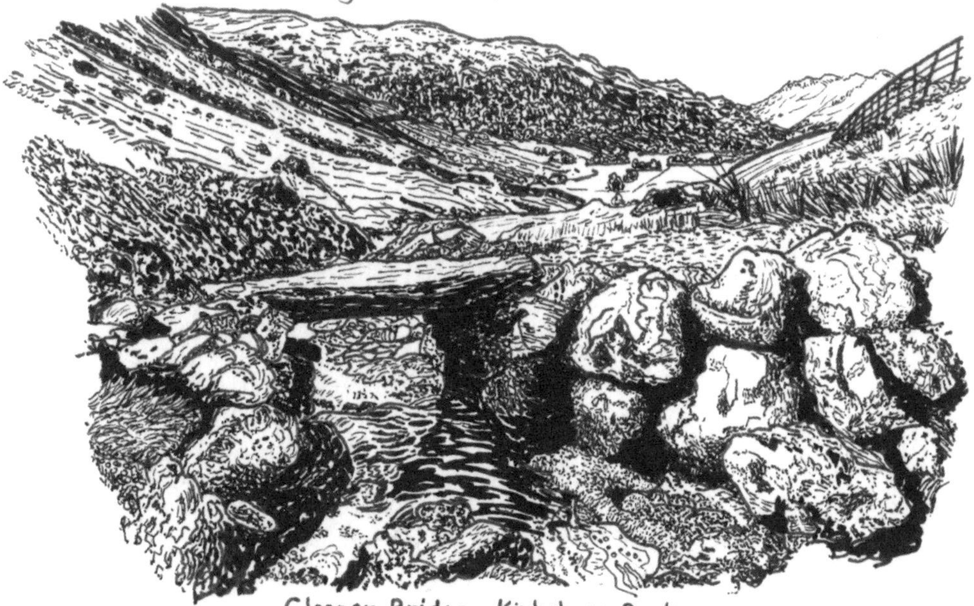

Clapper Bridge - Kirkstone Beck

The road and wriggling beck intertwine down the ravines' nadir,
The road surface and stone walls are constantly on the losing side of man versus nature,
Such is the hostility of the winters here.

One day like this... February 28, 2019

Eight degrees celsius, crystal clear skies, the mist on Ullswater stirs, swirls and slowly evaporates in the weak Spring morning sun. Flask, compass, cheese and pickle sandwiches, flapjack, Pooley Gingerbridge, foil blankets, emergency food, map, waterproof coat, gloves, buff, water. Stopped off at Granny D's in Pooley Bridge for a coffee, waiting for the mist to rise. Physically excited at the prospect of a day rambling, bimbling and exploring.

Drove slowly and mindfully beside the lake, Sandwick Bay (Sannick - local pronunciation) across the the water was stunning; like a theatre set with the mist separating the planes of land. Stopped off at Patterdale Post office to buy a paper. Parked at Cow Bridge with the honesty box; passed two people, then that was it, no one else until Priest's Hole two hours later. Took photos of the gnarled trees enveloping Dovedale Beck; then climbed the valley leaving the treeline behind, taking the stone staircase elevating me to the foot of Priest's Hole. No signs on the fells, went the wrong way; found the right route thanks to 3G and a Youtube video. Ideas, thoughts, flowing and coursing through the mind.

Priest's Hole, an eagles' eyrie of a cave; protected, safe, a commanding vista, and a shovel to assist with the conveniences. Continued up to the crest heading to Dove Crag, hitting a ceiling of cloud before the summit. Visibility nil. Stopped: turned around dropping back into Dovedale and clarity. What good fortune, I had missed so much; the stunning staircase weaving its way down past huge erratic rocks shrouded in cloaks of Klimt like lichen. Emerald pools jewel the crystal stream down to the valley floor and the safety of home.

(written to the soundtrack of Van Morrison's 'Coney Island' playing in my head)

Dovedale

724'

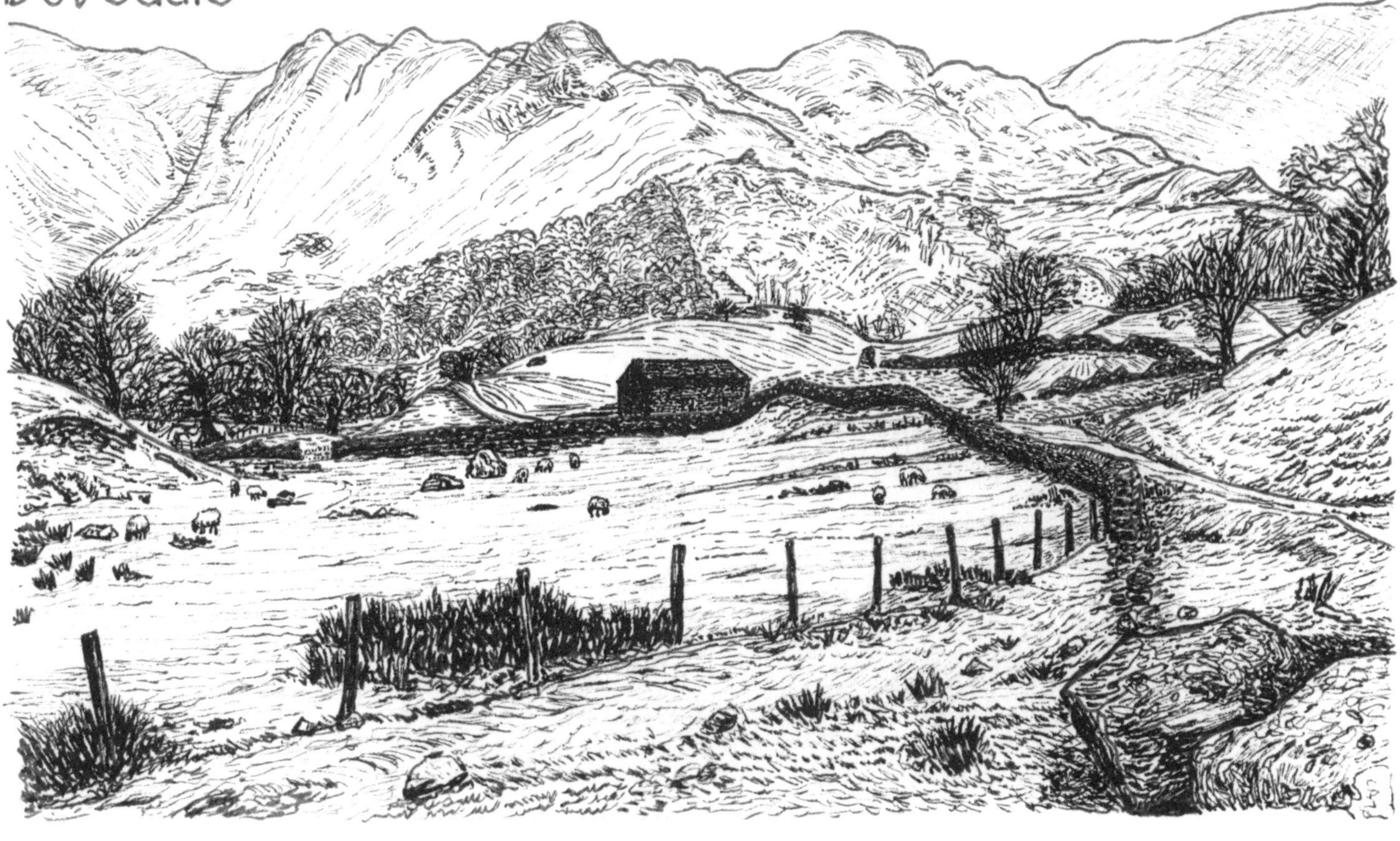

Dovedale

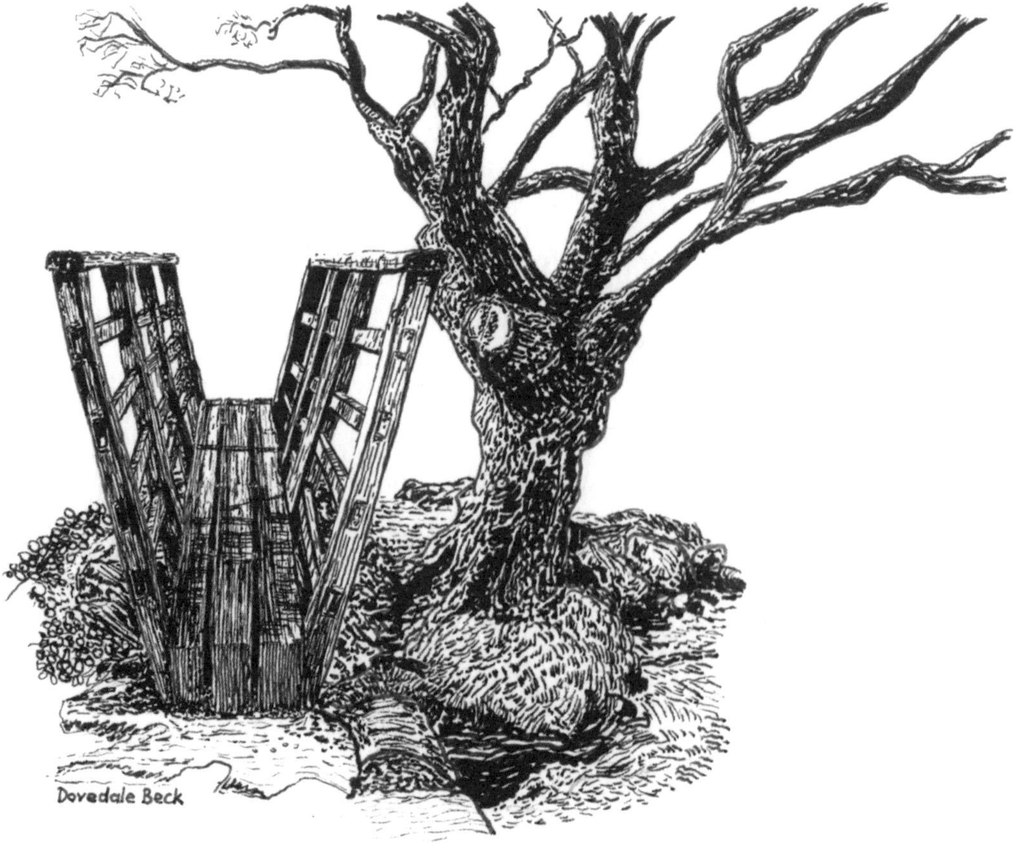

Dovedale

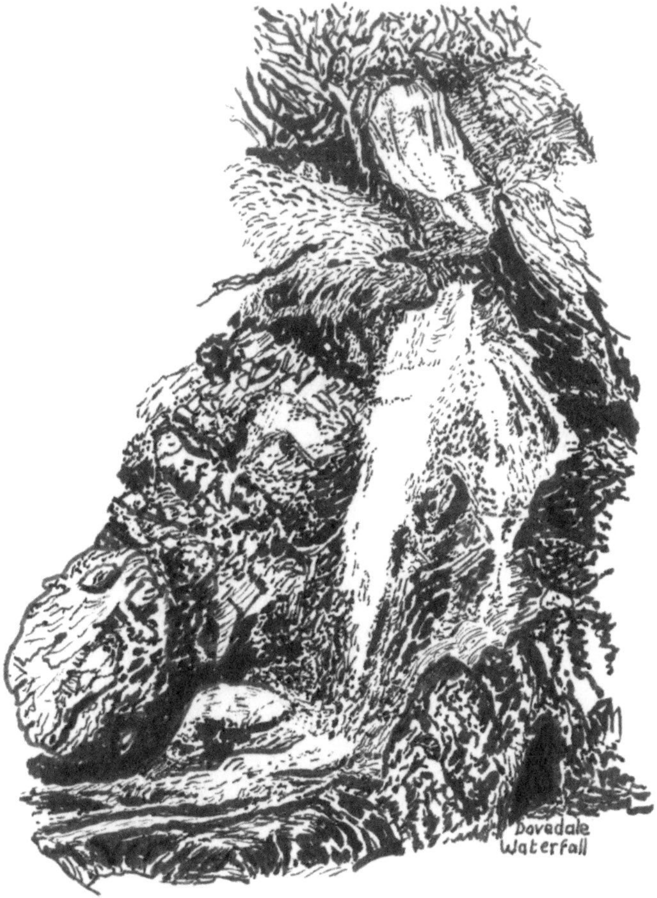

Priest's Hole - Dove Crag

2262'

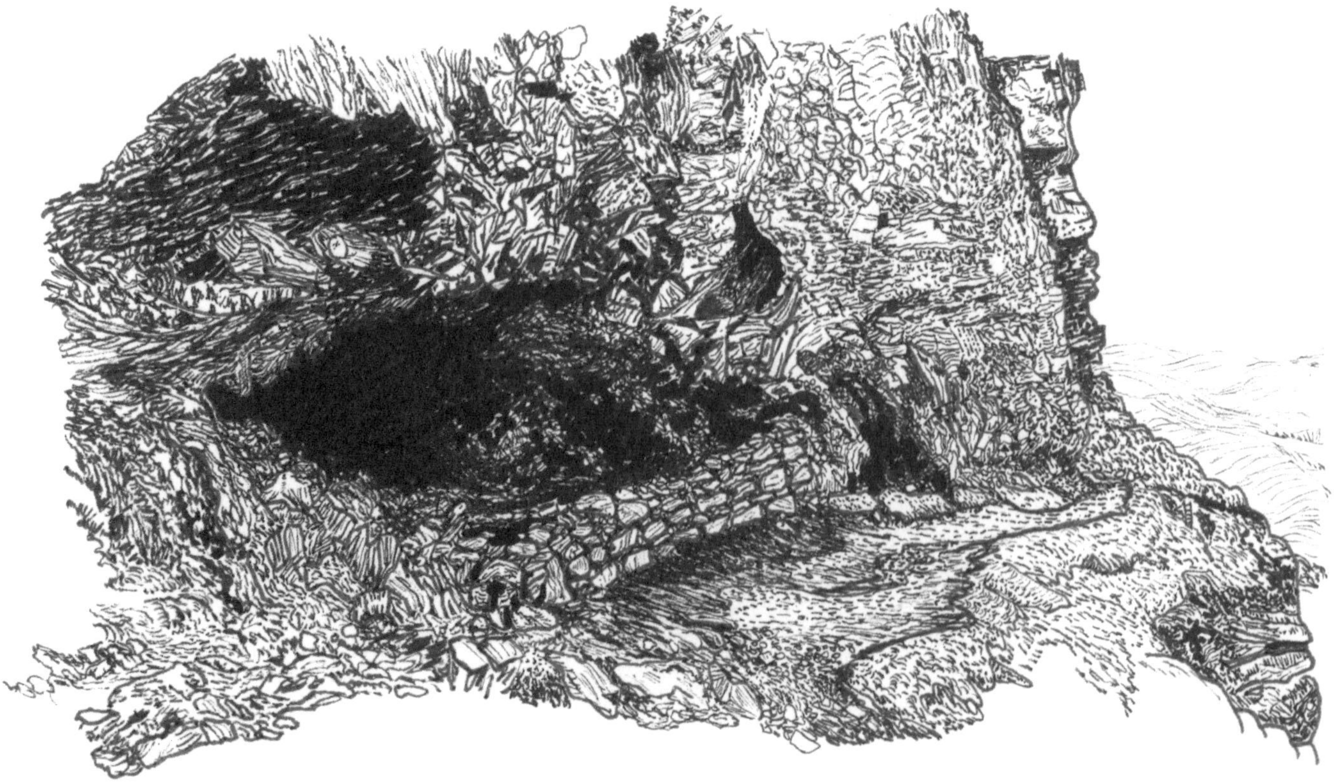

Dove Crag - East of Summit

2495′

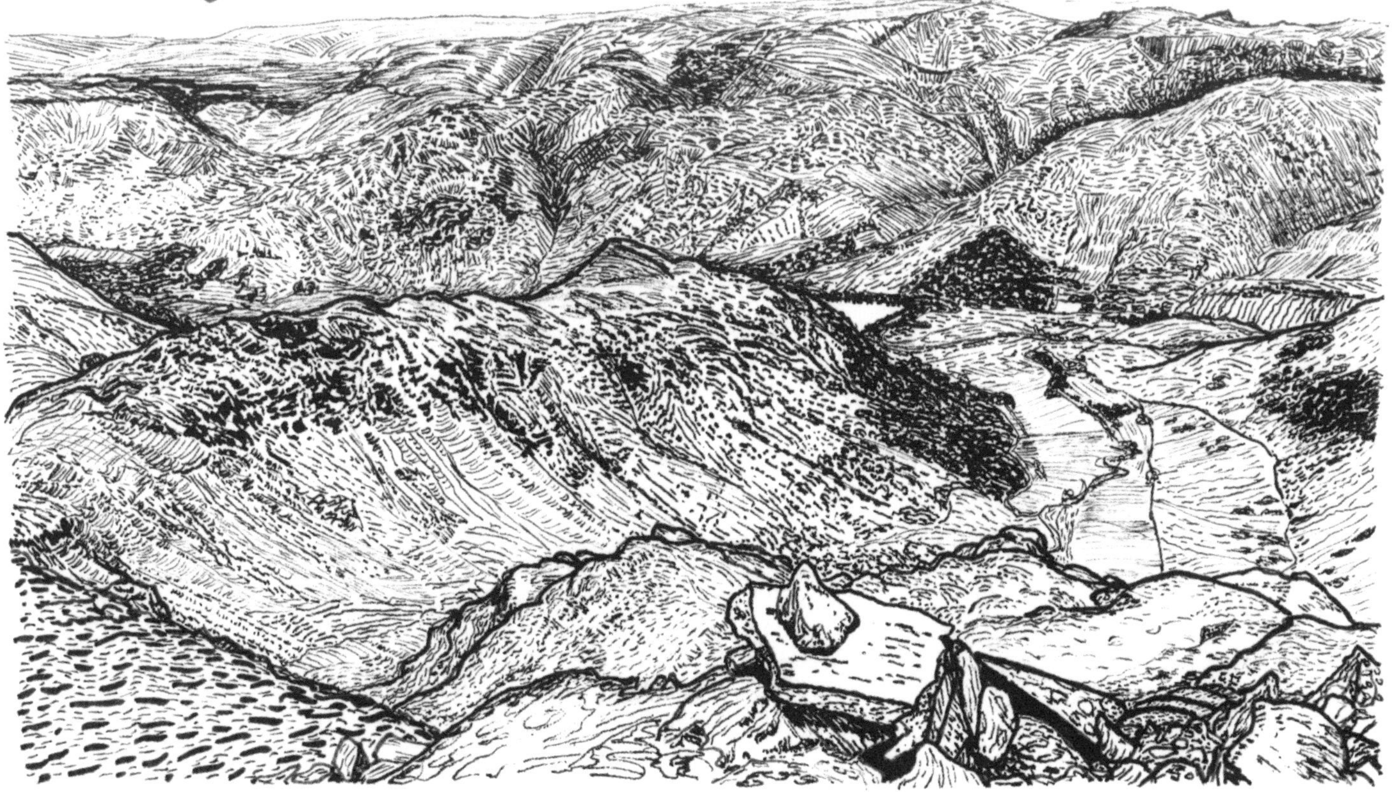

Patterdale

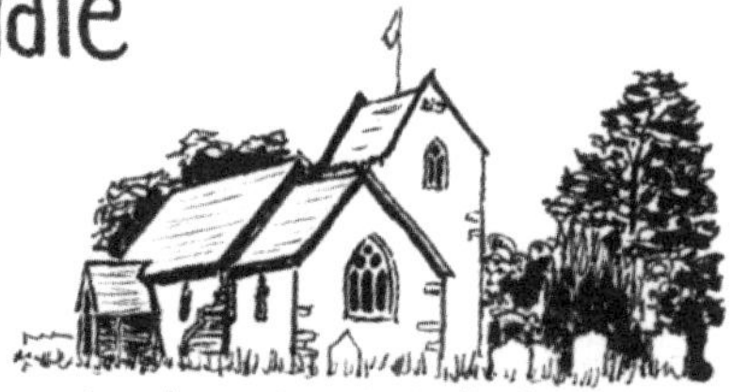

St. Patrick's Church built in 1853

Wainwright based himself at the Old Water View Hotel here whilst researching his Coast to Coast route.

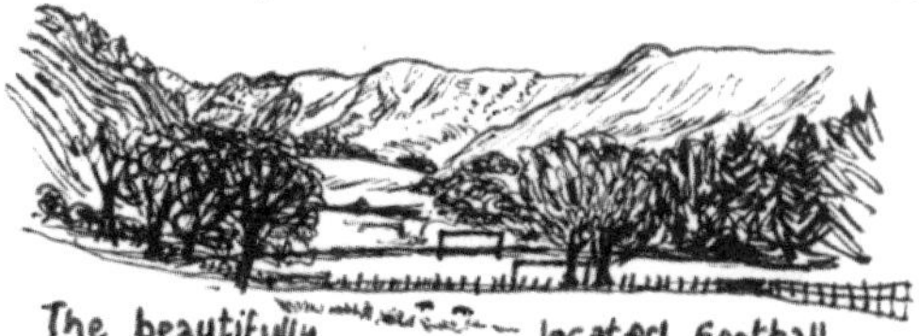

The beautifully located football pitch nestled in Grisedale valley bottom behind St. Patrick's church.

Wordsworth stayed at the White Lion Inn on 10th November 1805, "At the breakfast table tidings reached us of the death of Lord Nelson, and of the victory at Trafalgar... we were shocked to hear that the bells had been ringing joyously at Penrith to celebrate the triumph."

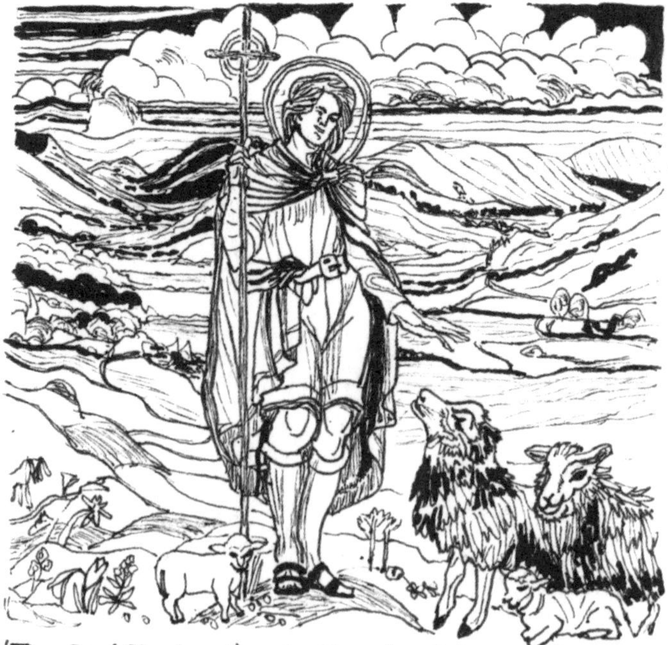

'The Good Shepherd' embroidered wall hanging featuring local scenery in St. Patrick's Church Patterdale. This is by Ann Macbeth who lived in the area from 1920-1948. Also hanging in the Church is a copy of Ann Macbeth's internationally acclaimed Nativity embroidery. Ann is named on The Artist's Seat installation nearby.

Patterdale

♿ 485′

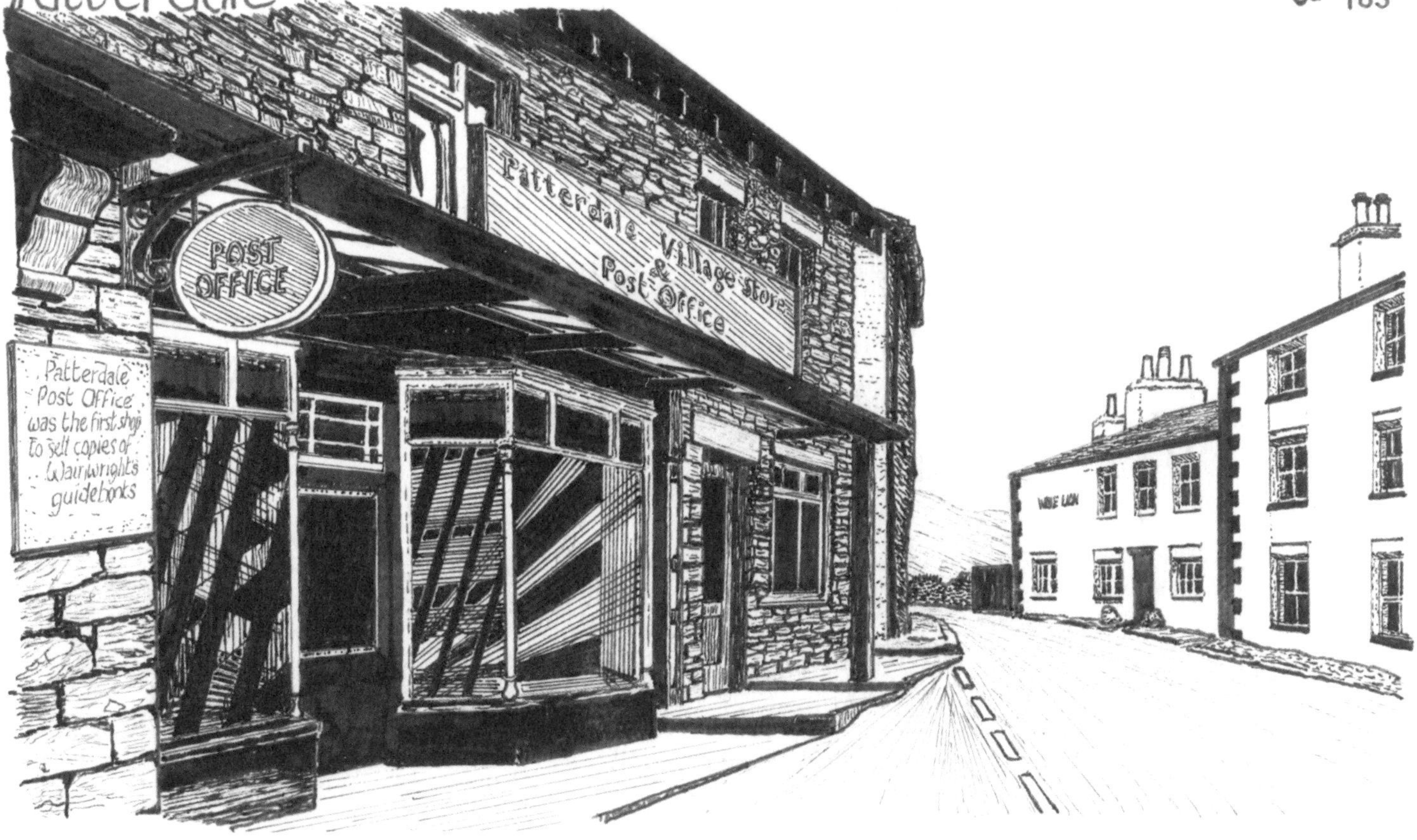

Arnison Crag - North of Oxford Crag

787′

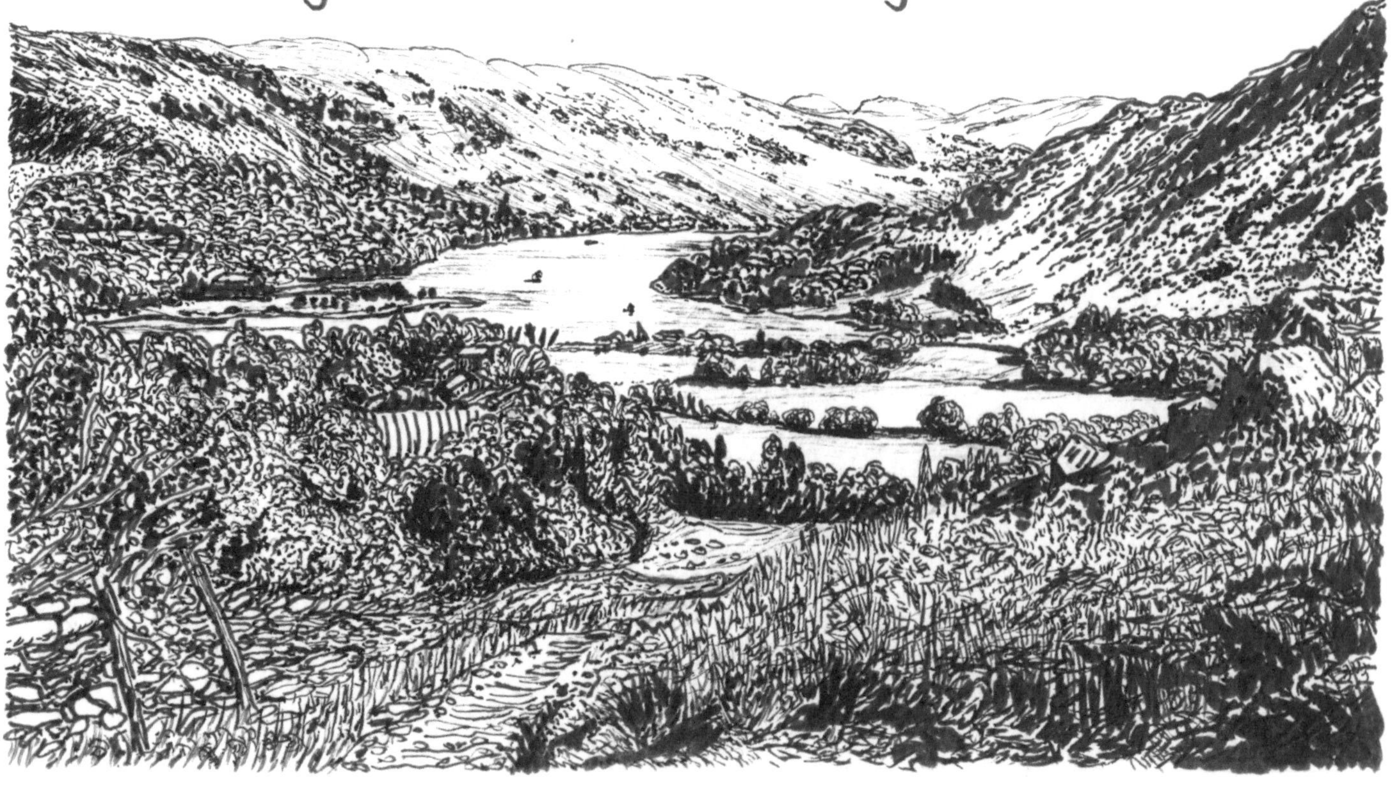

Arnison Crag ~ north west of summit

1344′

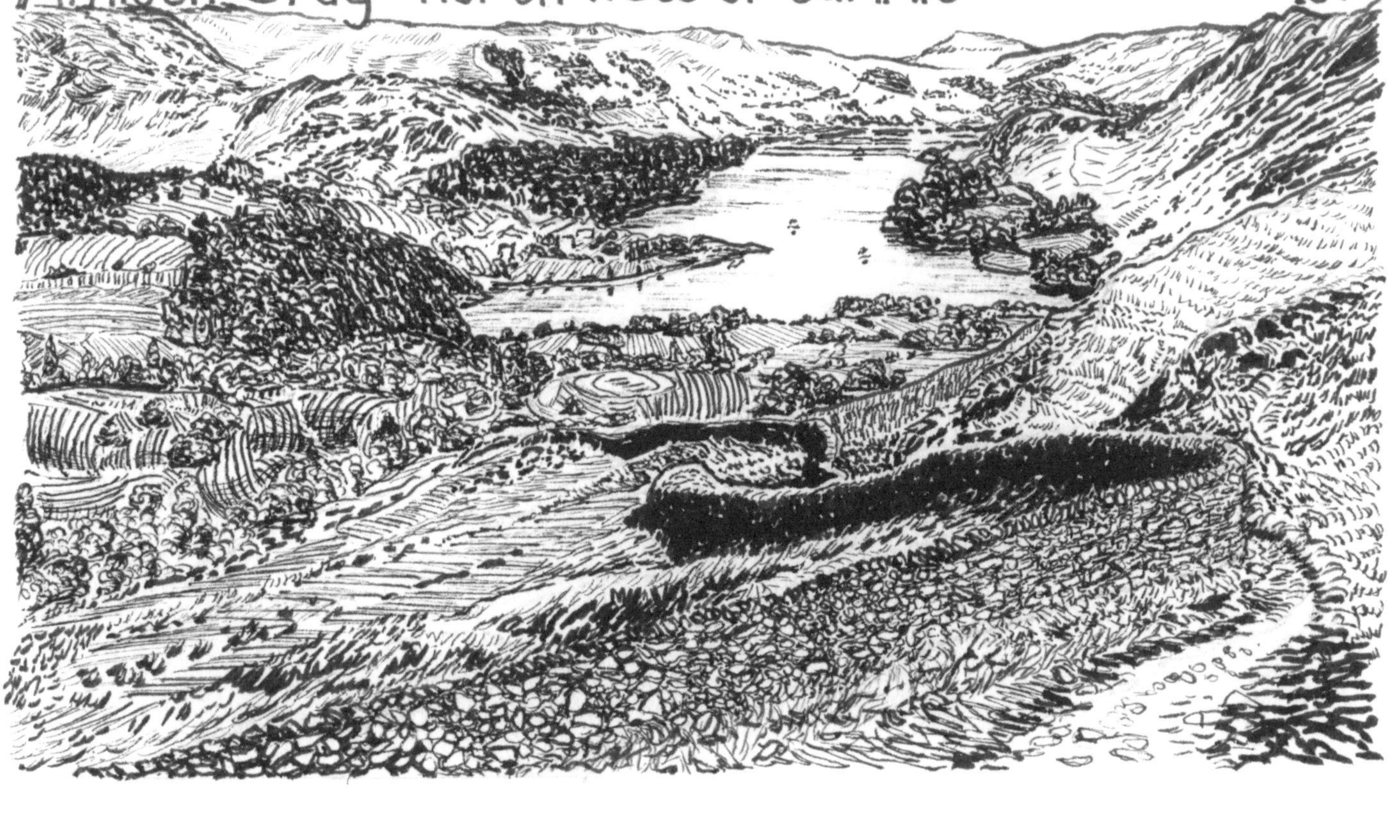

St. Sunday Crag - north ridge

2571'

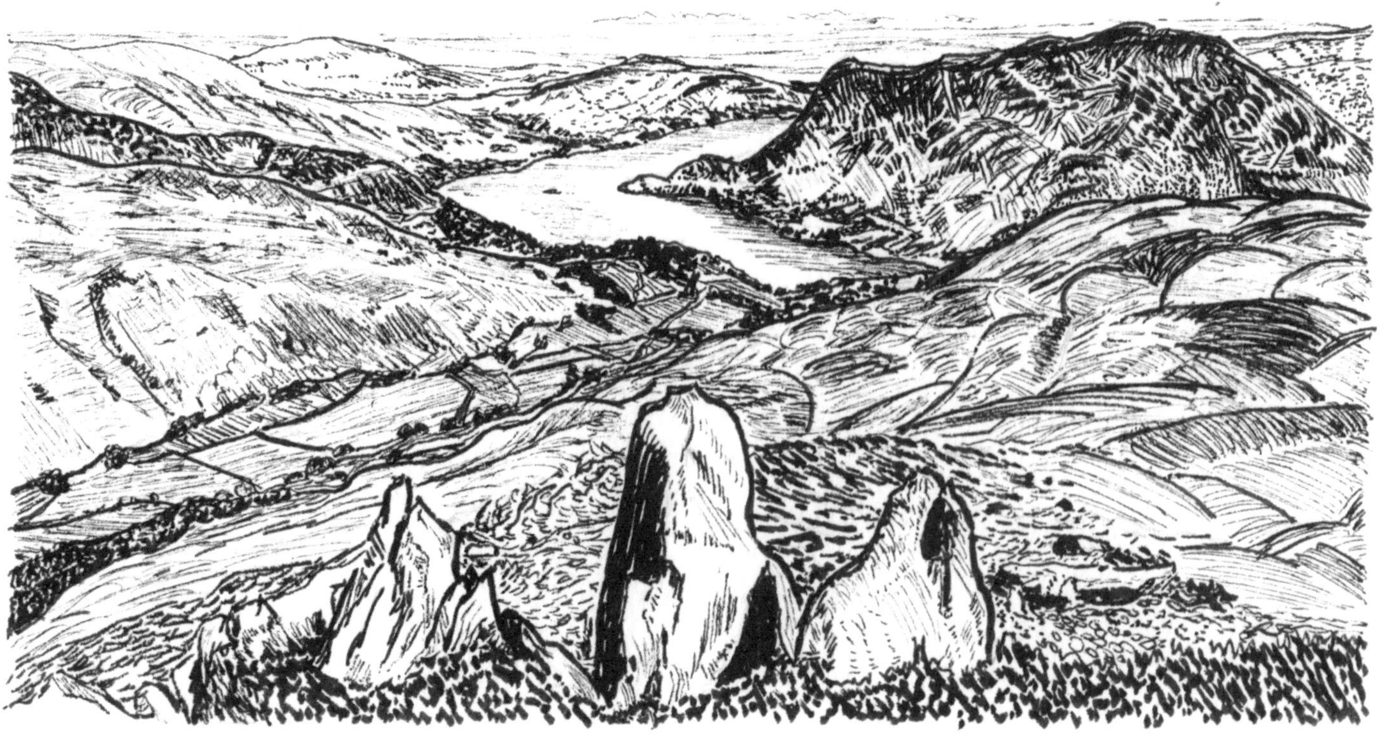

Deepdale Hause

2426′

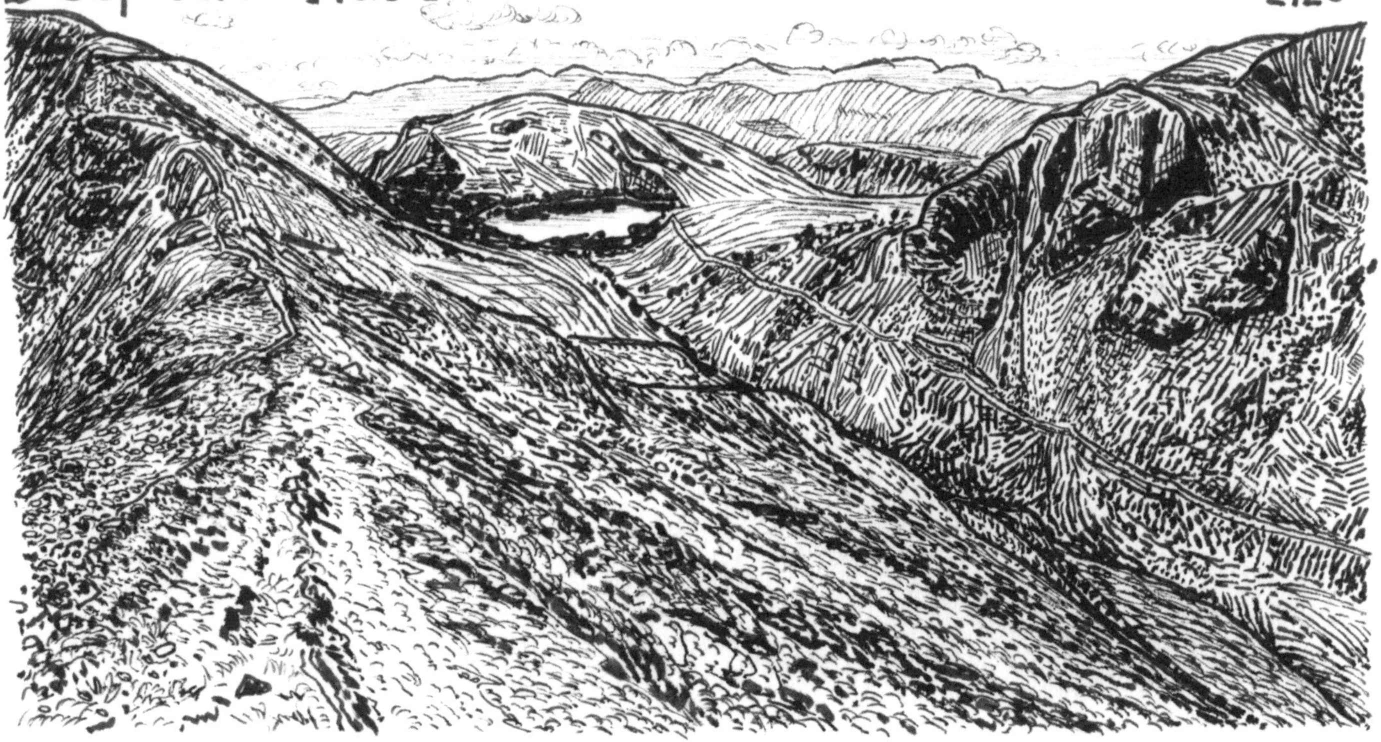

Patterdale / Glenridding

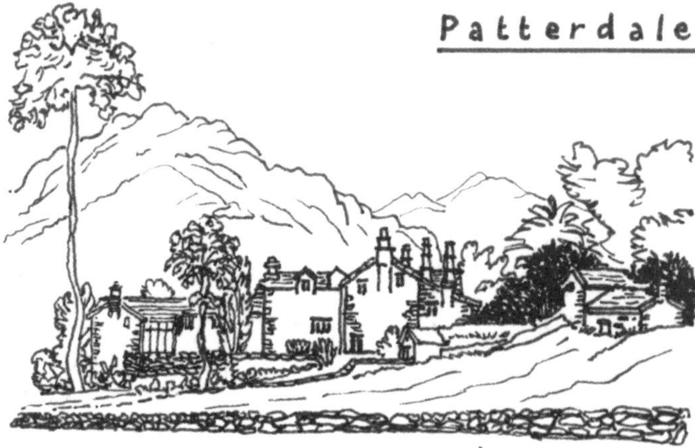

The 'Palace of Patterdale'

(from an original watercolour by Joseph Farrington (1747-1821))

John Mounsey purchased Patterdale Hall in 1624. Later, during the Civil War of 1642-51 he led a band of (Patter) Dalesmen to Stybarrow Crag to repel the Scots who were on route to fight Charles I in Preston. Henceforth Mounsey and their first born male descendants were known as 'The King of Patterdale'. The property stayed in the family until 1821.

The Patterdale Hall site is now used as a centre for children's education.

St. Patrick lived at some time between AD390 and 540. The legend is that he was shipwrecked on the Duddon sands, made his way to Ullswater and performed baptisms at the Well here. Thereafter it was known as St. Patrick's Dale, and subsequently Patterdale. The Well Spring now seen was built in 1787 making use of four of the original stones to preserve its Christian antiquity.

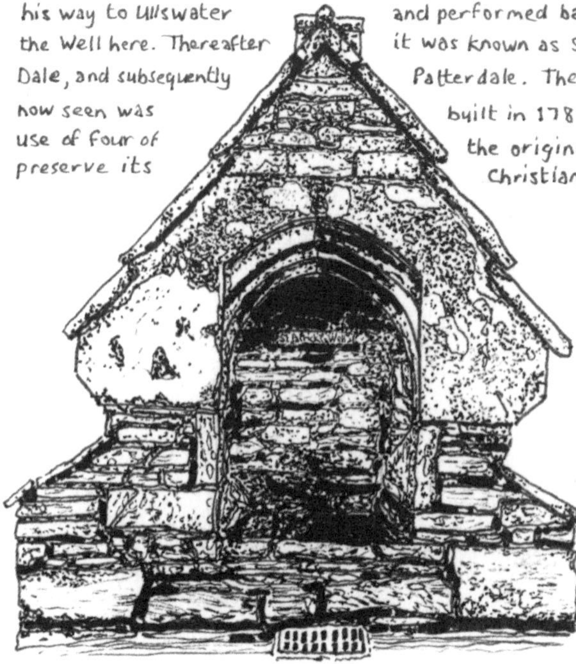

St. Patrick's Well

Patterdale to Glenridding Path

♿ 482′

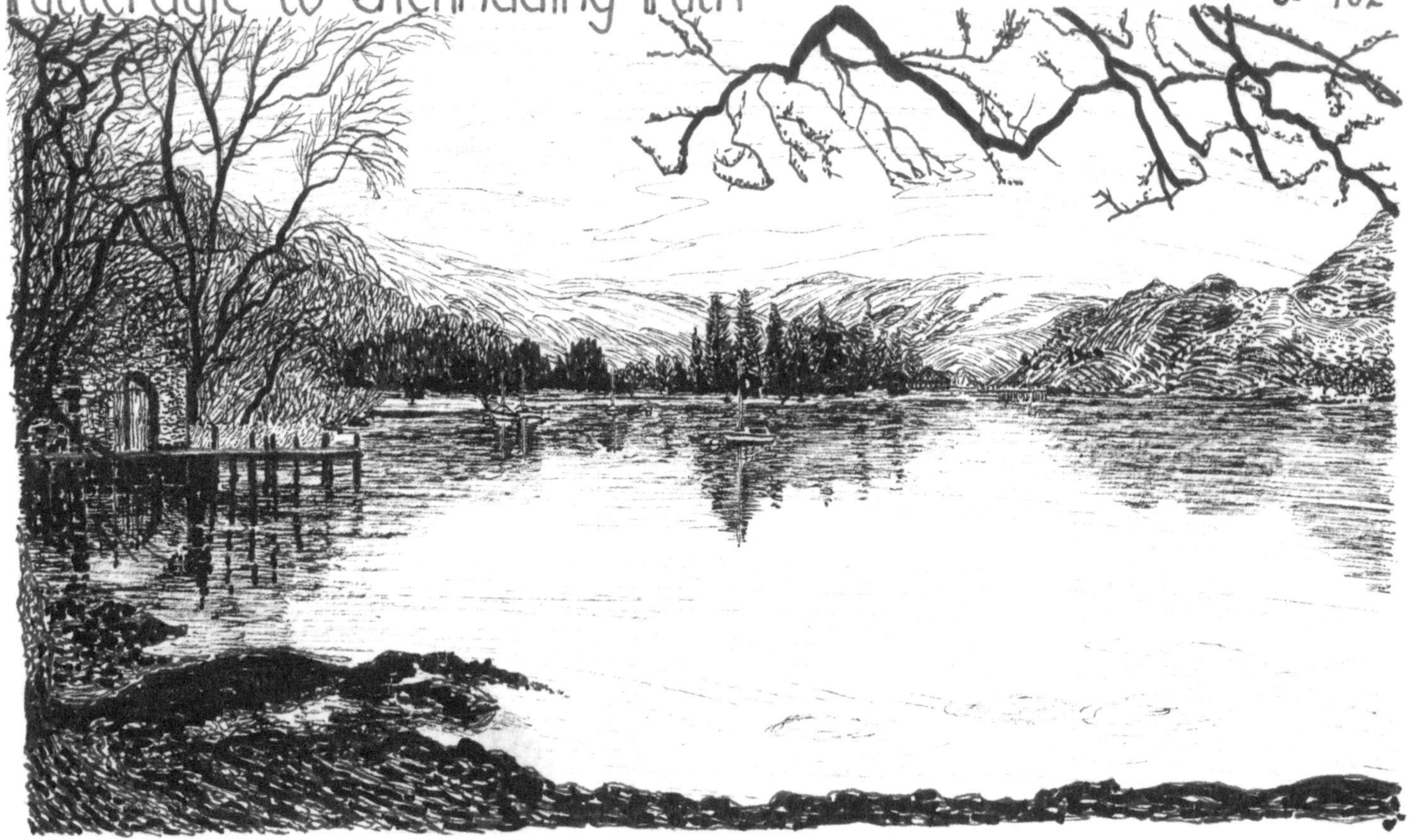

Mankind

Mining

The unique geology of the Lake District created many valuable deposits, a massive array of metals, minerals and fuels; the most notable being Iron, Copper, Lead, Silver, Coal, Graphite, Slate, Wolfram, Gold, Jasper and Garnet. Mankind has exploited these resources since the Stone Age. It was the 1500's when mining started to have a huge impact on the district. The famous Seathwaite wad mines began in the 1540's; wad was also known as black lead, plumbago and graphite; it is an incredibly versatile form of carbon, highly-prized for casting cannon balls, for crucibles in metal production, rustproofing, sheep marking and pencil production. Seathwaite was the best wad mine in the world. By the 1560's Keswick had six smelting plants and was the largest mining town in Britain. In 1564 Queen Elizabeth I granted a charter allowing skilled German miners to exploit the metal rich Newlands Valley. As mining boomed so did the demand for charcoal and wood for smelting, and tree trunks for pit props; in a few decades the whole area was denuded of trees. In the 1700's the gas flares from the west coast under sea coal mines became tourist attractions. Farming like mining was booming in the 1700's; the Enclosure Acts heralded the start of stone walling in the valley bottoms and beyond throughout Lakeland.

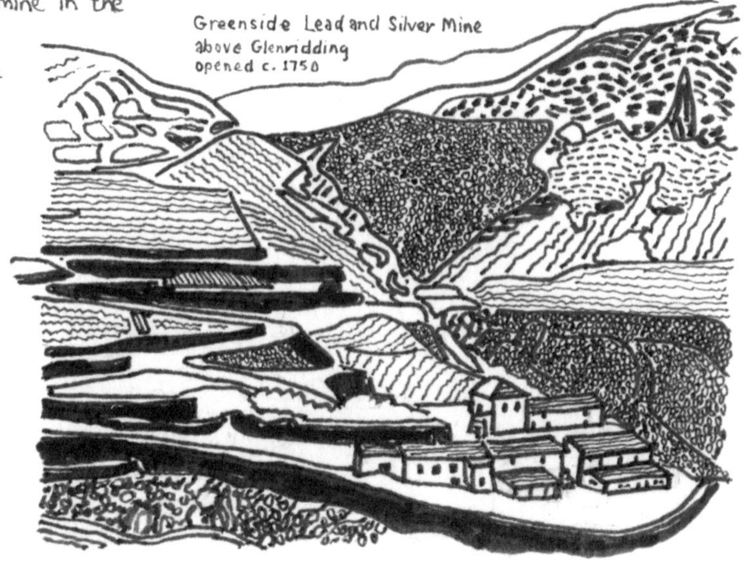

Mankind

1700 to 1775 The 'Lakers'

In the early 1700's travel writing came from the viewpoint of the productivity of the land, and the difficulty or ease of travel; there was no tourism. The Lake District was universally perceived with a mixture of horror and uselessness. Daniel Defoe (author of Robinson Crusoe) described the area in his 1727 'Tour of Britain' as "all barren and wild, of no use to man nor beast.... all the pleasant part of England was at an end". The roads through the Lakes were pack horse trails, too narrow for a carriage. The boom in roadbuilding in the mid 1700's made the journey to the edge of the Lakes much easier; the coach journey from London to Penrith cut from nine days to three. The first tourists in the 1770's were drawn to Ullswater and Derwent Water to hear and feel the 'echoes'. Boats were fitted with cannon, they were fired and the 'Lakers' could hear the reverberations between seven and twenty times depending on the stillness of the day. This popular pastime continued until the 1930's.

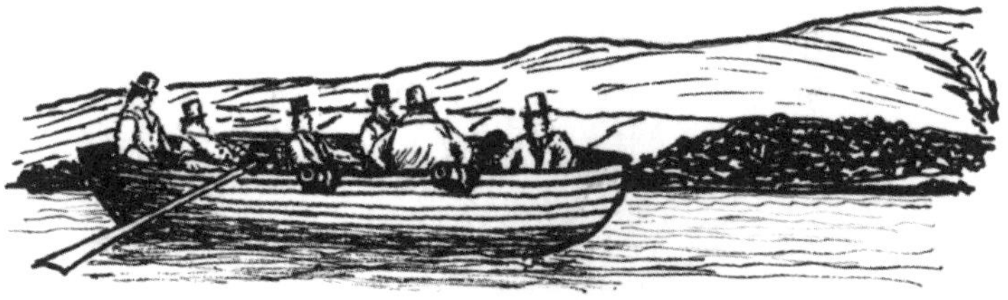

The upper class tourist trend of the time was the 'Grand Tour' of Europe. Encountering the Alps on the journey to Italy and Greece began the fashion for appreciating mountain scenery. In this time before cameras the must have accessory to appreciate the landscape was the Claude Glass; a blackened convex mirror which created a more picturesque image of the view. The Napoleonic Wars of the early 1800's made travel in Europe dangerous and brought the Grand Tour to an abrupt halt. The attention of the leisured classes then switched to England's own mini Alps, the Lake District.

Mankind

1775-1860: Guide Books, the Picturesque and Romantic Movements

The Romantic Movement made the Lake District fashionable, a new way of looking at the landscape, the idea that natural wonders and scenery would nourish the soul; an antidote to the Industrial Revolution. Thomas Gray in his 1775 'Journal of a visit to Lakeland' was the first to write about the district appreciatively; here about Grasmere, "an unsuspected paradise; all is peace, rusticity and happy poverty, in its neatest and most becoming attire".

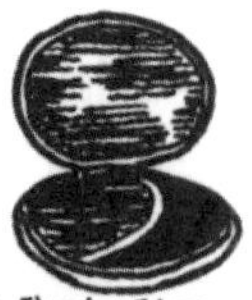
A Claude Glass

Thomas West's 1778 'Guide to the Lakes' started the idea of scenic tourism, he identified viewing stations for the public to find and enjoy with their Claude glass. The stations were of modest height, enough to view the lake, and near to the road; tourists followed the guide to bag the stations and give opinions on them; it became hugely popular. William Gilpin took it to another level in his 1786 "Observations... on Cumberland and Westmoreland" setting quasi scientific rules on Picturesque Correctness, composition, perspective and form. This became 'the' rulebook for Picturesque tourism, introducing a new terminology into the national vocabulary, even King George III was a fan. For example Jane Austen's novel Northanger Abbey of 1817 features a conversation on foregrounds, second distances, sidescreens, perspectives and light and shade.

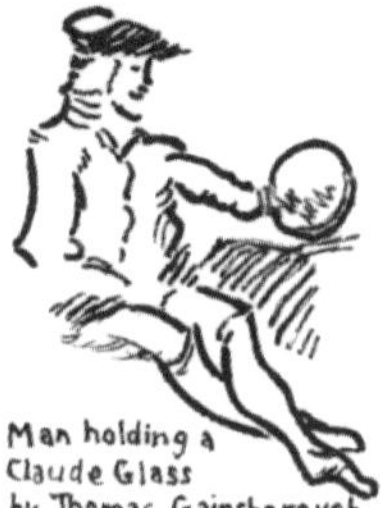
Man holding a Claude Glass by Thomas Gainsborough

The first to describe walking the fells for pleasure was Joseph Budworth in his 1792 240mile ramble which included all of the major peaks. Lyrical Ballads Volume 1 (1798) by Wordsworth and Coleridge was the first poetry written in everyday language about the natural world and normal people. The next year William and Dorothy Wordsworth moved to Grasmere.

Mankind

1775-1860: Guide Books, the Picturesque and Romantic Movements

In 1805 Wordsworth and his fellow poet Robert Southey, Walter Scott the pioneer of the historical novel and Humphry Davy, inventor of the Davy Lamp and discoverer of nitrous oxide all walked up Helvellyn together; it was a seminal high point of the Romantic movement. Later that year Charles Gough fell to his death climbing Helvellyn; it was two months before his body was found with his loyal terrier Foxey beside him, along with two Claude Glasses. The story of Foxey's devotion caught the public imagination; the Romantic Movement had its first martyr also. Wordsworth was inspired by it to write the poem 'Fidelity', Walter Scott wrote the novel 'Helvellyn', and Landseer painted 'Attachment' with Foxey's paw on the chest of a fully clothed Gough. The truth that Gough's body was stripped of its flesh and his head never found didn't get in the way of Romantic interpretation.

'Attachment' - Edwin Landseer 1829

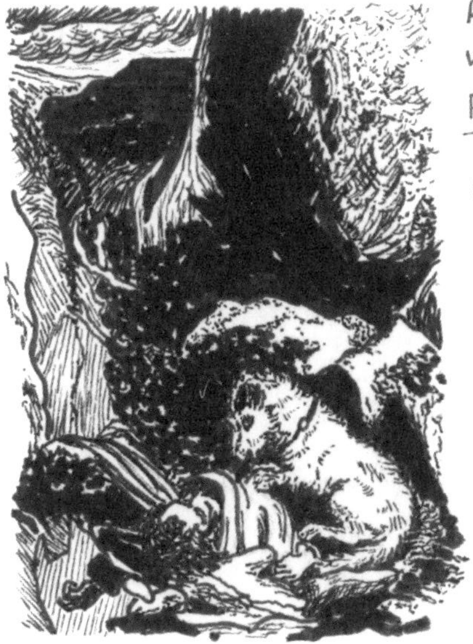

From 1815 Wordsworth published his popular 'Guide to the Lakes', using it and lots of letters to the press to publicise his conservationist ideas. He despised the swathes of Larch and Fir trees planted after mining had deforested the district; he thought new buildings painted white were vulgar, ruining the view of a whole valley; and later he was a fierce critic of the railways intrusion. However, the Industrial Revolution was in its pomp and he could do nothing to stop a line coming to the shores of Windermere. By 1860 railways were established around the perimeter of the whole district; and by 1859 Windermere, Coniston and Ullswater had all launched pleasure cruises on their lakes. The Victorian tourism boom was here.

Section 3: Dollywaggon Pike to Glencoyne Park

55.	Dollywaggon Pike - The Tongue		2748′
56.	Nethermost Pike - from Lad Crag		2951′
57.	Keldas - North West of Summit		856′
58.	Birkhouse Moor - Little Cove		1082′
59.	Birkhouse Moor - Nab Crag		2197′
60.	Birkhouse Moor - North of Summit		2230′
61.	Hole-in-the-Wall - towards Helvellyn		2328′
62.	Striding Edge - High Spying How		2769′
63.	Striding Edge		2754′
64.	Helvellyn - Striding Edge		3118′
65.	Helvellyn - Trig Point		3112′
66.	Helvellyn - Swirral Edge		3118′
67.	Helvellyn - towards Lower Man		3082′
68.	Catstycam		2917′
69.	Glenridding Dodd - East of Summit		1377′
70.	Glenridding Dodd - East Flank, looking SE		1148′
71.	Glenridding Dodd - East Flank, looking NE		1148′
72.	Glenridding Dodd - North Flank		1279′
73.	Heron Pike - looking North East		1935′
74.	Heron Pike - looking South East		1935′
75.	Mossdale Bay		492′
76.	Mossdale Bay	&	525′
77.	Glencoyne Wood		1262′
78.	Mossdale Bay - Ullswater Way		498′
79.	Glencoyne Wood -		1344′
80.	Glencoyne Wood - West Entrance		1036′
81.	Glencoyne Bay (with duck)	&	479′
82.	Glencoyne Bay	&	479′
83.	North Glencoyne Bay	&	479′
84.	Swineside Knott - looking North East		1813′
85.	Swineside Knott - looking South East		1813′
86.	Glencoyne Bay - North Shore		492′
87.	Glencoyne Park - Ullswater Way	&	557′

This section is the most intense, spectacular and challenging swathe of the Ullswater Valley, bringing us full circle back to Glencoyne Park at Aira Force. It starts with the stunning ridge walk from Dollywaggon Pike to Helvellyn; then highlights the delights of the best route up Helvellyn via Birkhouse Moor and Striding Edge. Whole lake panoramas and gorgeous shoreline and woodland glimpses complete the picture.

Section 3: Dollywaggon Pike to Glencoyne Park

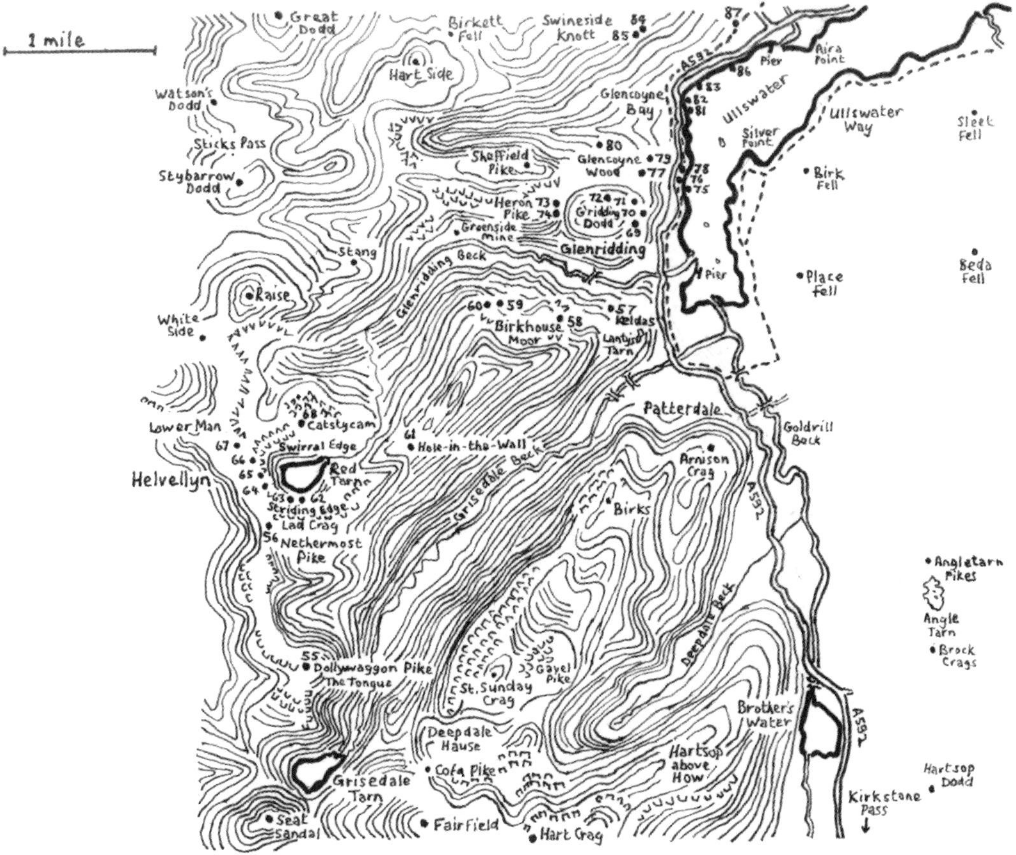

Words are few in Section 3; the 'wow' views dominate; they speak more than words. The only suggestions here are;

explore

linger

embrace

and enjoy...

Dollywaggon Pike - The Tongue

2748′

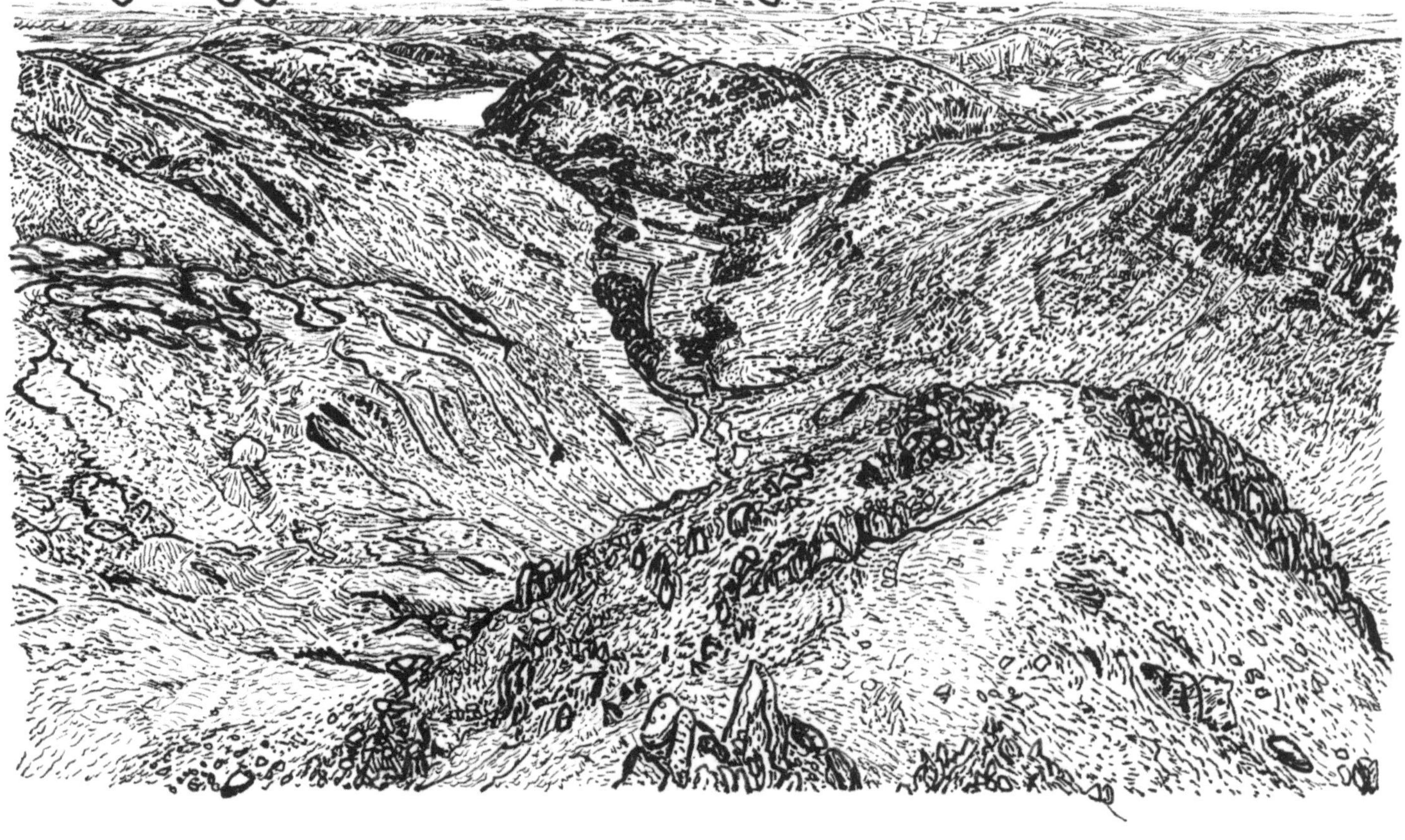

Nethermost Pike - Striding Edge from Lad Crag 2951'

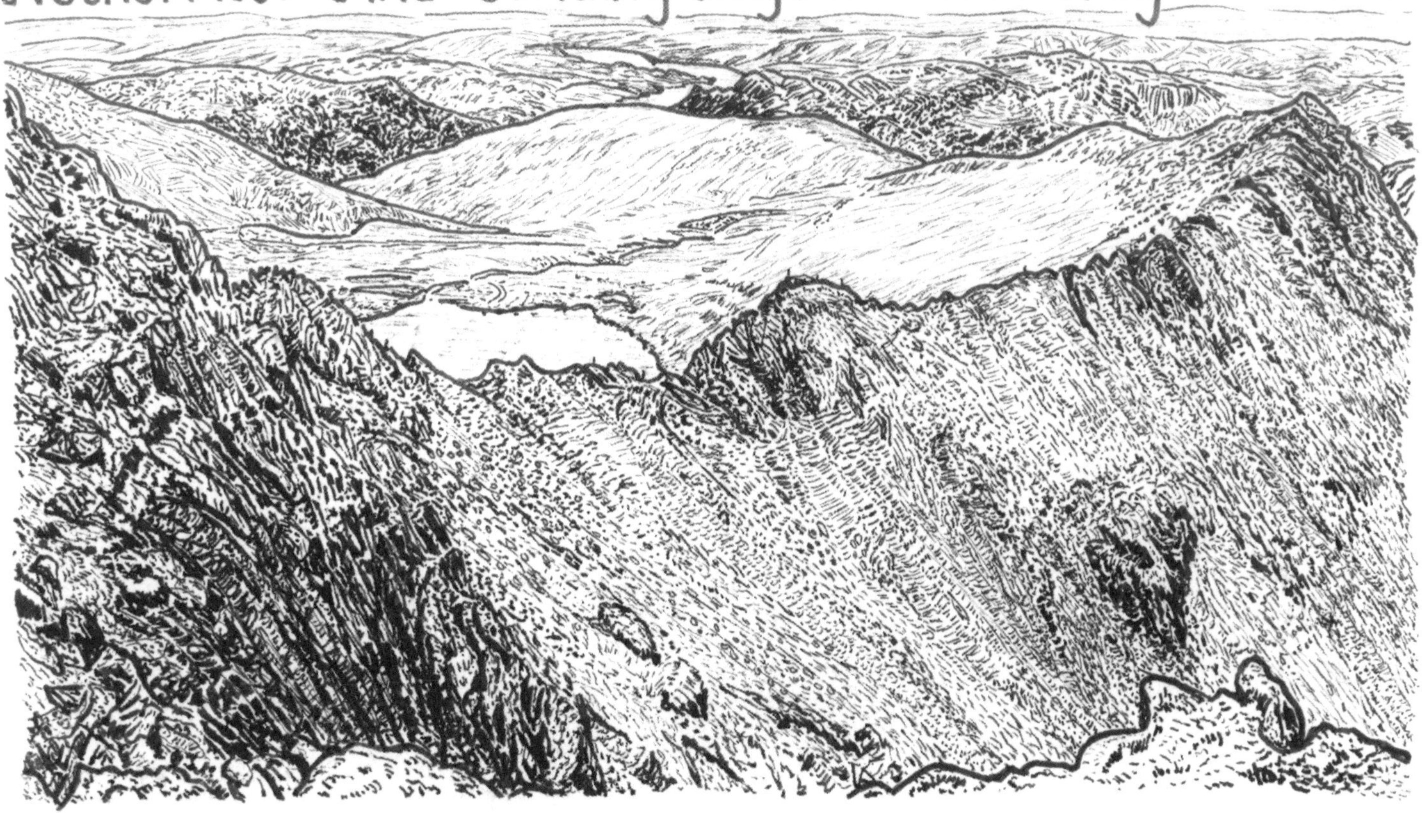

Keldas - North West of Summit

856'

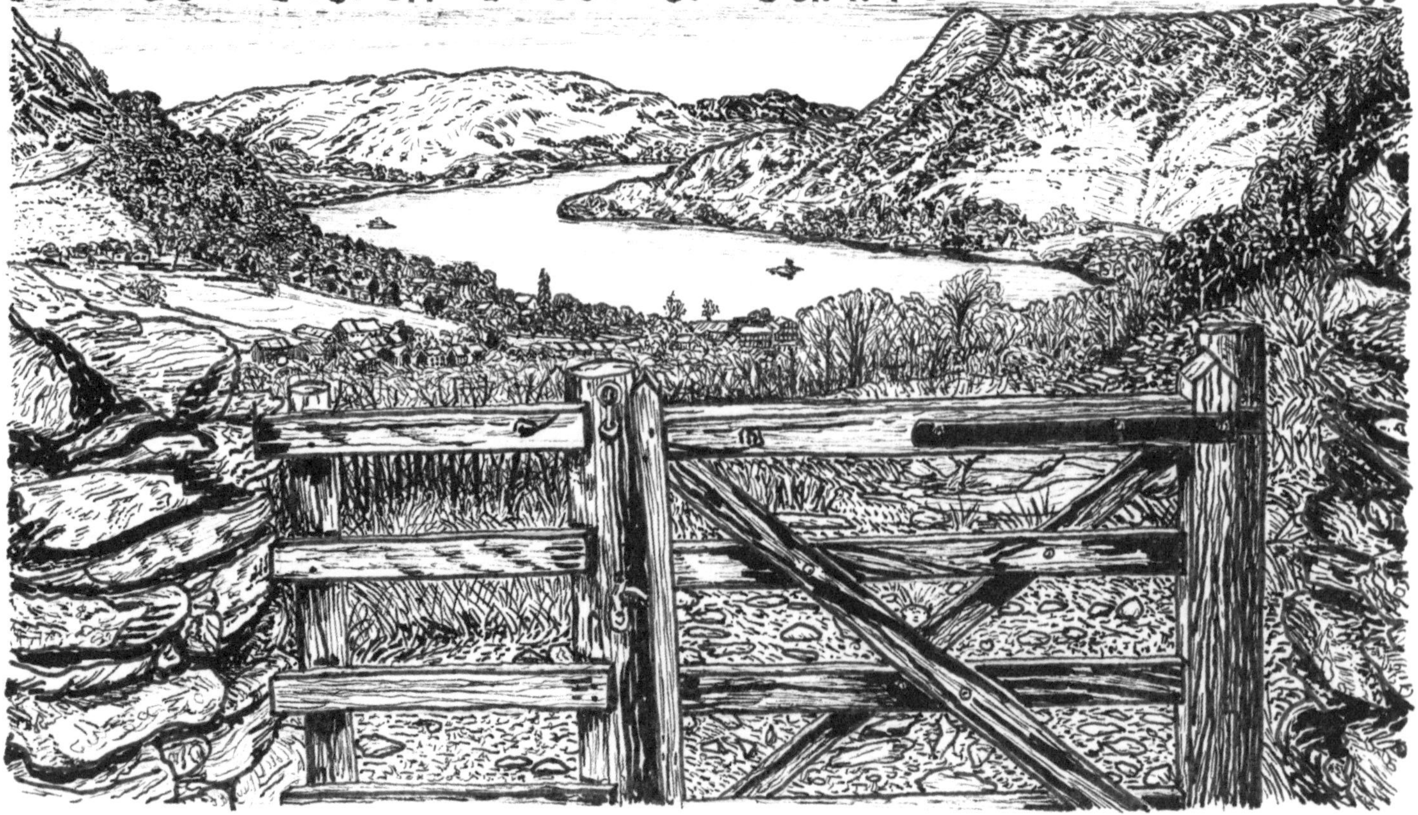

Birkhouse Moor ~ Little Cove

1082′

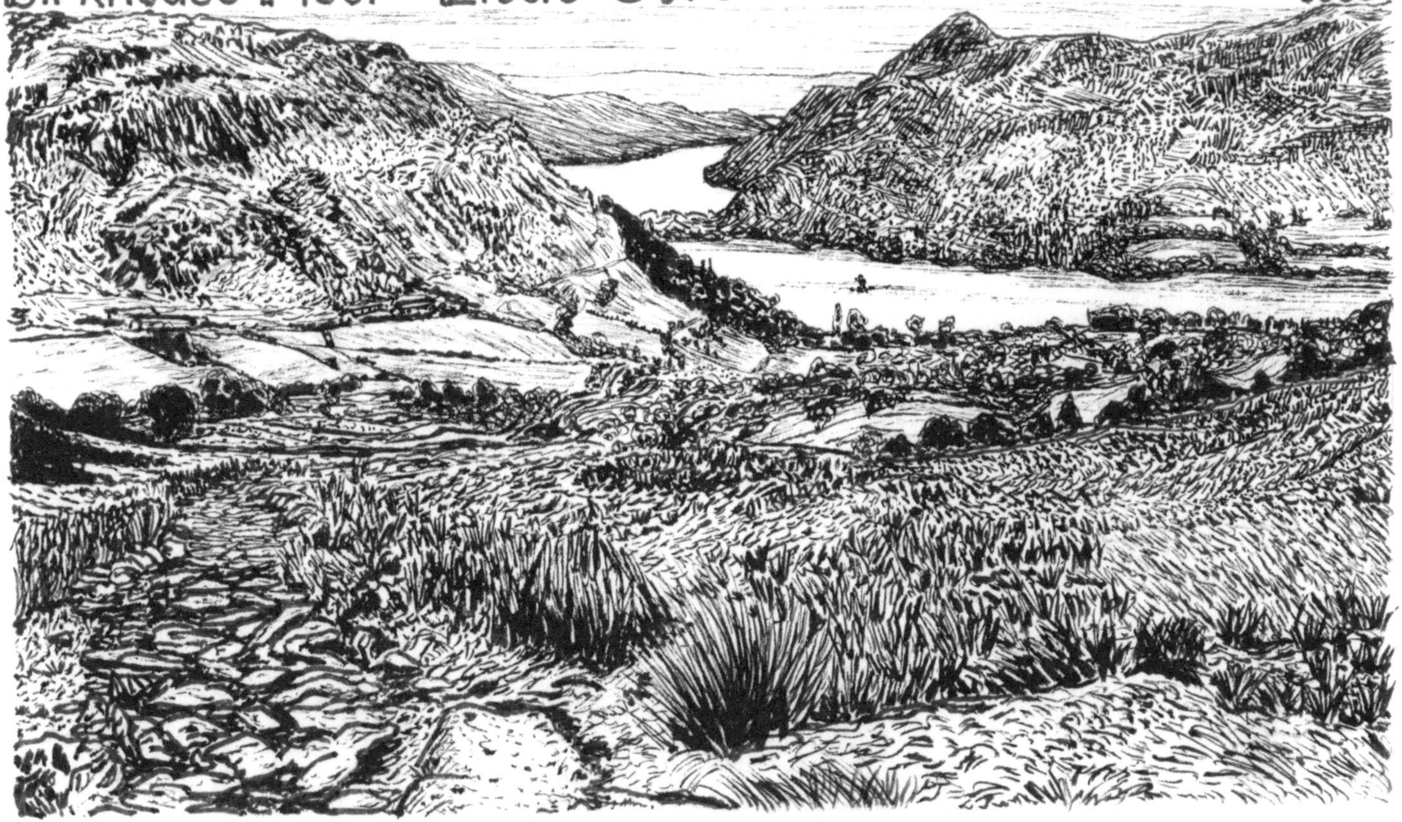

Birkhouse Moor ~ Nab Crag

2197′

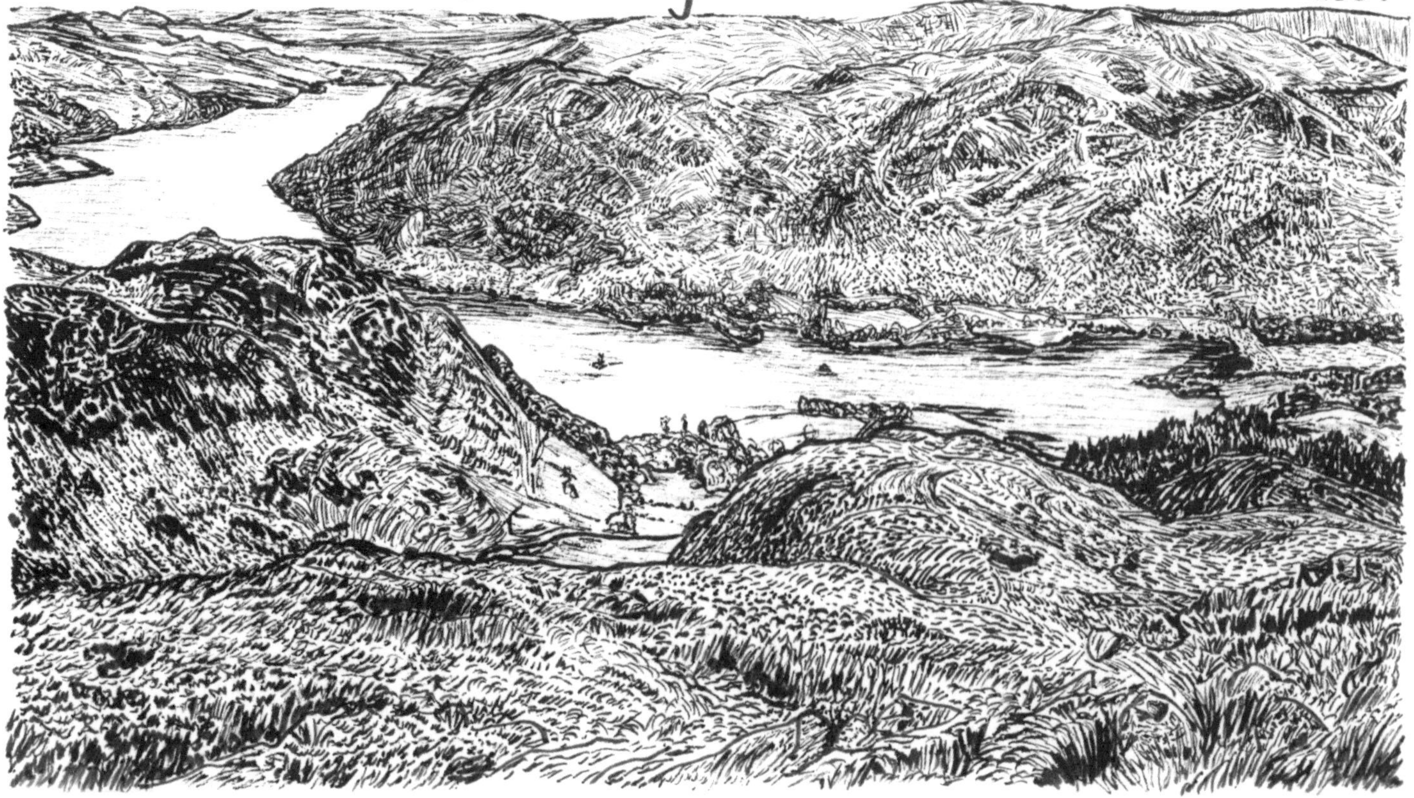

Birkhouse Moor - North of Summit

2230′

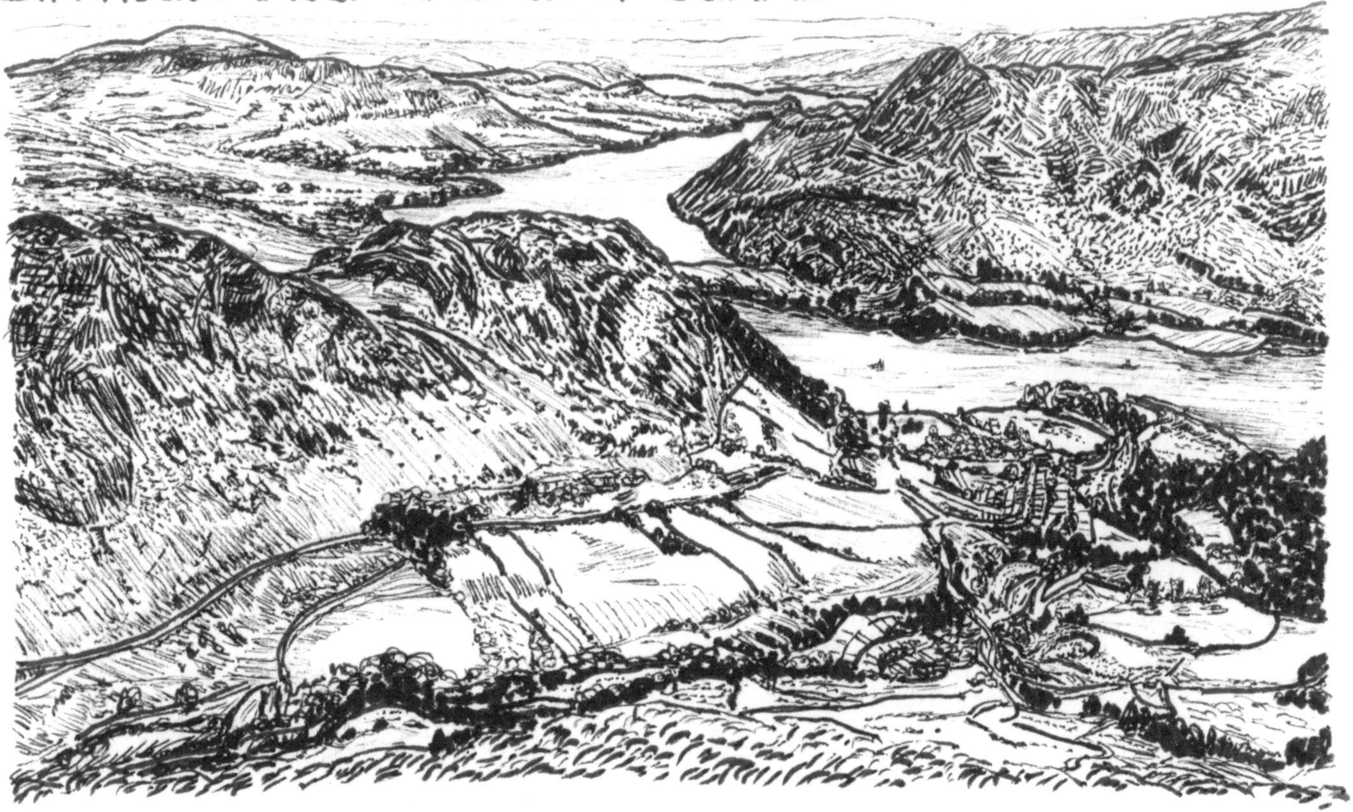

Hole-in-the-Wall - towards Helvellyn 2328′

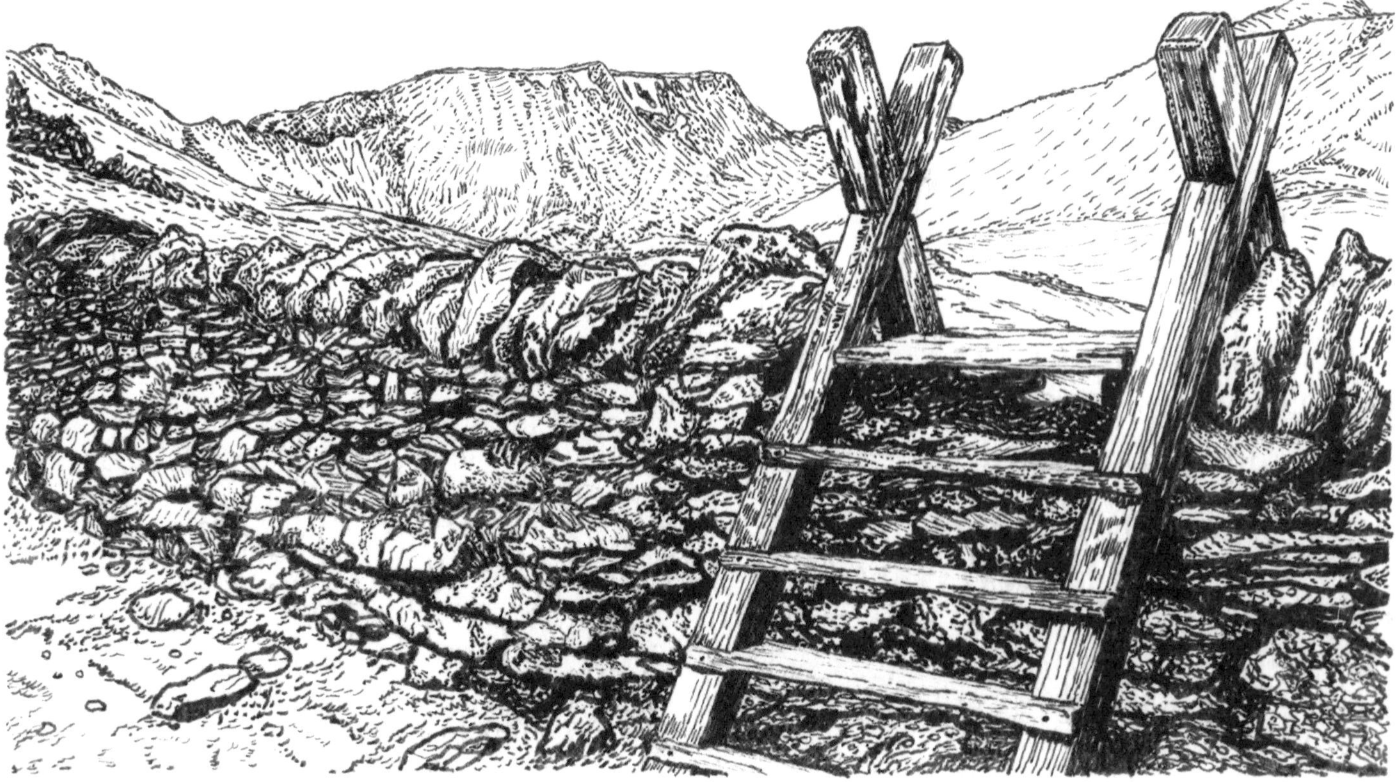

Striding Edge - High Spying How

2769'

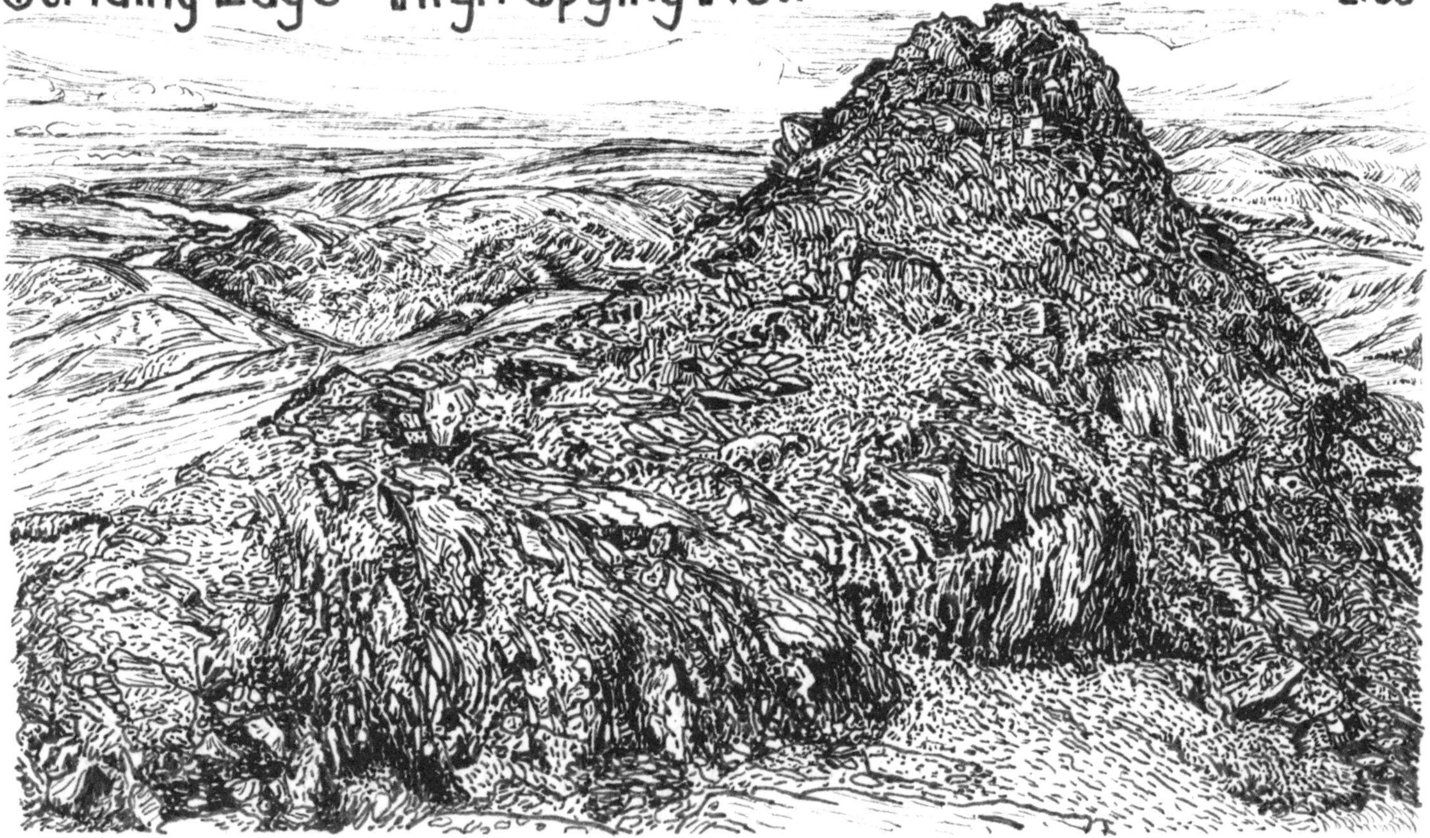

Helvellyn

Inspiringly named; the most climbed; Britain's Favourite walk (voted No 1 in the 2018 ITV programme of that name). The route from Glenridding via Birkhouse Moor, taking in Red Tarn, Spying How, Striding Edge, the panoramic plateaued summit; descending Swirral Edge, having the bonus of Catstycam, winding down by Red Tarn Beck and Greenside mine make for an utterly world class day's walk; it is the best in lakeland. Drama, jeopardy, danger, reward and according to the Father of Lake District Cartography, Jonathon Otley (1766-1856), it gives "a more complete view of lakeland than any other point."

Helvellyn massif north to south is nine miles long and four and half miles wide, a massive natural barrier and boundary. It is the watershed between Thirlmere and Derwent Water to the west, and Ullswater and the river Eden to the east. The name derives from a mixture of Norse and Celt:

'hel - gival - lyn'

'hill - well - lake'

'the hill containing a lake (Red Tarn) that is like a well.'

Behind Scafell Pike and Scafell it is England's third highest mountain; it is the most climbed because of its proximity to the major lakeland villages, and that it can be climbed from all directions.

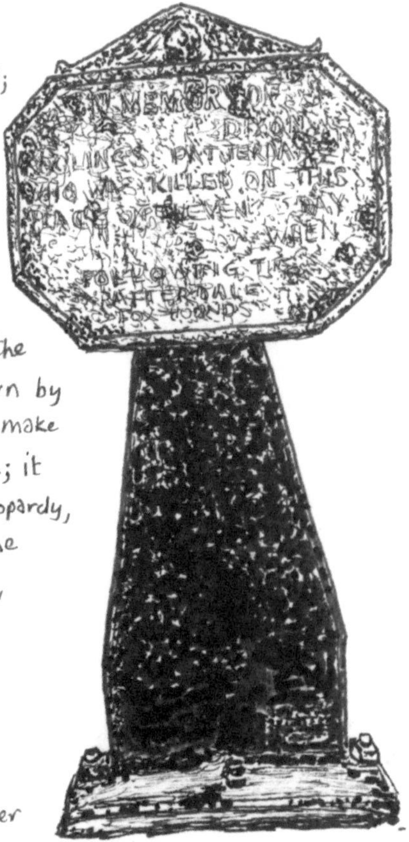

The 1858 Dixon Memorial on Striding Edge overlooking Nethermost Cove - he fell to his death whilst trailing the Patterdale hounds

> The mountains have no signs, no warnings, many people fall foul of the real dangers of sudden weather changes and not being prepared. Helvellyn claims several lives every year. In Winter it should not be climbed without crampons and an ice axe. The Mountain Rescue Teams are unquestioning highly-skilled volunteers; try not to have to call them out. As Wainwright said; 'watch where you are putting your feet.'

Striding Edge

2754′

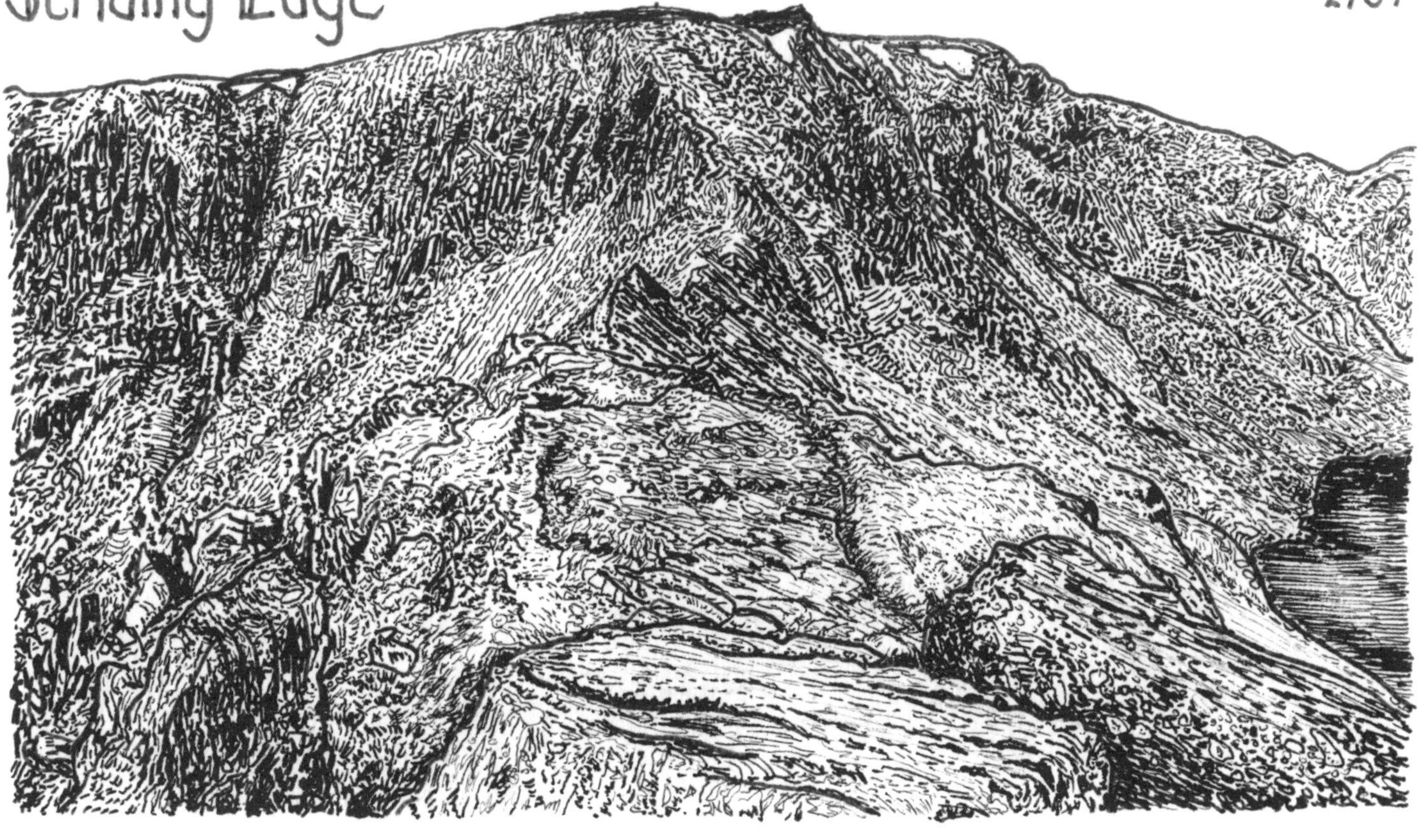

Helvellyn: at the north west of the summit plateau is Lower Man (shown a few pages ahead) with views north to Bassenthwaite Lake, Skiddaw, the Solway Firth and Dumfries and Galloway beyond. There are extensive and glorious vistas west to Scafell and south to Windermere, Coniston and Morecambe Bay; they will appear in Volume 2 of this series.

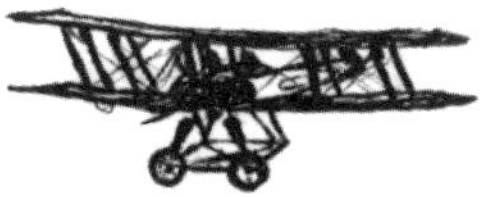

In 1926 an Avro 585 (left) was audaciously landed on the summit with 30 yards to spare before Striding Edge.

Glenridding and Greenside

'Glenredyn' in Cymric meaning 'valley overgrown with bracken' first appeared in records in 1290. It developed as a mining community from the 1600's when lead was discovered at Greenside. The mine closed in 1962 by which time it had produced 159,000 tons of lead and 45 tons of silver. It was the world's first mine to be electrified in the 1890's. Tragedy was miraculously avoided at 1·30 am on 29th of October 1927 when Keppel Cove Dam (which fed Greenside) burst, sending sheep and cattle through the village, across the valley floor to Side Farm in a 6 feet high tsunami; mercifully no one was killed. The spit of land where the Steamers' Pier and car park now sit was created by the dam burst. In 2015 Glenridding suffered devastating flooding three times in one month; resilience and flood prevention initiatives are ongoing. Glenridding is now a mountain village mecca with world class walking on its doorstep.

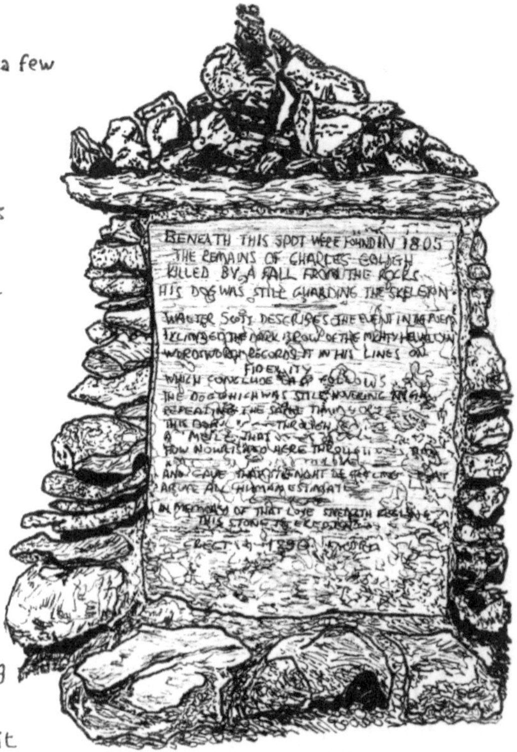

The Charles Gough Memorial; martyr of the Romantic Movement, fell from near the summit in 1805. Cannon Rawnsley, conservationist and champion of Beatrix Potter organised its installation in 1890.

Helvellyn ~ Striding Edge

3118′

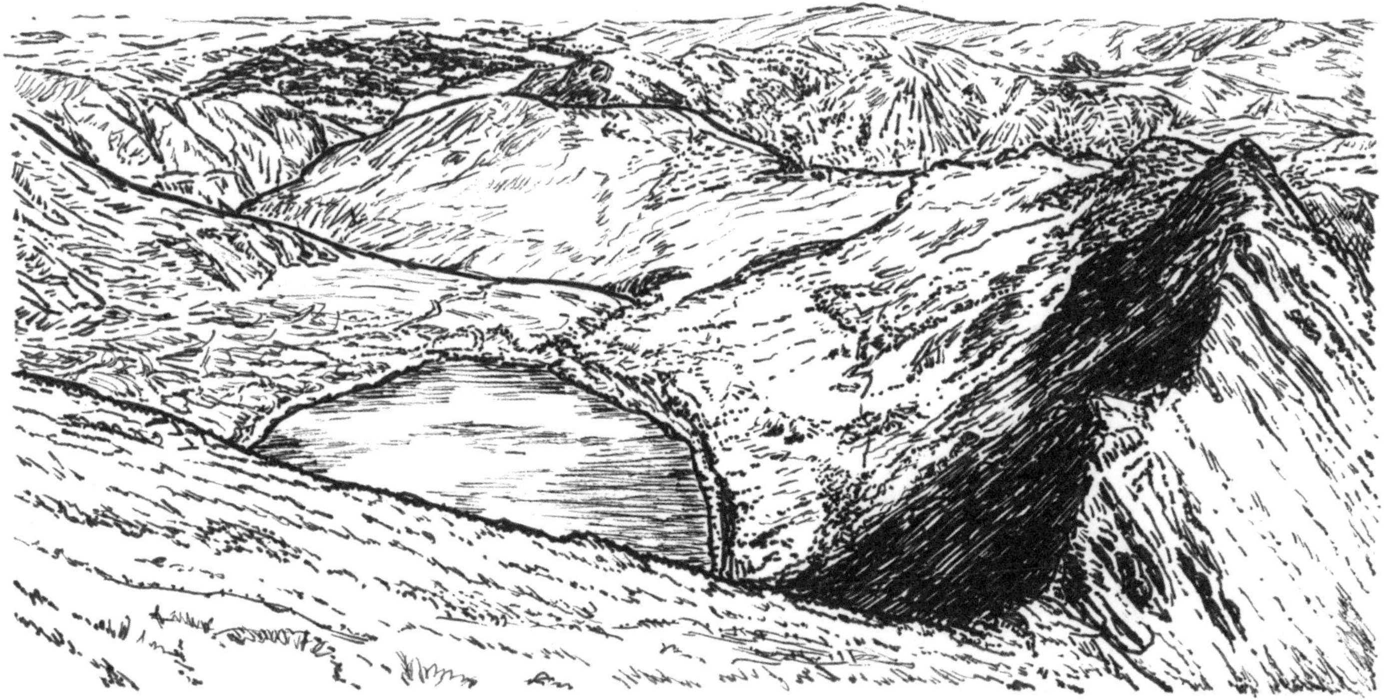

Helvellyn - Trig Point

3112'

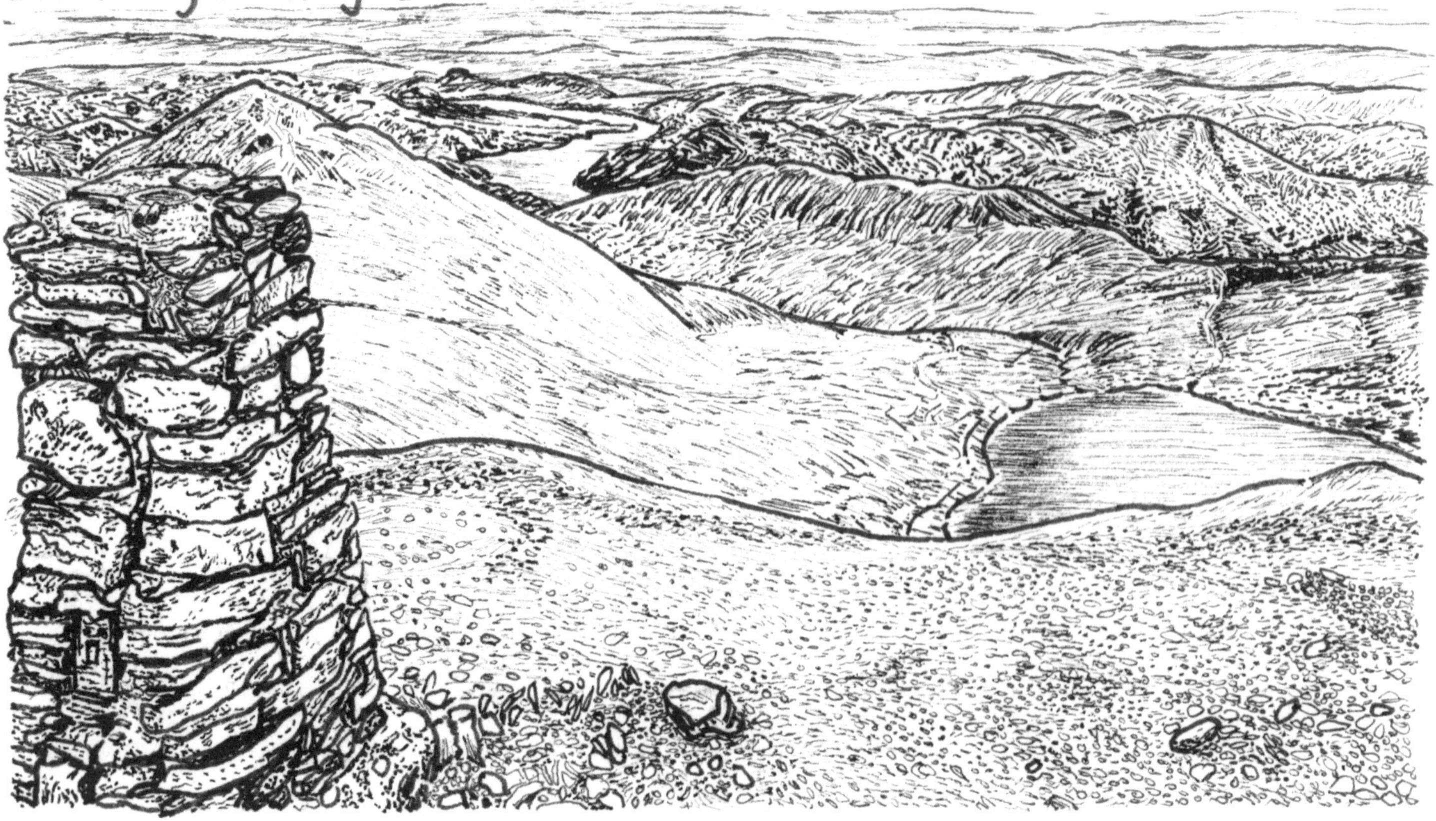

Helvellyn ~ Swirral Edge 3118′

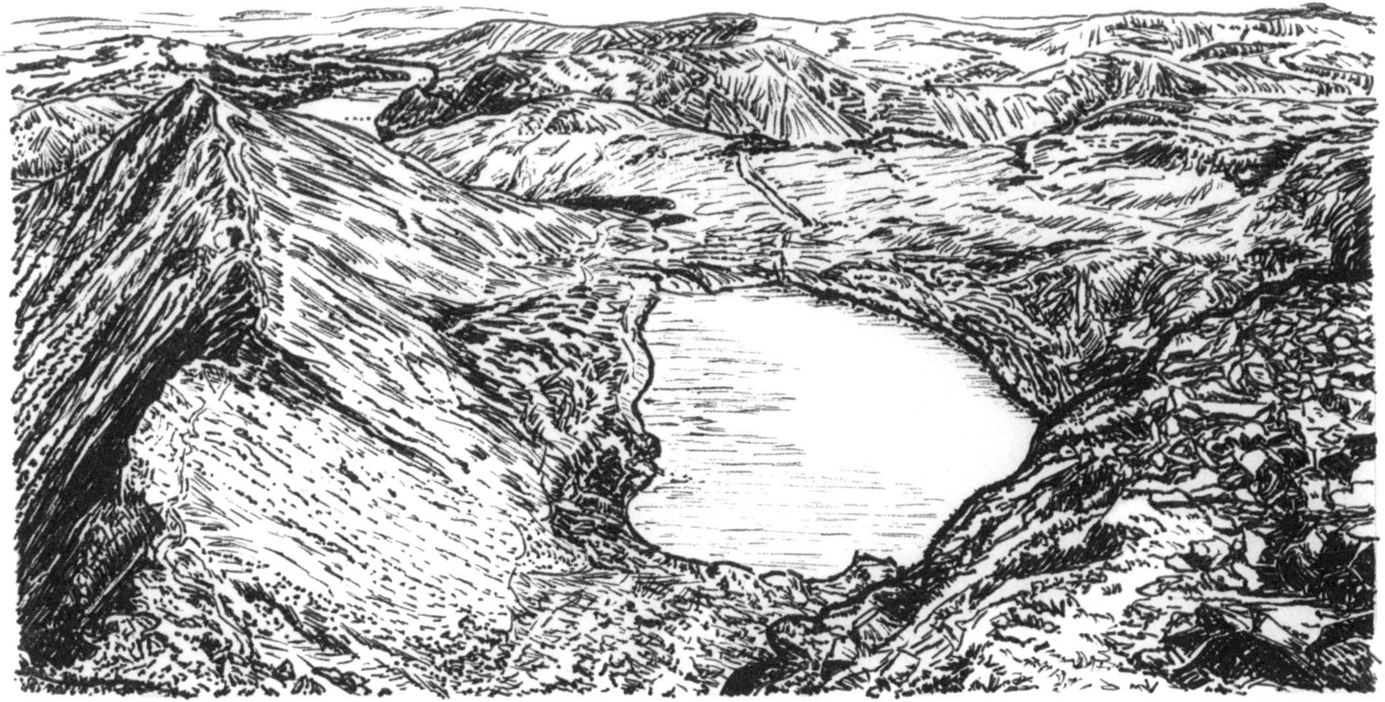

Helvellyn - towards Lower Man

3082'

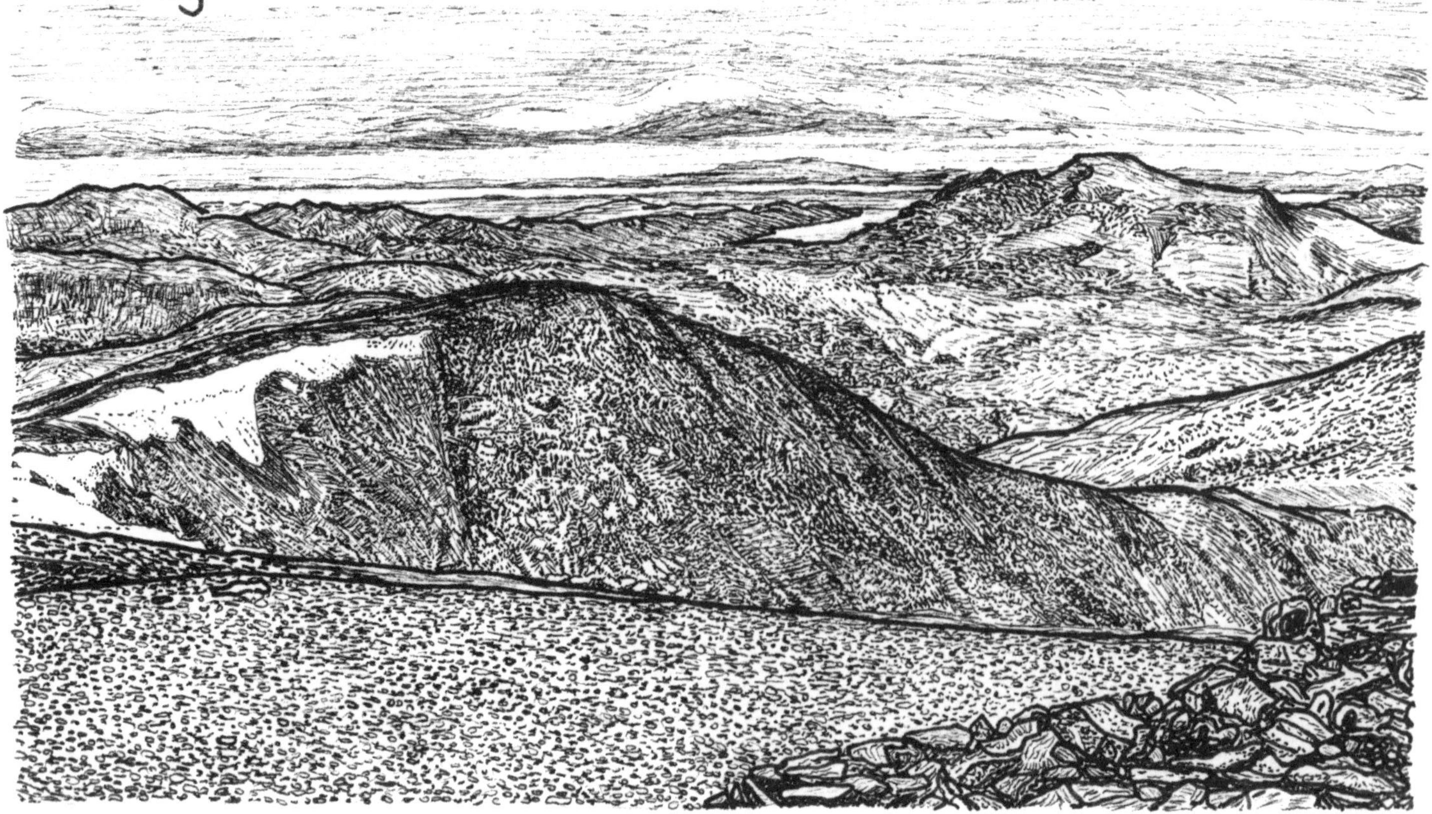

Catstycam

2917'

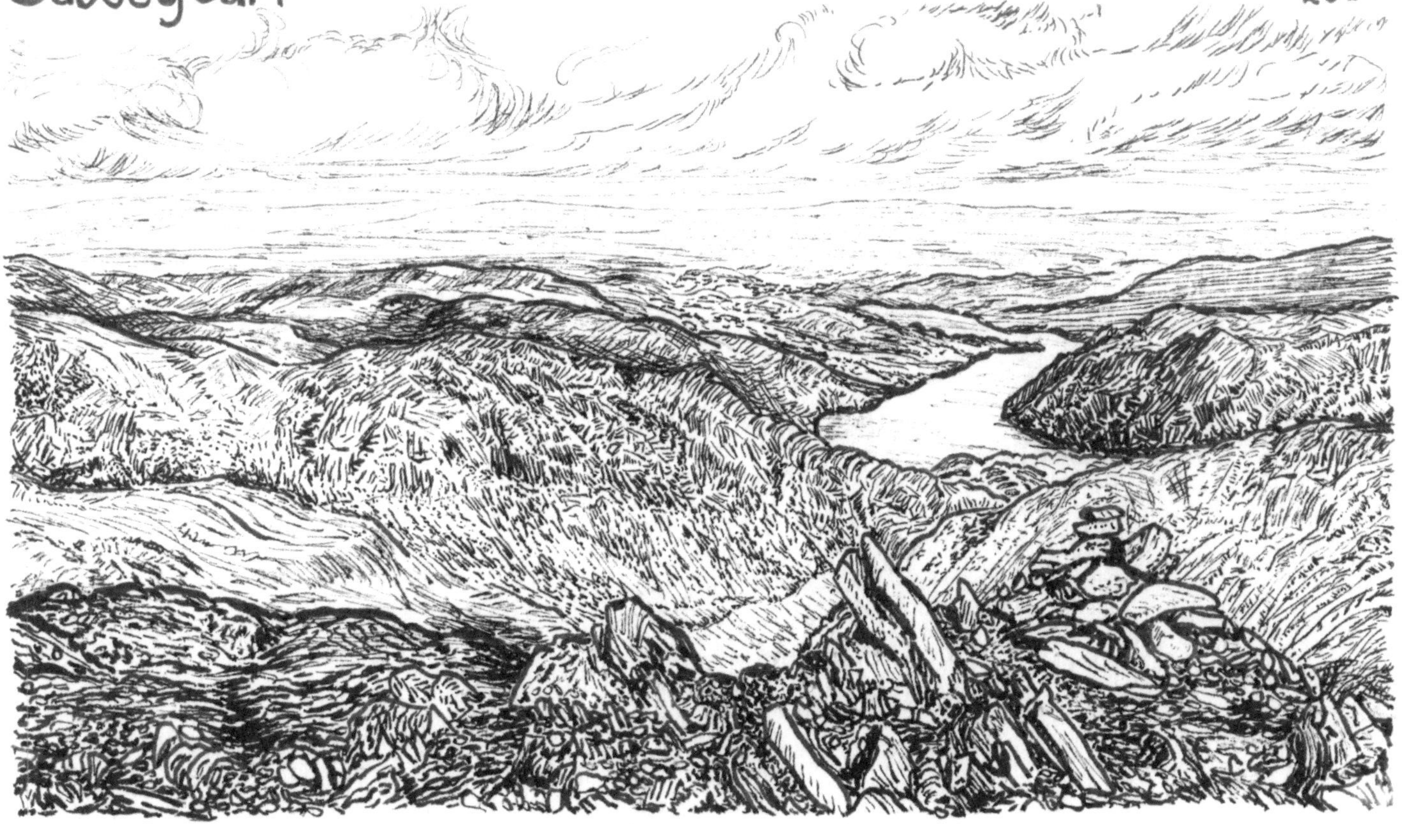

Glenridding Dodd - East of Summit

1377′

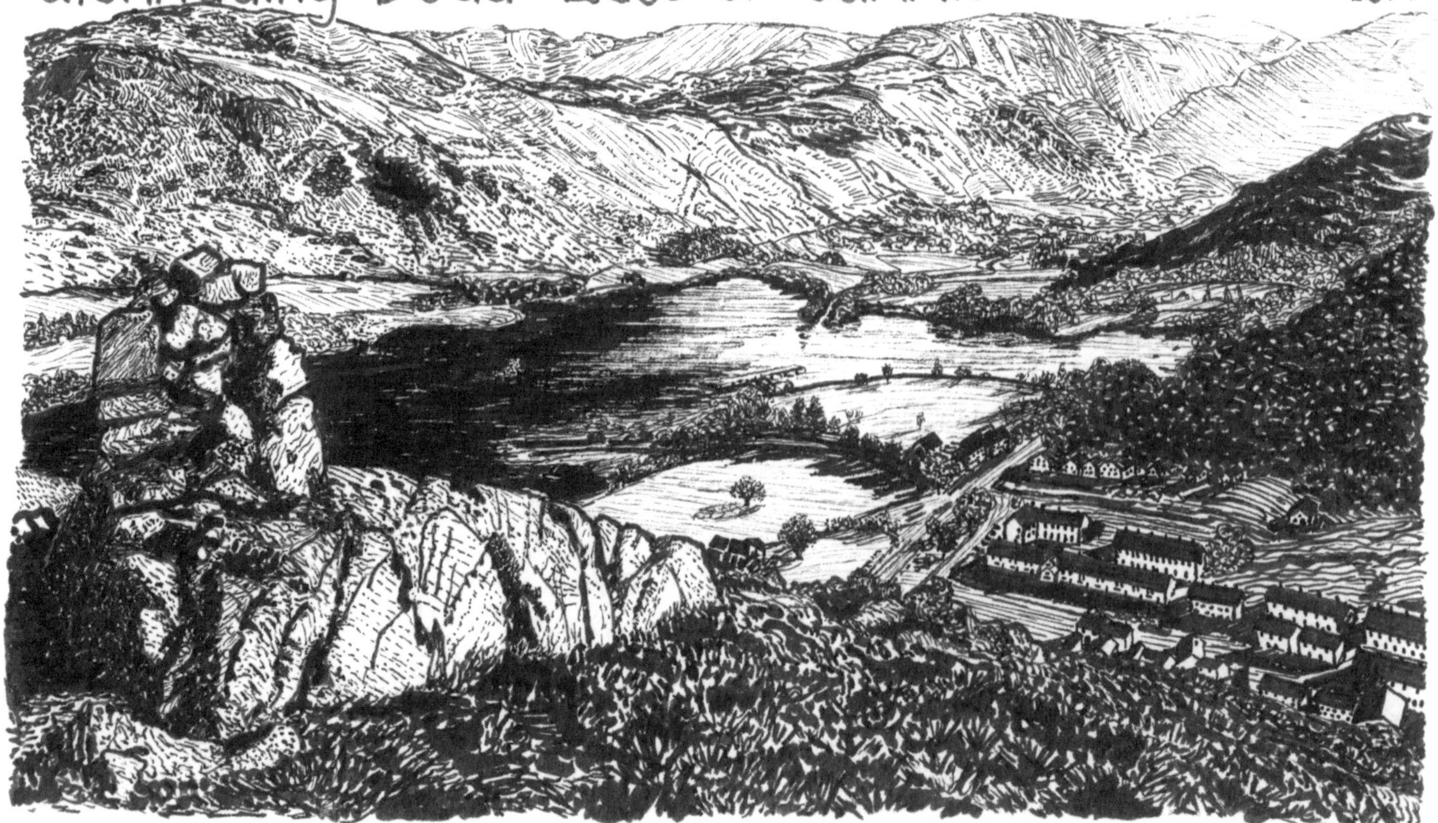

Glenridding Dodd - East Flank

1148′

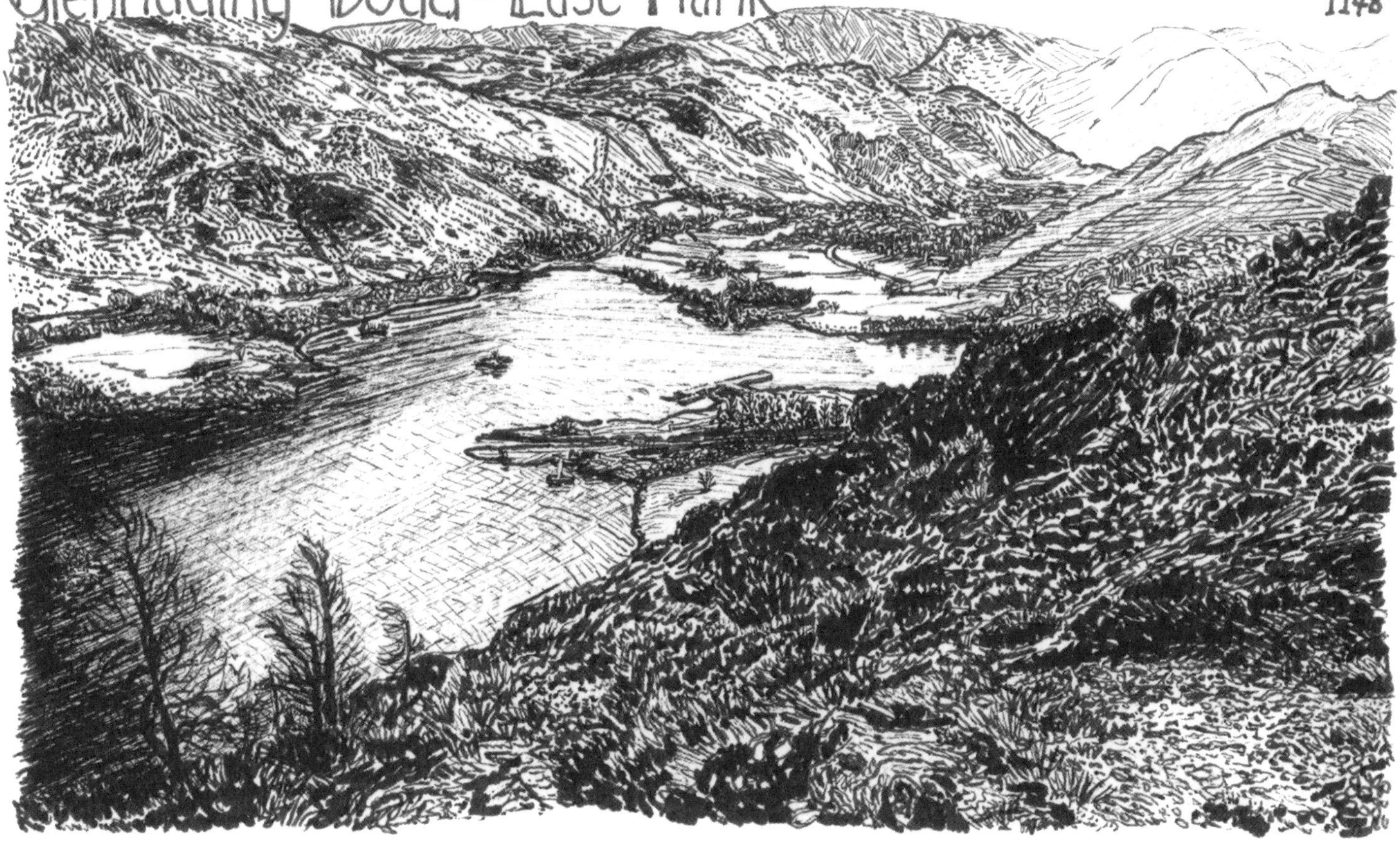

Glenridding Dodd - East Flank

1148′

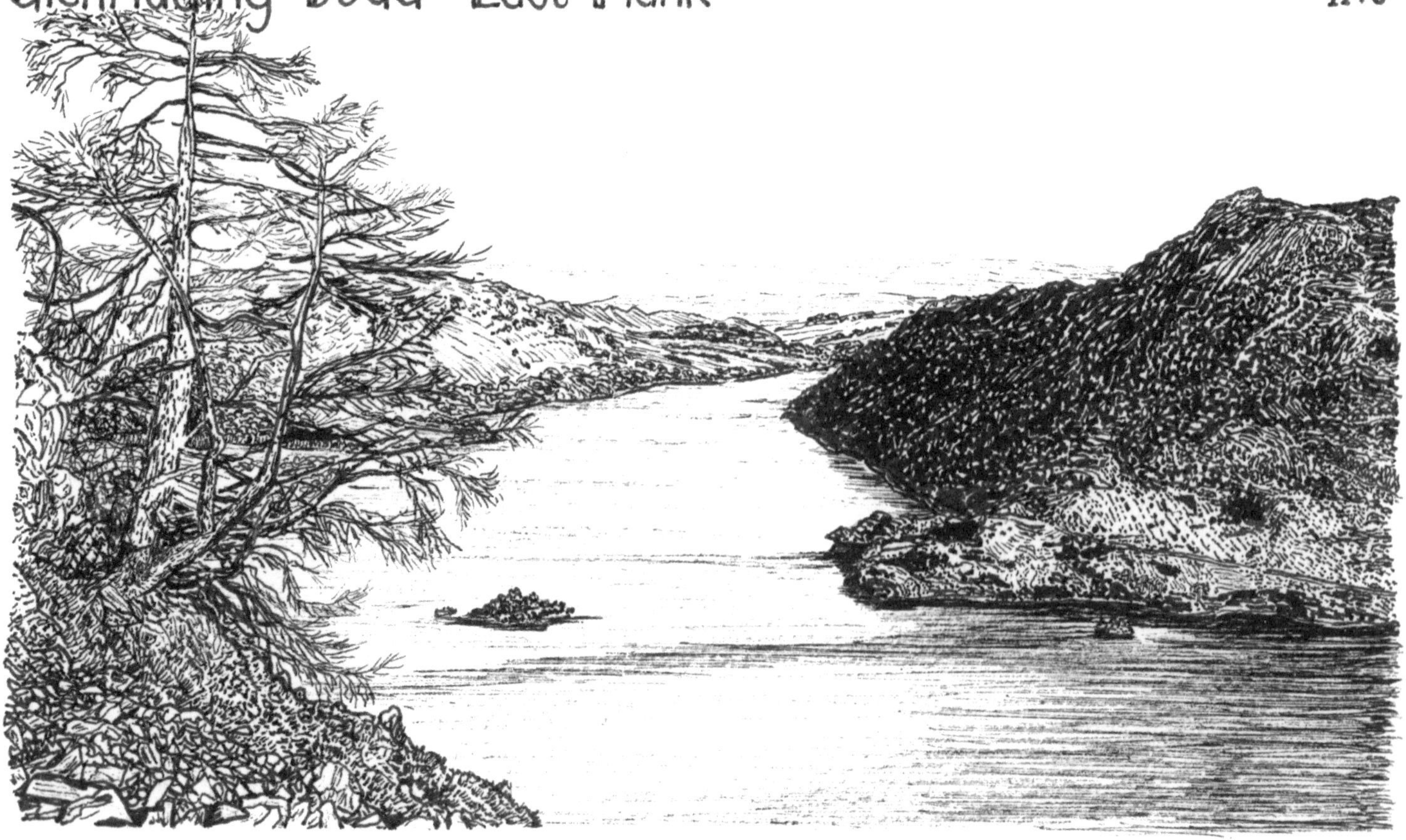

Glenridding Dodd - North Flank

1279'

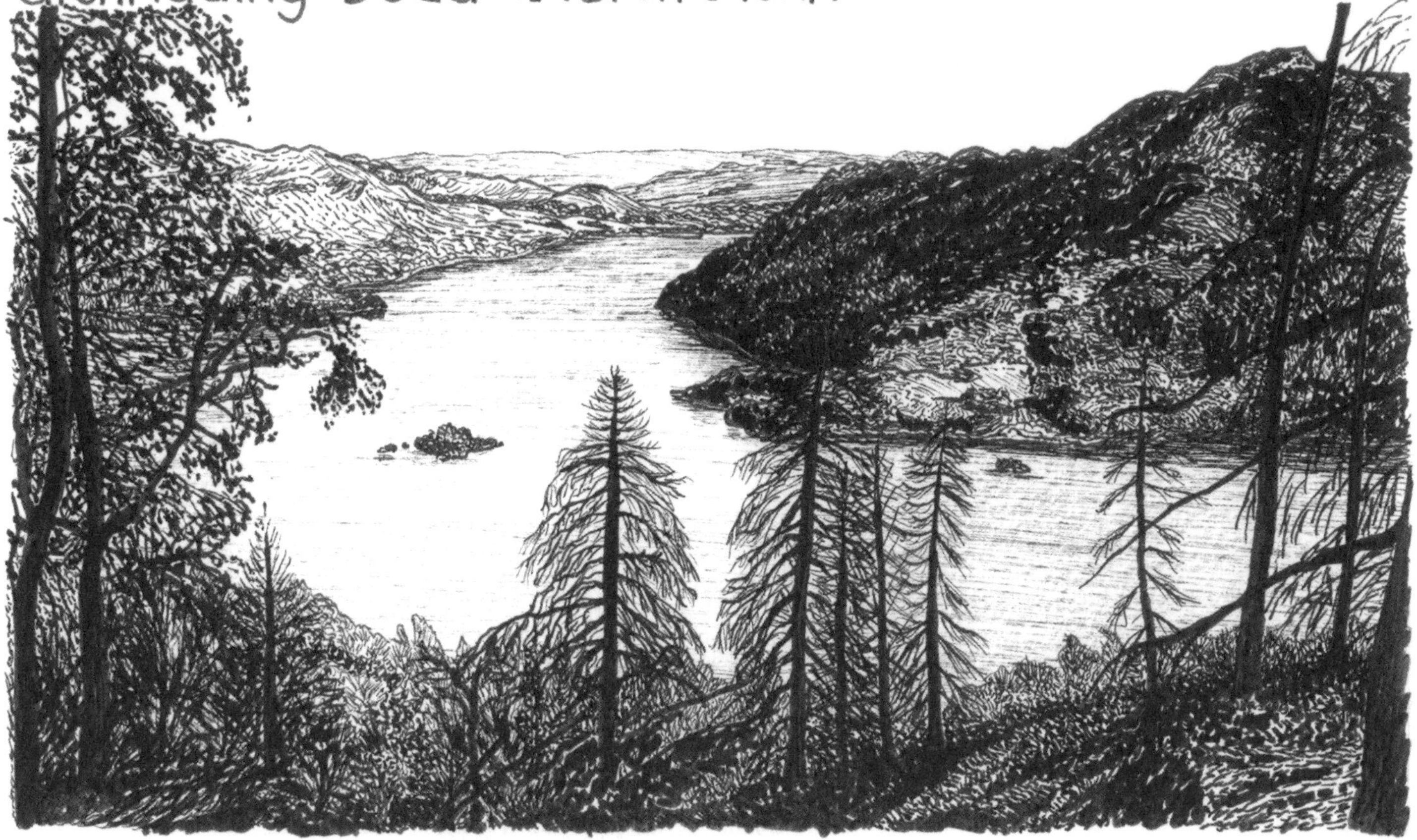

Heron Pike ~ looking North East 1935

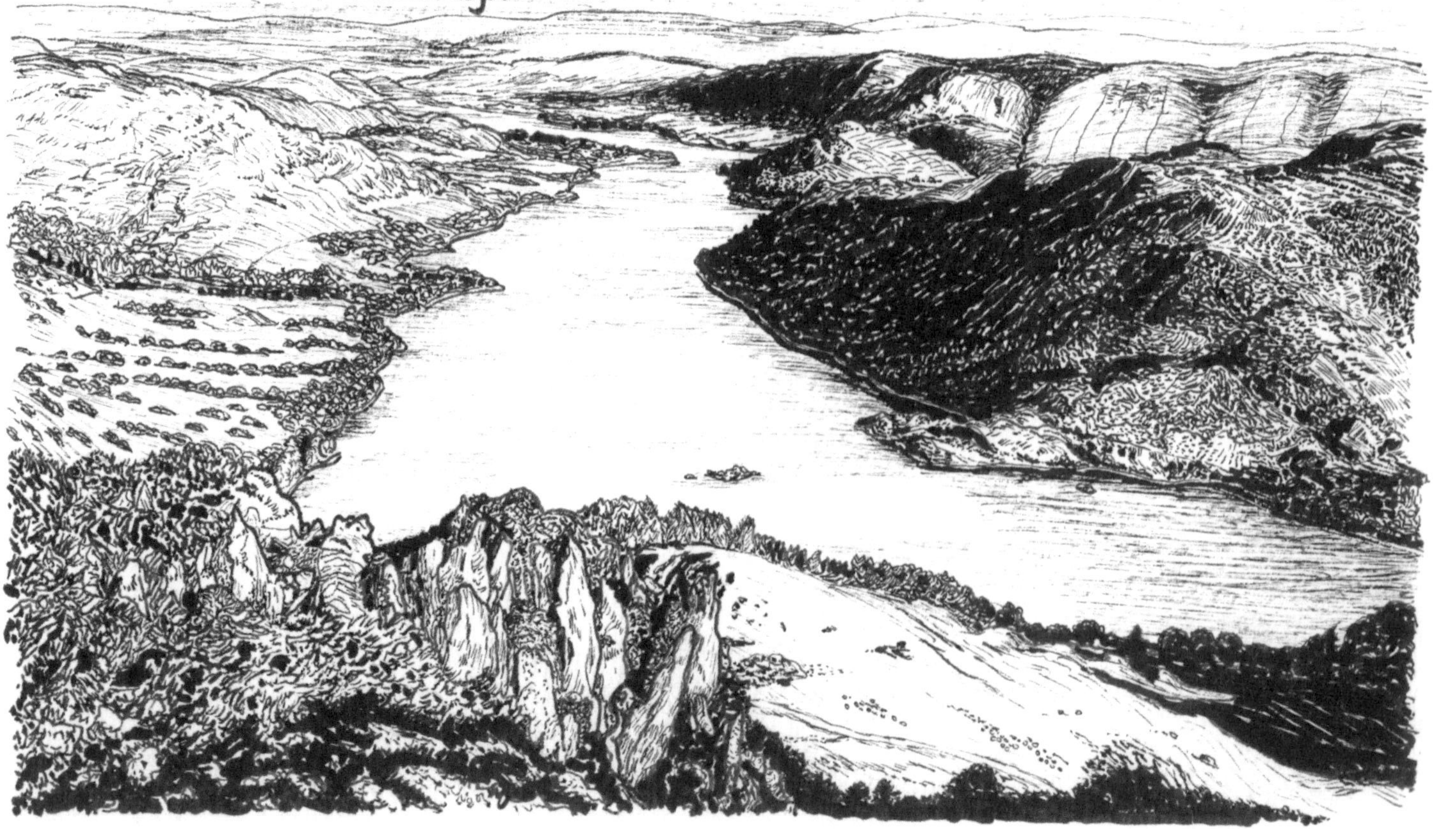

Heron Pike - looking South East 1935

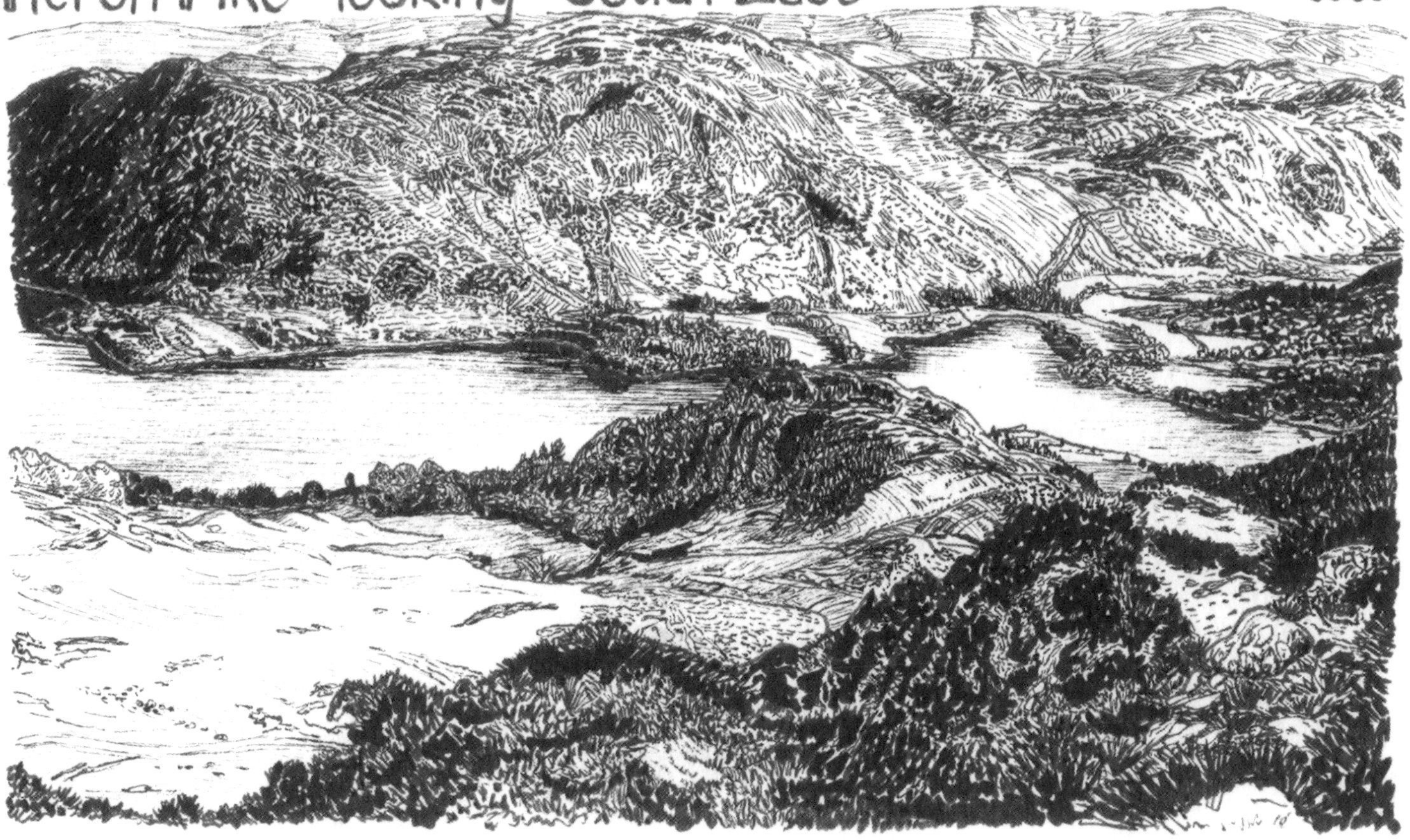

Mossdale Bay

492'

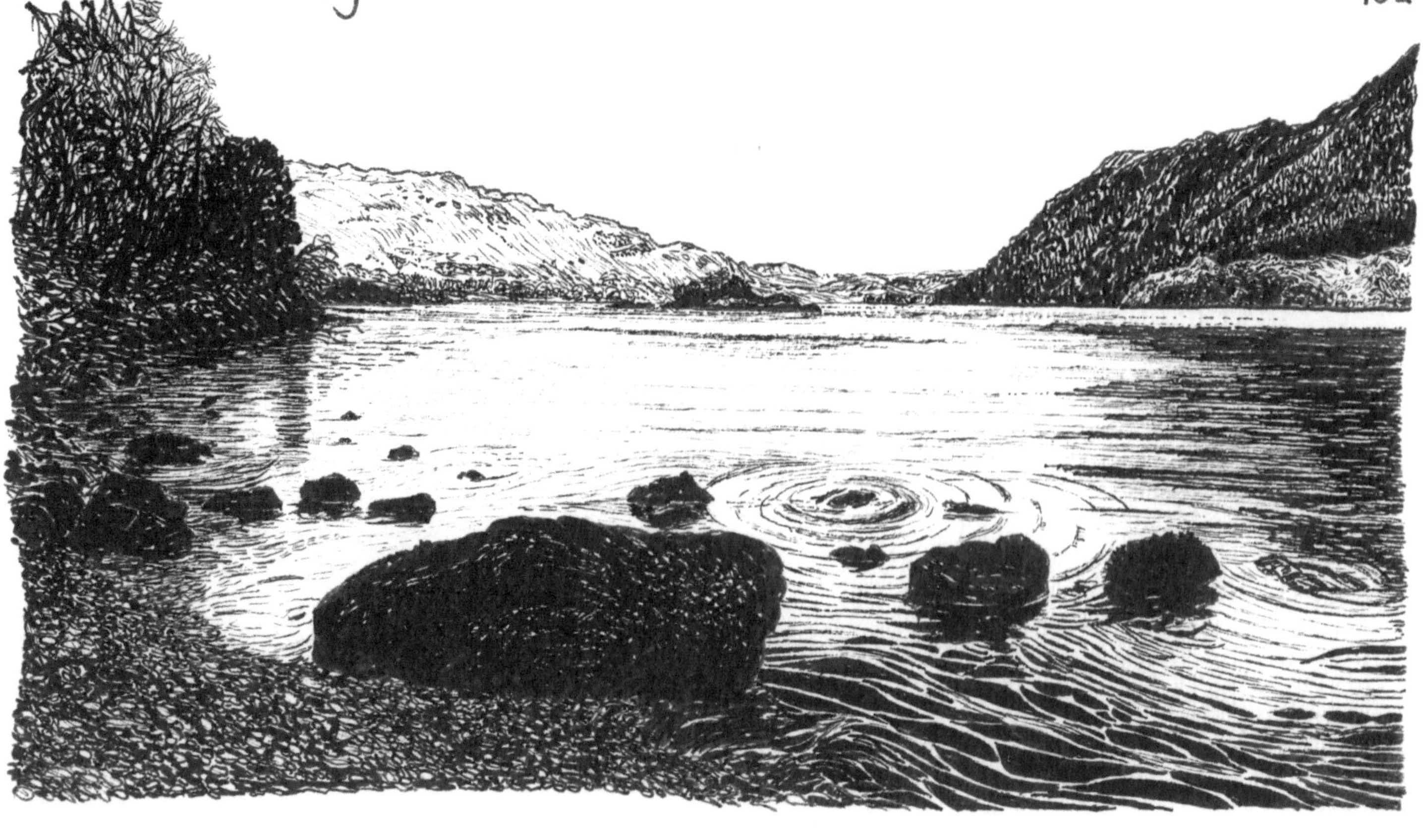

Mossdale Bay

♿ 525′

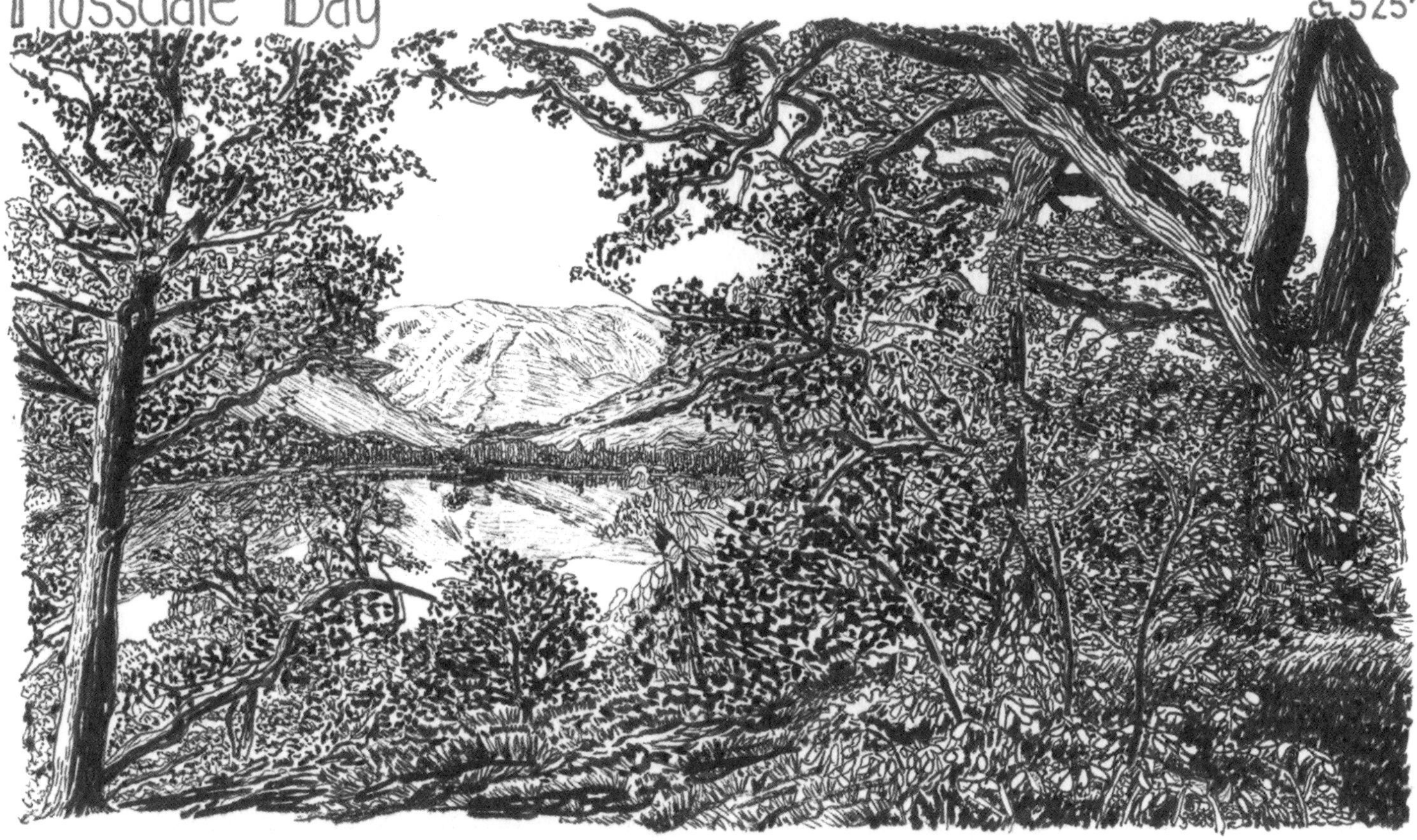

Glencoyne Wood

1262′

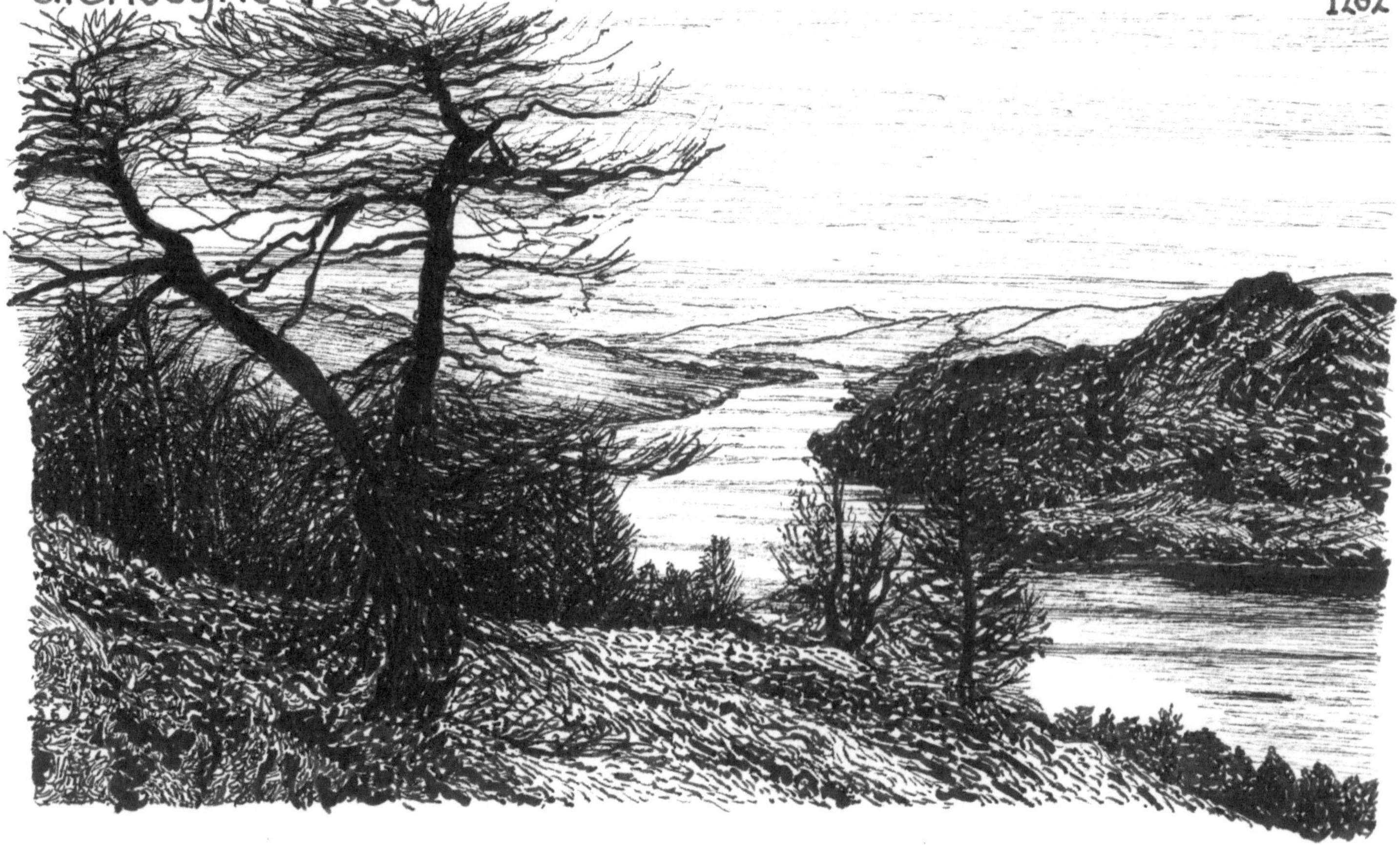

Mossdale Bay - Ullswater Way

498´

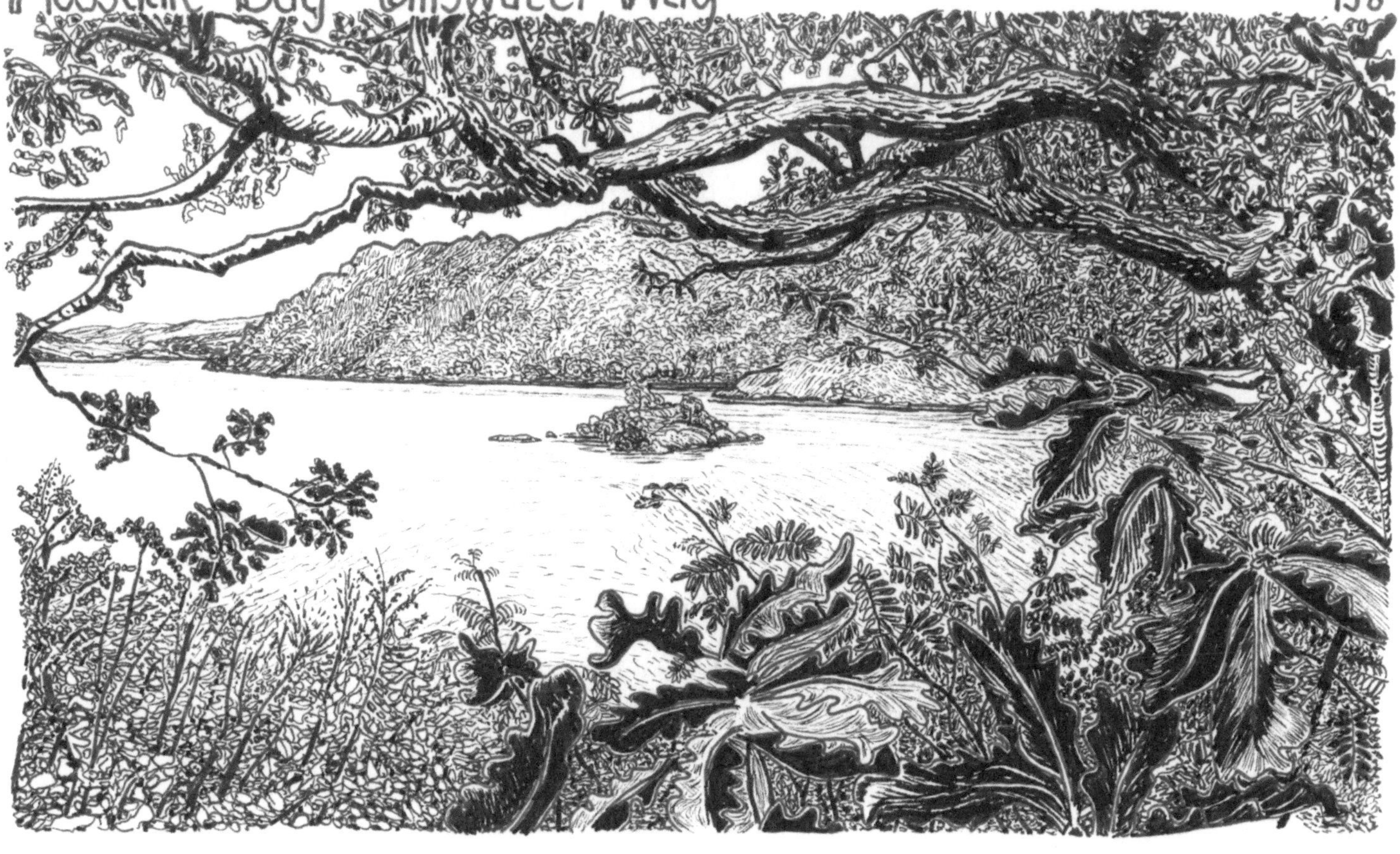

The Ullswater Way : Glenridding to Aira Force

The section from Glenridding to Aira Force is the most enchanting and rewarding three miles of the twenty-one mile trail. Exquisite woodland shoreline gives way to the grandeur of Glencoyne Bay with its 180° views of Ullswater's second and third reach, culminating in the evergreen charm of Aira Force and Gowbarrow Park.

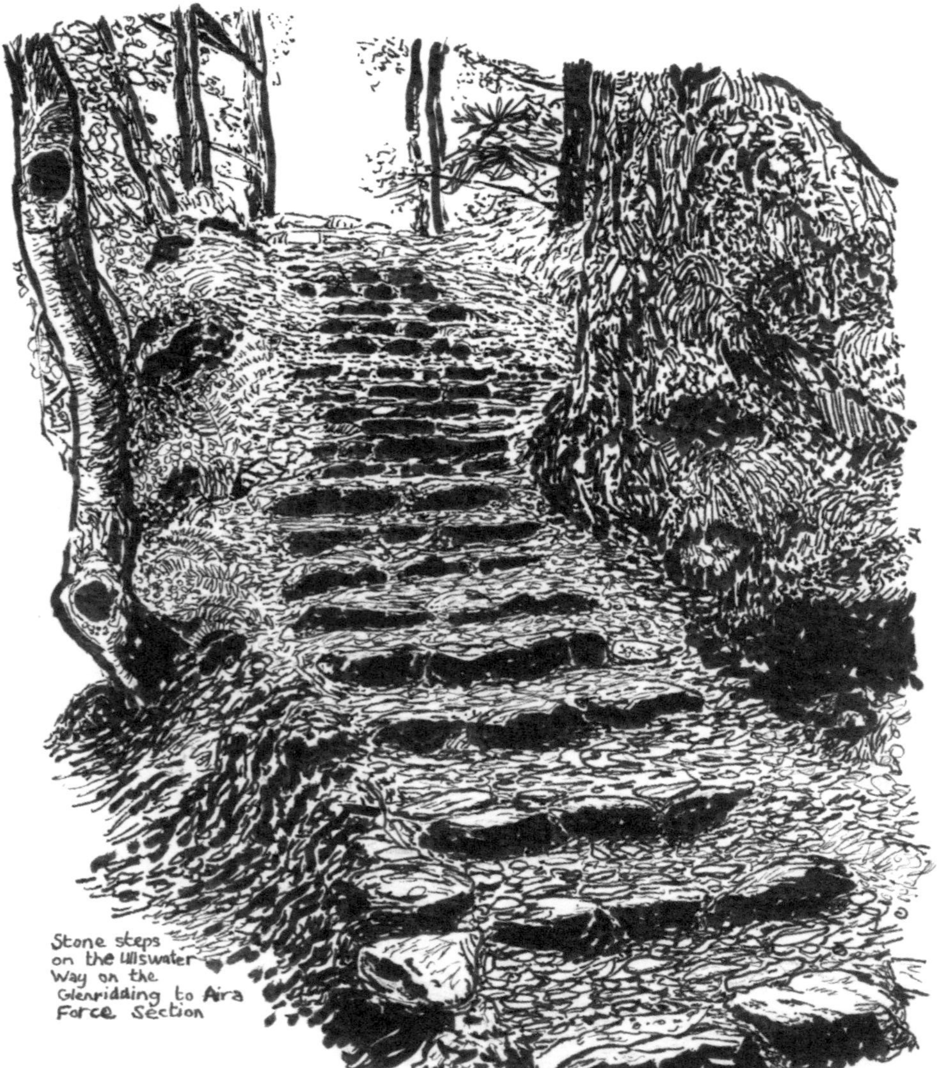

Stone steps on the Ullswater Way on the Glenridding to Aira Force Section

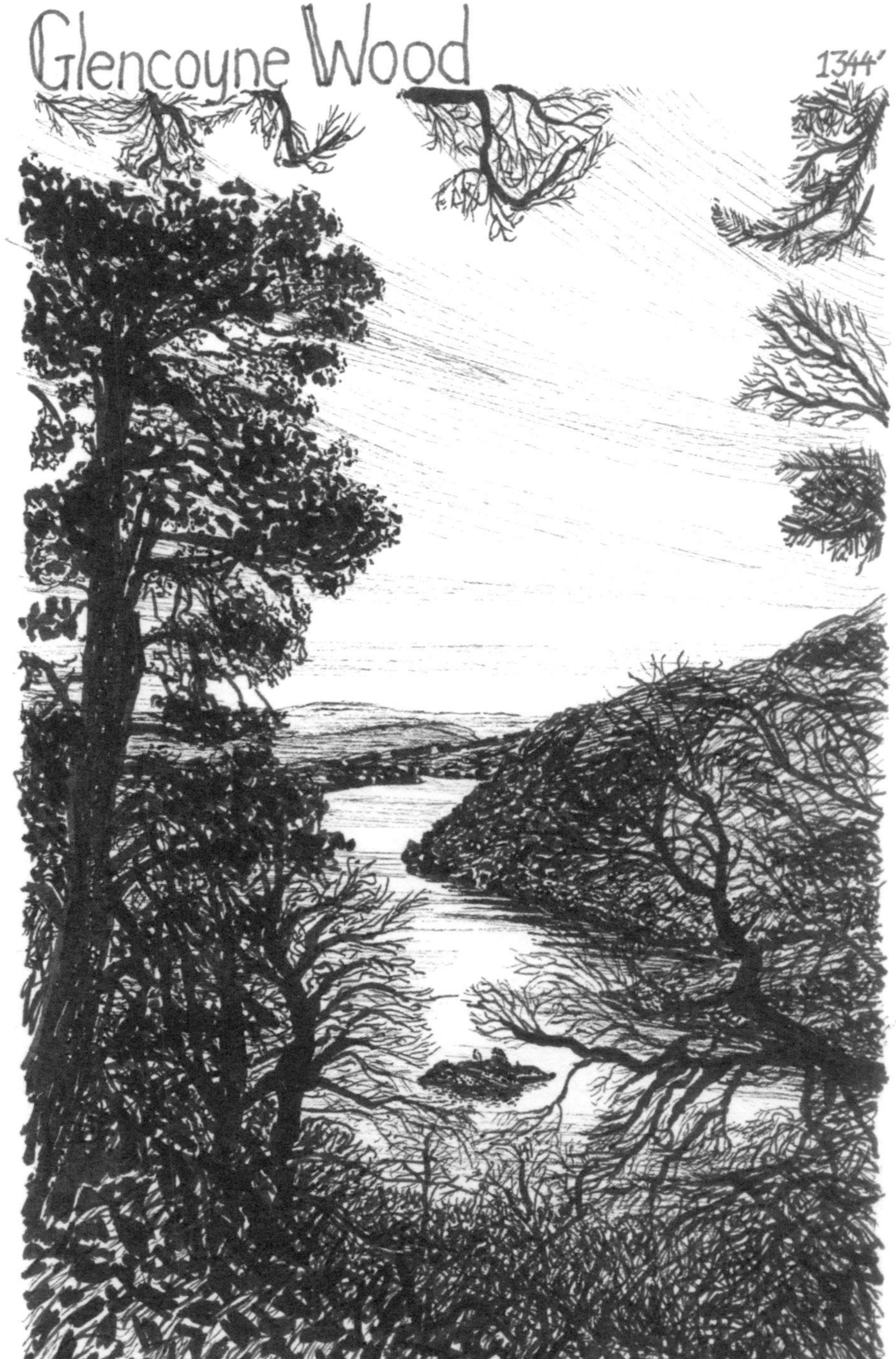
Glencoyne Wood
1344'

Glencoyne Wood - West Entrance

1036'

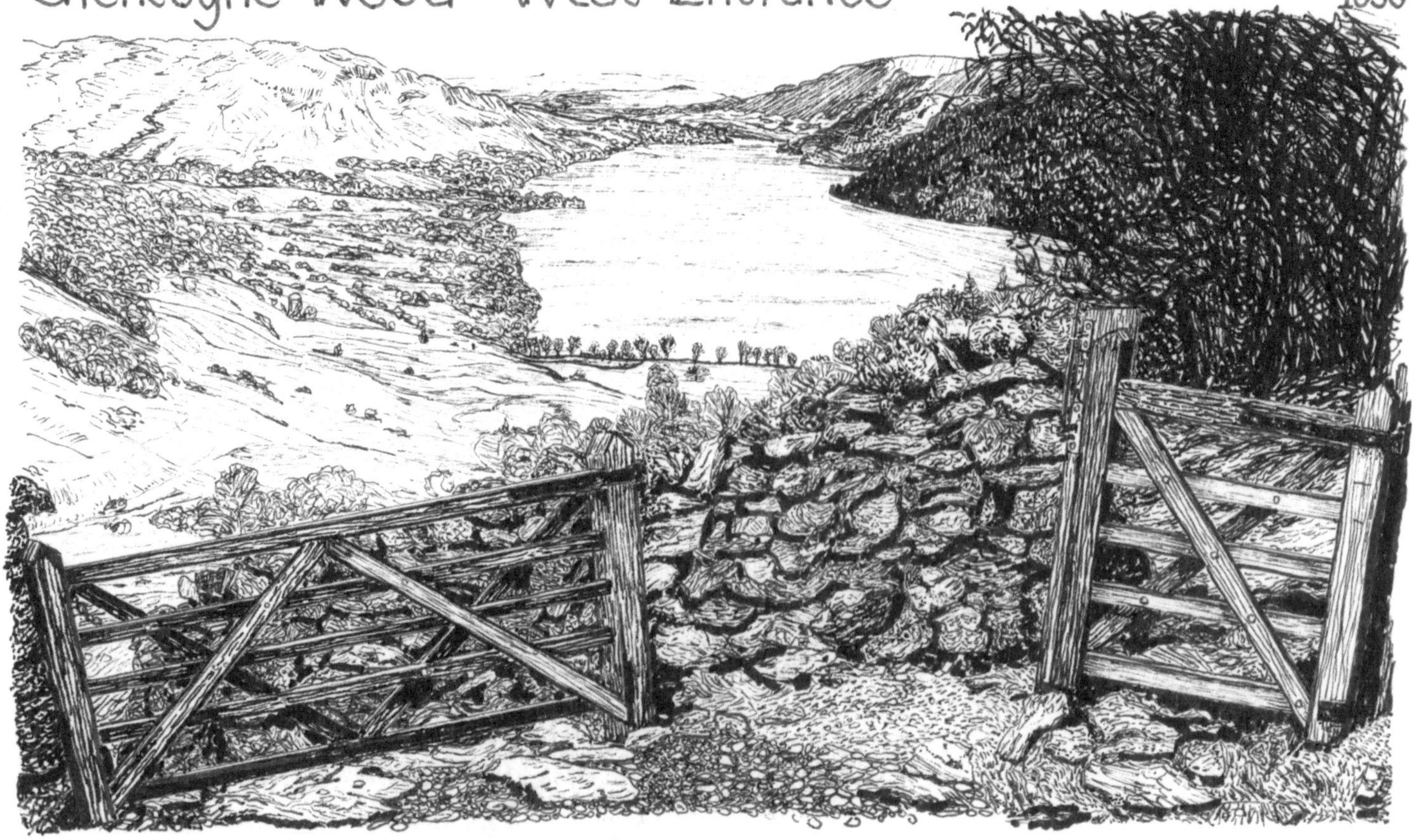

Glencoyne Bay

♿ 479'

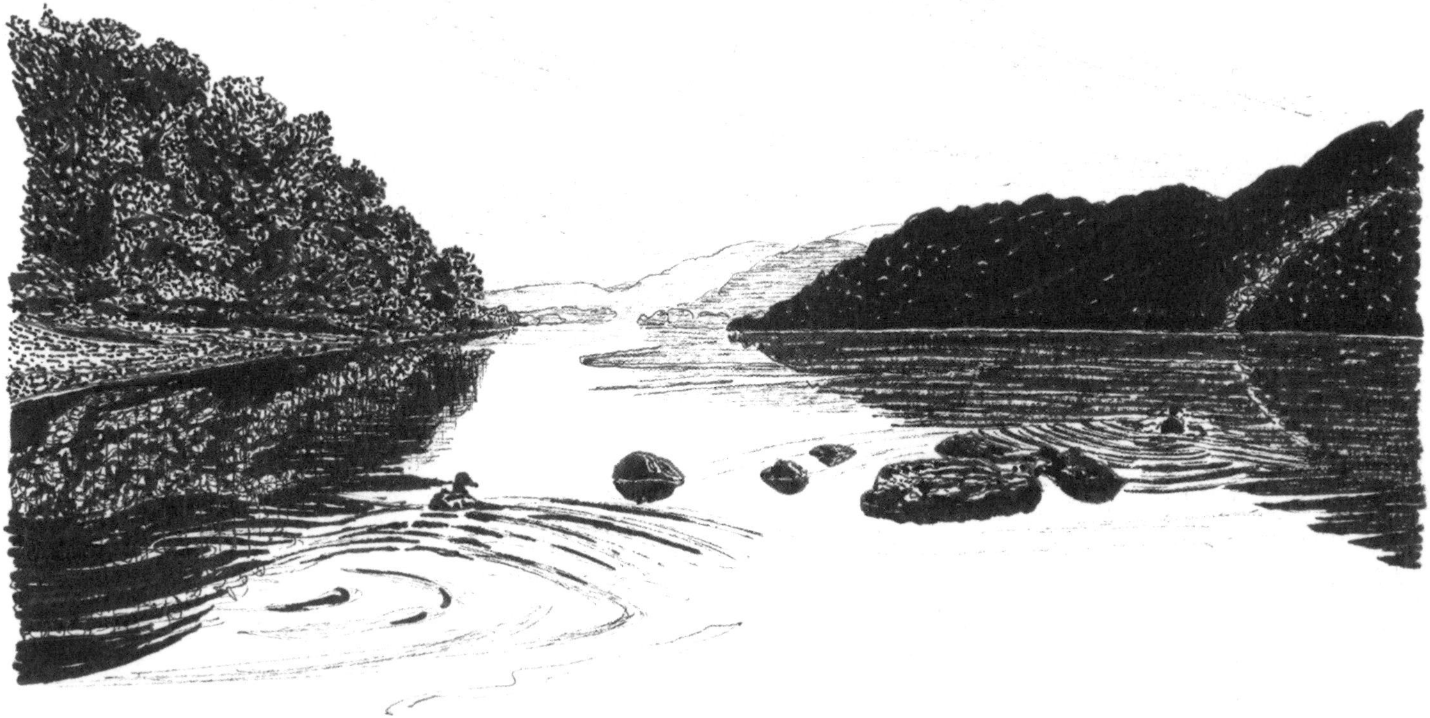

Glencoyne Bay

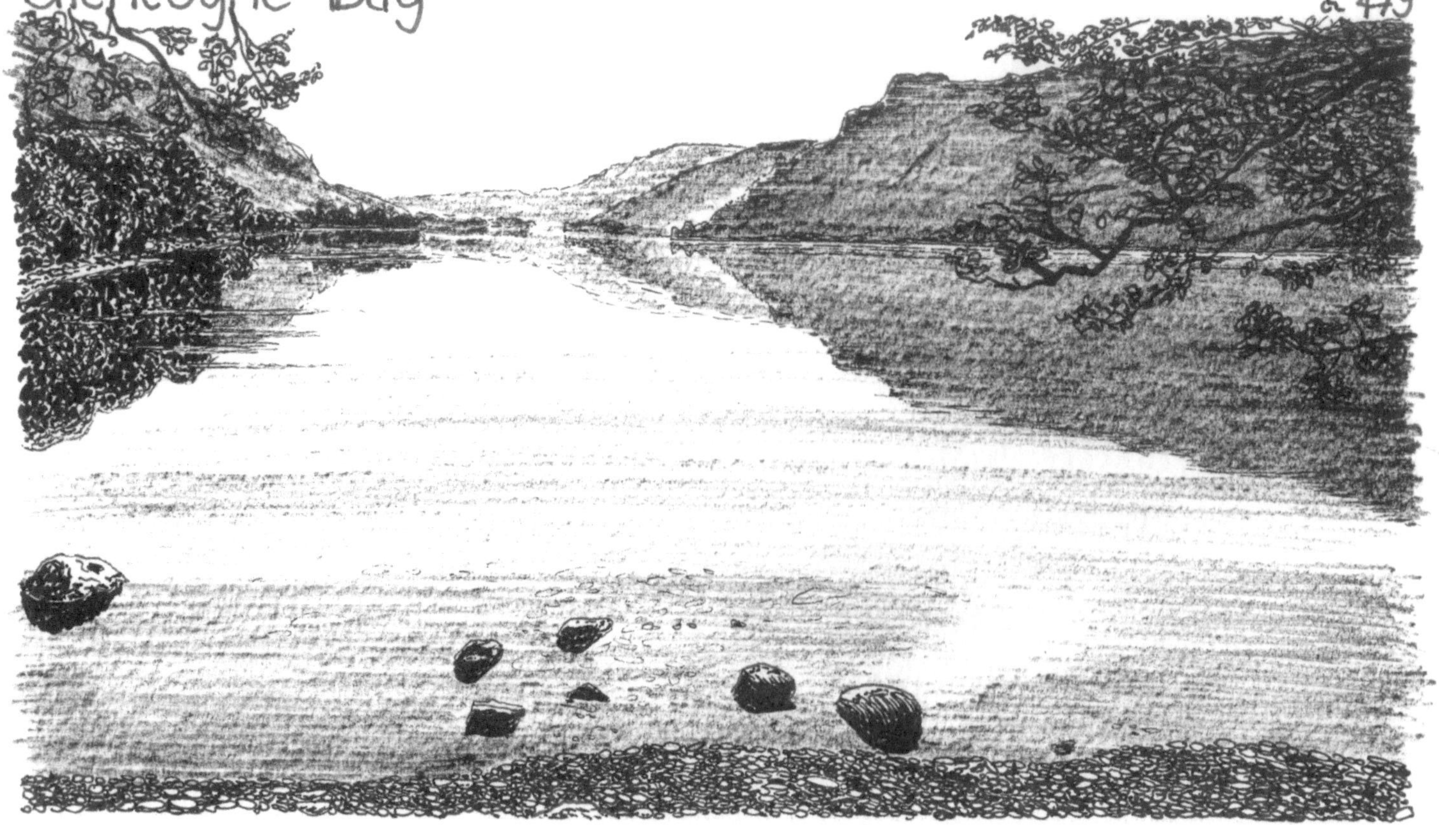

North Glencoyne Bay

♿ 479'

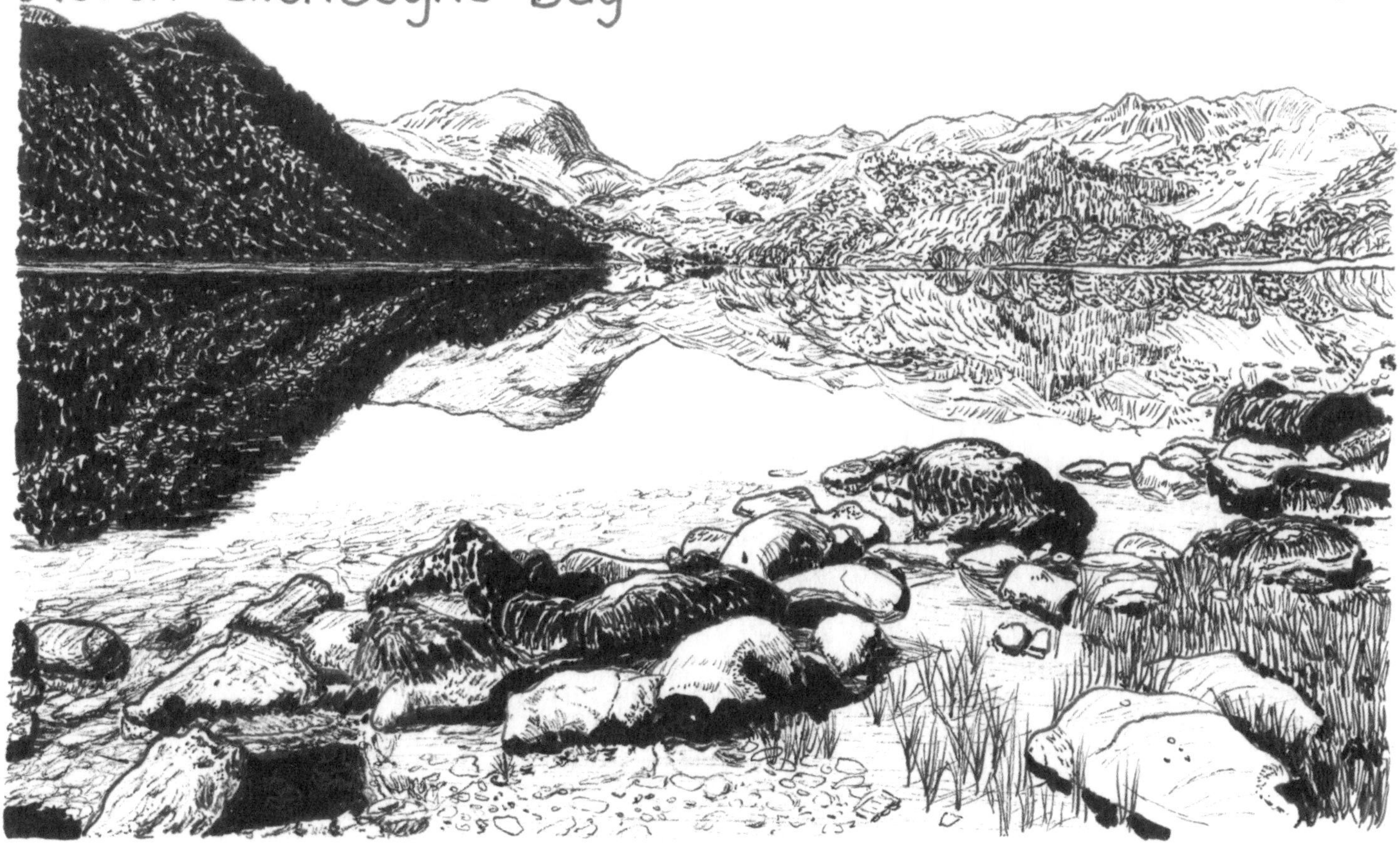

Swineside Knott

1813′

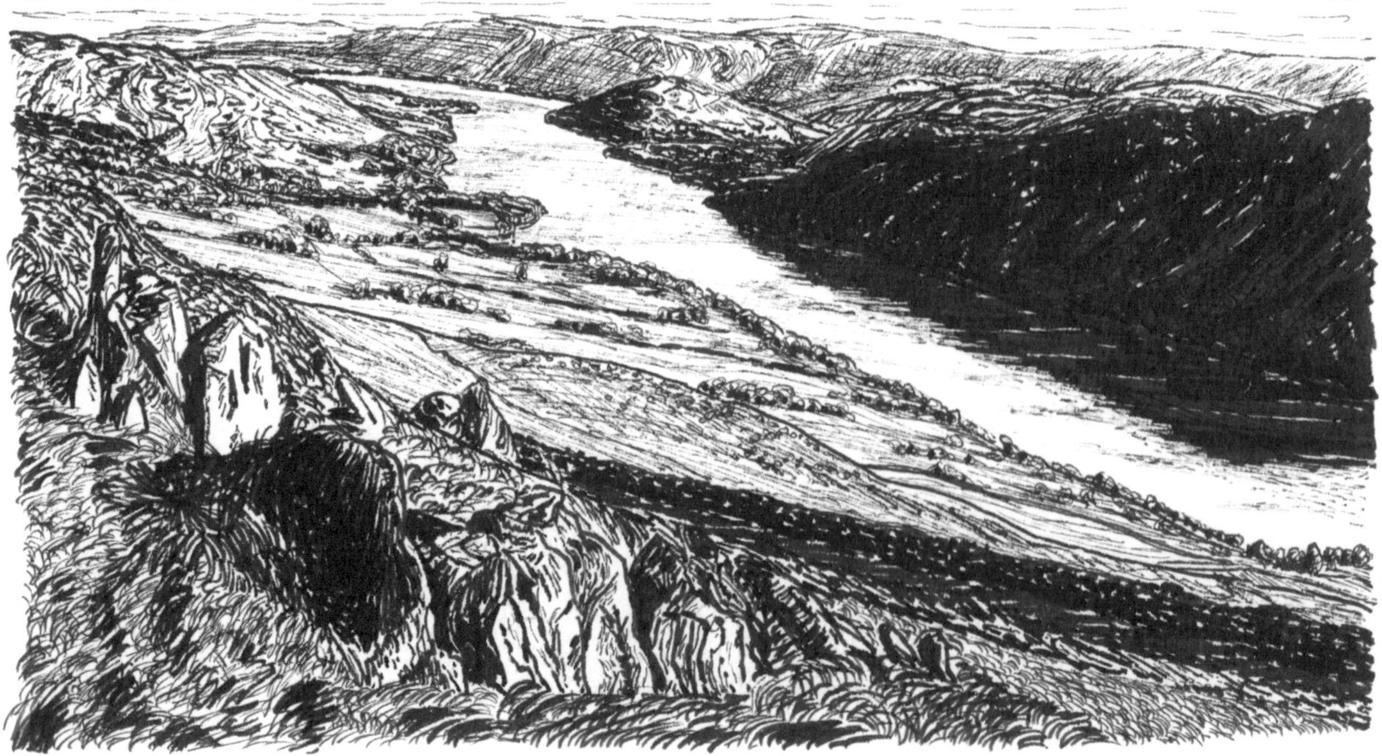

Swineside Knott

1813'

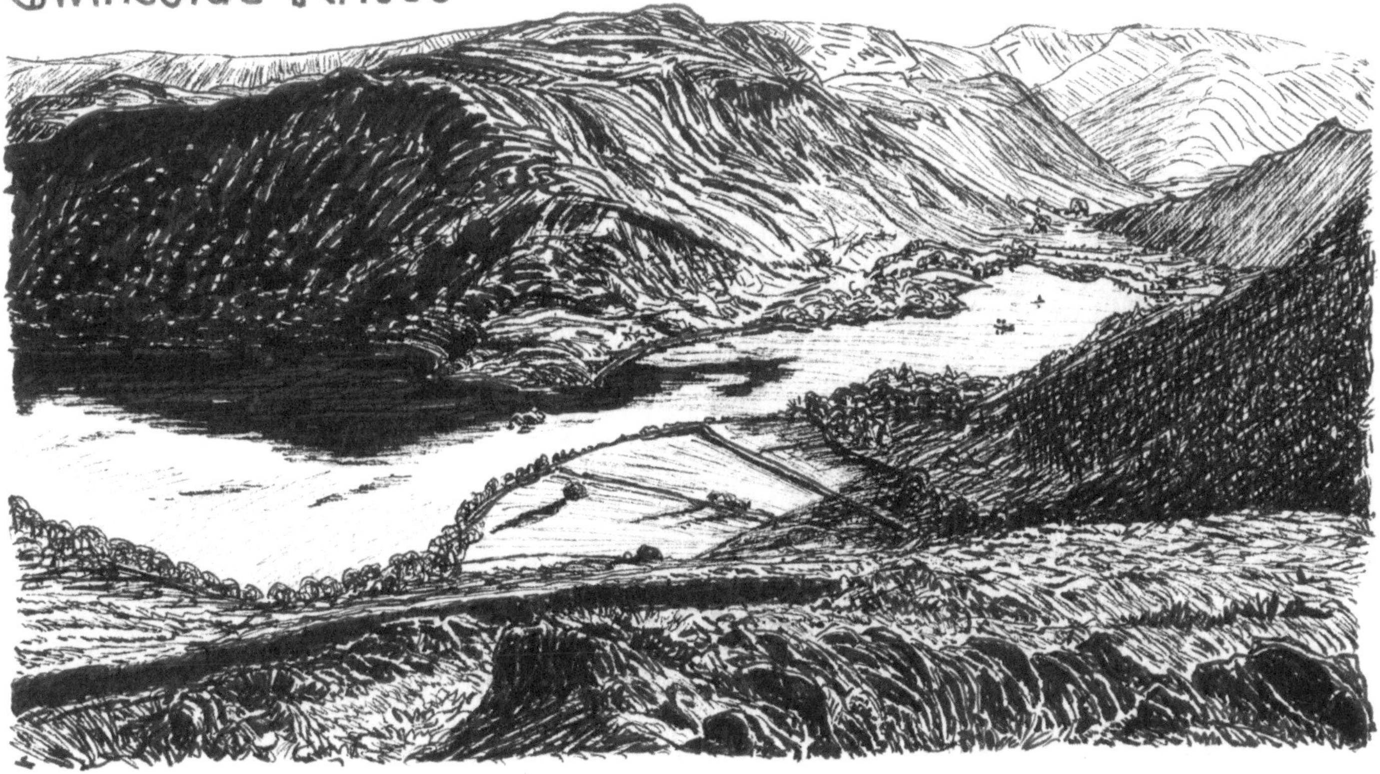

Glencoyne Bay - North Shore

492′

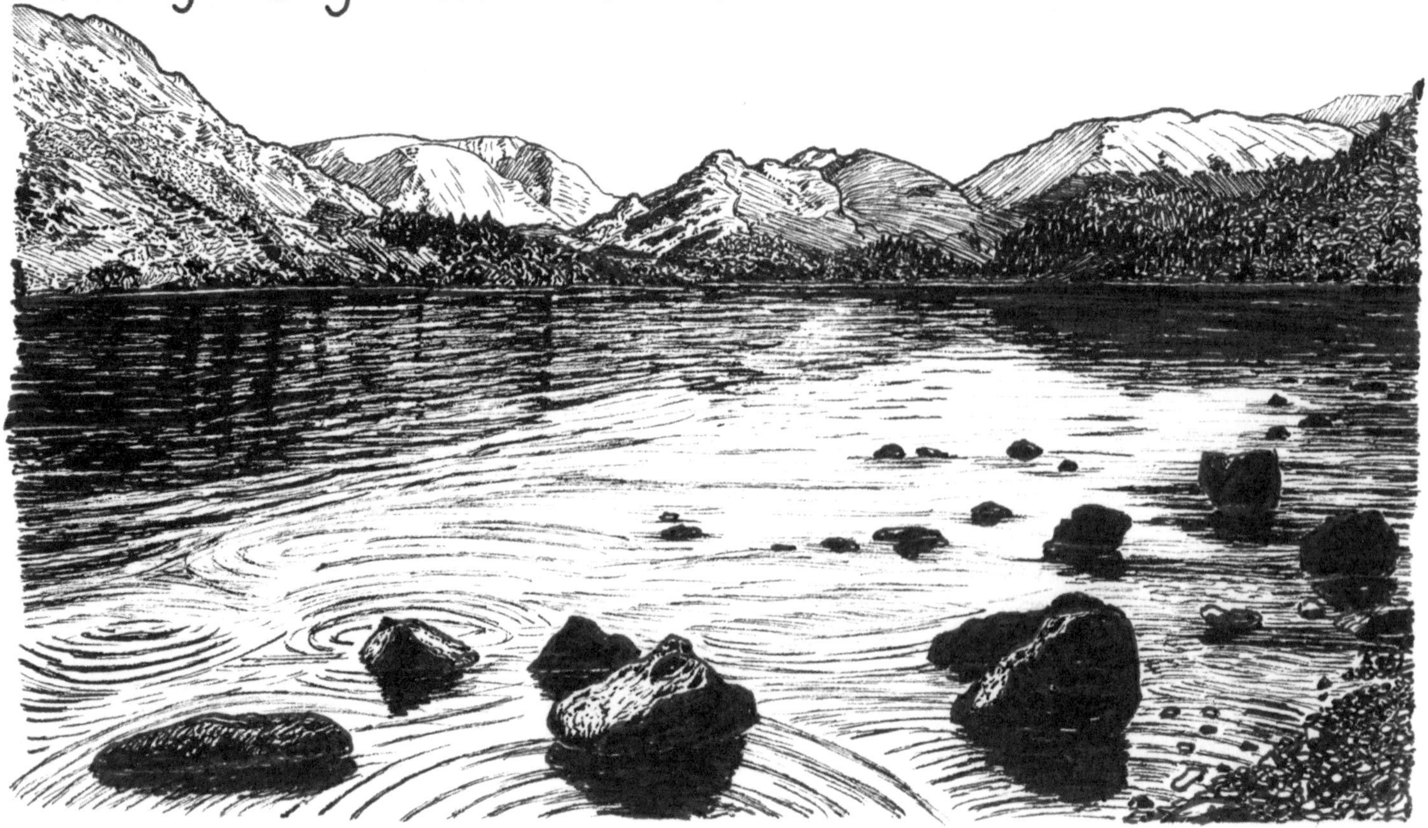

Glencoyne Park - Ullswater Way

♿ 557′

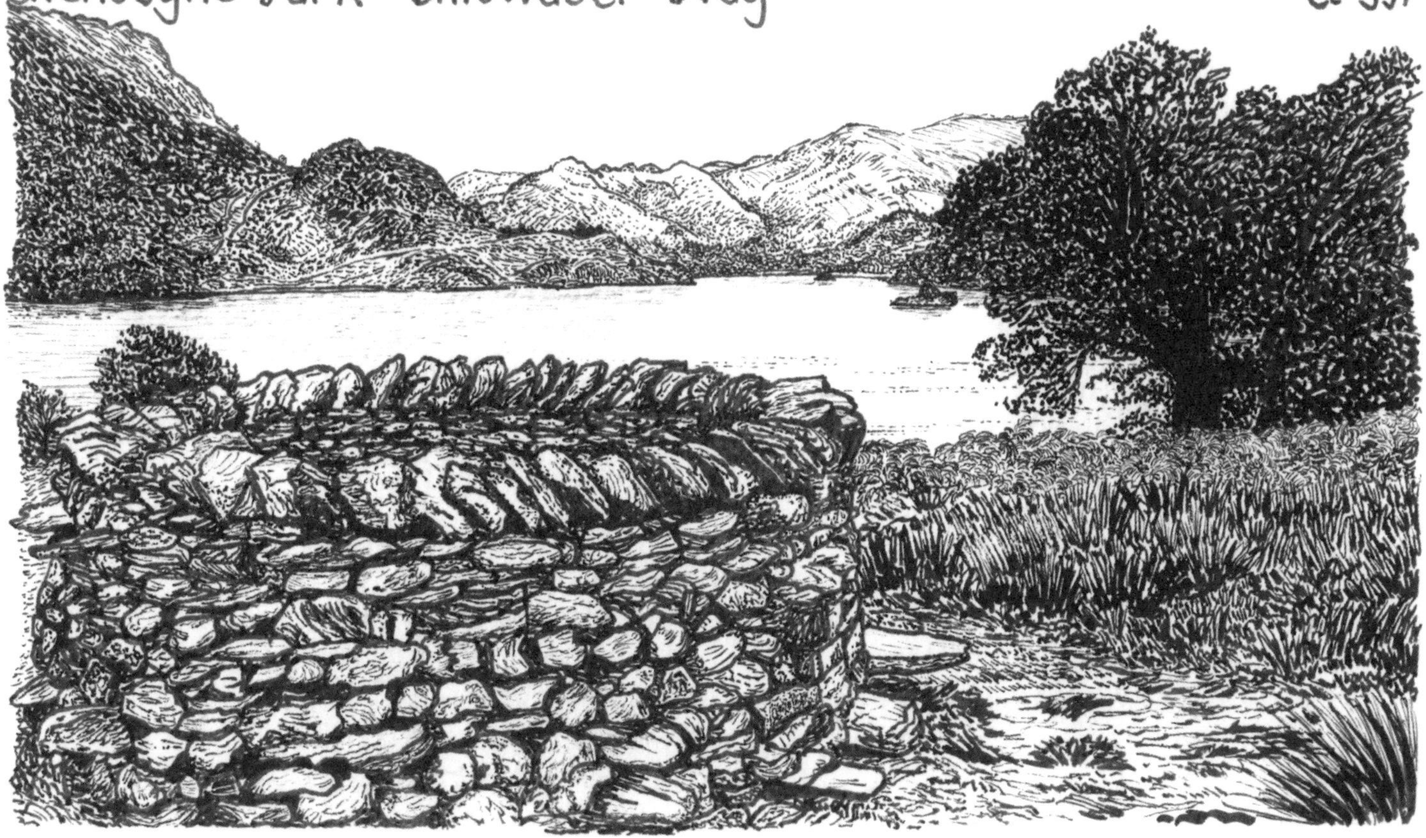

The Conservation Movement

The National Trust

Wordsworth believed that the Lake District should be "a sort of national property, which every man has a right to perceive and a heart to enjoy". This was the first time the concept of national ownership of a landscape had been published and why Wordsworth is considered the founder of the Conservation movement. He created the climate of opinion, carried on by subsequent generations that made the formation of the National Trust and later the National Park possible. In the second half of the 1800's tourism boomed and mill owners raced to build grand villas on every knoll with a lake view, whilst the villages were overlaid with inns, hotels, boarding houses, shops and restaurants.

The passing of the Thirlmere Act in 1879 forced the conservationists into being better organised. Cannon Rawnsley (1851-1920) led the way in standing up to the juggernaut of Victorian industry. In 1883 he founded the Lake District Defence Society recruiting the great and the good as members, such as William Morris, Octavia Hill and John Ruskin. They prevented two new railways being built, in Borrowdale and Ennerdale. In 1887 he organised a mass trespass of Fawe Park on Derwent Water and Latrigg fell whose private owners had blocked off public rights of way; the Society won a legal battle for their reinstatement. In 1893 Lodore Falls and Grasmere Island were put up for sale. Rawnsley was frustrated that there was no legal way of buying these for the nation.

Wythburn and Leathes Water which became Thirlmere in 1894

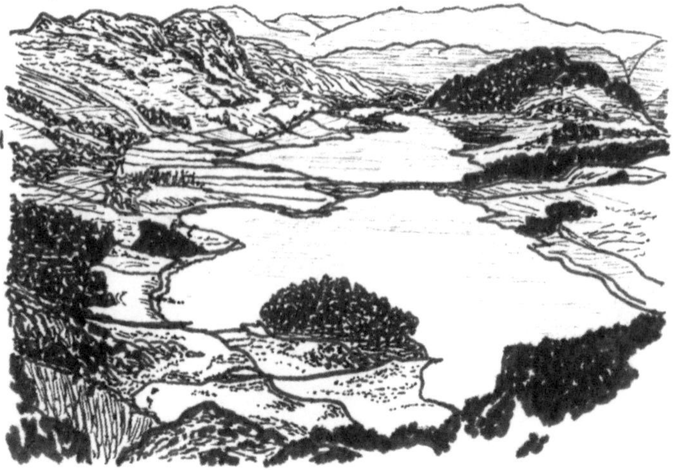

The Conservation Movement

The National Trust

So, in 1895 he co-founded the National Trust for Places of Historic Interest or Natural Beauty, Rawnsley became Honorary Secretary, and his friend Rupert Potter (father of Beatrix) became the first Life Member. The Trust's first actions were defensive; to rescue the charming double humped bridge at Grange in Borrowdale from being replaced, and to prevent the building of a tramway from Windermere to Bowness. The next priority was to secure prime lakeside land; the first success was the Brandelhow estate, 108 acres on the shores of Derwent Water underneath Catbells which was under threat of becoming a housing development. Vigourous fundraising enabled the Trust to secure it in 1902. The magnificent 750 acre Gowbarrow Park followed in 1906, safeguarding both where Wordsworth's daffodils danced and the stunning Aira Force. In the years after World War 1 the Trust was gifted many significant fells as memorials to the fallen. At the time of Rawnsley's death in 1920 the Trust had 1387 acres in the district. Rawnsley had been instrumental in helping Beatrix Potter become published. Her books were a huge success, enabling her to buy Hill Top at Sawrey; she is easily in the top 100 best-selling authors of all time. After she stopped writing she dedicated her life to farming, Herdwick sheep breeding and buying additional land and farms. When she passed in 1943 she gifted over 4,000 acres and many cottages to the Trust, with one stipulation; that Herdwicks continue to be bred on them. By the end of World War 2 the Trust owned a staggering 122,000 acres; a quarter of what would become the Lake District National Park.

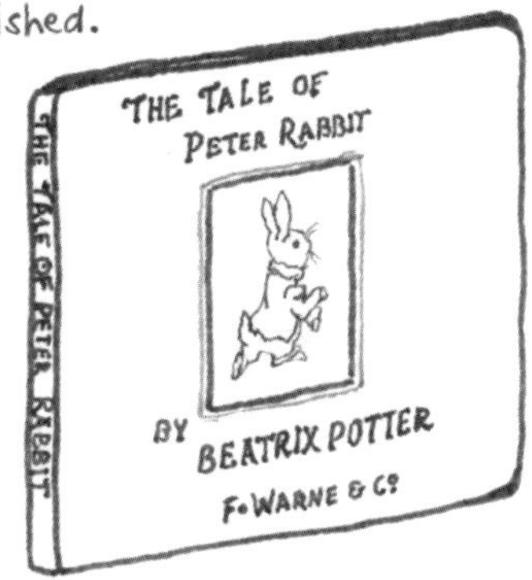

The Conservation Movement

Friends of the Lake District

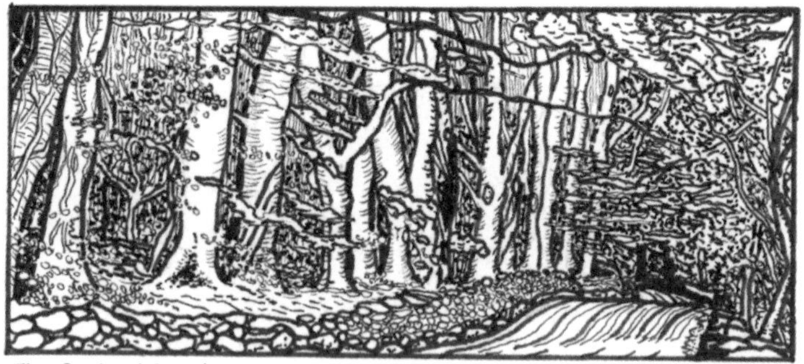

The Rusland Beeches - saved by Friends of the Lake District in 1956

Britain was ravaged economically after World War One; national demand for electricity, coal and the new telephone system meant that wood was desperately needed for pit props and telegraph poles. In 1919 the Forestry Commission was formed; there were no constraints on where, how or what it planted. The Lake District was seen as prime planting ground; by 1933 over 6½ million Spruce, Larch and Sitka had been planted in dense mono-blocks around Ennerdale and Thornthwaite. Further plans in 1934 for planting in Dunnerdale and Eskdale spurred Wordsworth's grandson, also called William, and Rev. Symonds into forming the Friends of the Lake District. They garnered the support of the novellist and Borrowdale resident Walpole, Keynes the economist, Collingwood the philosopher, Beveridge the architect of the Welfare State, and Birkett who went on to save Ullswater in 1962; they succeeded in establishing a 300 square mile exclusion zone for mass planting in the Lake District. Rev. Symonds had argued that the ideal future for the Lake District was to be a national park and not a national forest.

In 1937 the Friends' set up Lake District Estates to protect upland farming culture and prevent farms being bought by the Forestry Commission or as second homes. By 1977 they had 17 working farms and gifted them to the National Trust for their future safe keeping. Friends of the Lake District continues today with its own campaigns with its Kendal headquarters a few yards from the National Parks'.

The Conservation Movement

Lake District National Park Authority

In 1929 a Government Select Committee was set up to hear the case for National Parks; the argument for was compelling but came to nothing as the recession of the 1930's took hold. Frustration in the north of England in 1932 at the lack of access to the hills led to the mass trespass of Kinder Scout in Derbyshire; this was the spark to start the Ramblers' Association 'Right to Roam' campaign. The National Trust and Friends of the Lake District maintained their pressure but nothing happens until after World War Two with the passing of the National Parks and Access to Countryside Act of 1949. In May 1951 the Lake District National Park is established (one month after the Peak District National Park) with 912 square miles of protected landscape. Ever since the National Park has had to wrestle with at times two contrary objectives of preserving the landscape, protecting wildlife and heritage and those of amply providing access and facilities for the public's open air enjoyment. A 1974 legal review judged that where conflict arises, the conservation interest should take priority.

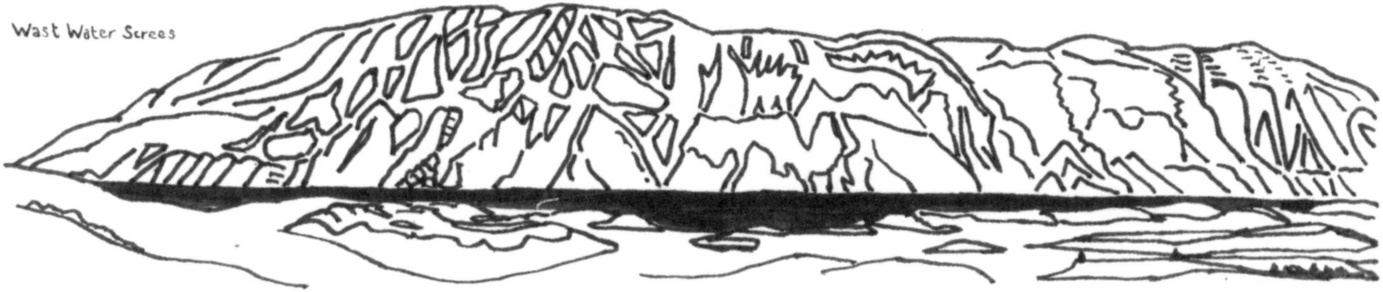

Wast Water Screes

Section 4: Lowther Park to Haweswater

88.	Lowther Park	& 623′
89.	Sleddale Beck	721′
90.	Old Corpse Road	1344′
91.	Old Corpse Road	951′
92.	Rowantreethwaite Beck	984′
93.	Branstree - West of Summit	2131′
94.	Harter Fell	2539′
95.	Nan Bield Pass - Harter Fell	2295′
96.	Nan Bield Pass Shelter	1967′
97.	Mardale Ill Bell	2492′
98.	High Street - Racecourse Hill	2692′
99.	High Street - East of Trig Point	2623′
100.	Rampsgill Head	2543′
101.	High Street - Riggindale Crag	2656′
102.	Caspel Gate Tarn	1967′
103.	Castle Crag - Haweswater	984′
104.	Haweswater - North Shore	967′

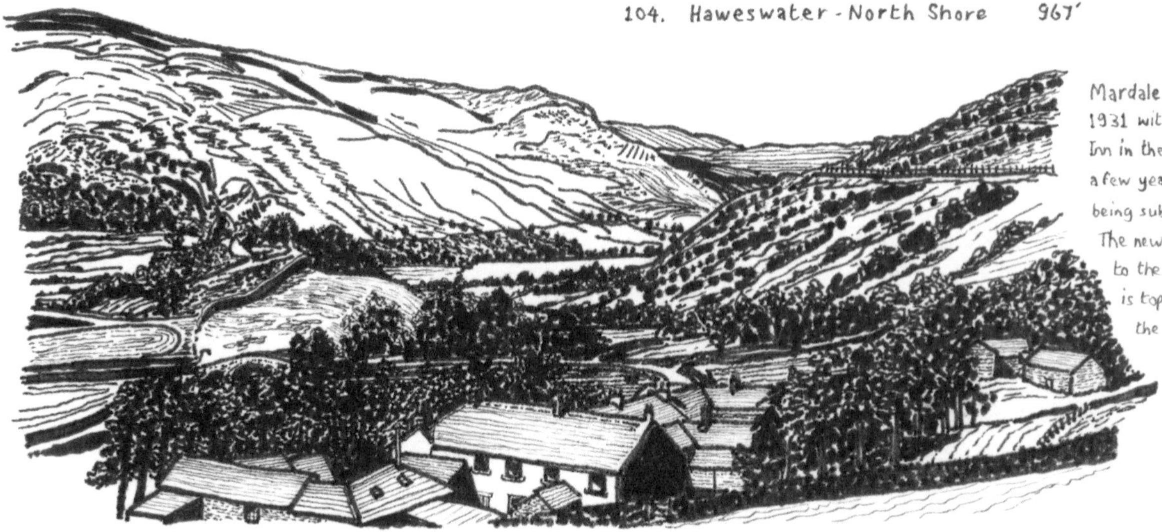

Mardale Green around 1931 with the Dun Bull Inn in the foreground, a few years before being submerged. The newly built road to the valley head is top right in the picture.

Section 4

Lowther to Haweswater

This final section starts in the elysian pastures of Lowther Park; then down to the unspoilt rugged charm of Sleddale. West next on the Old Corpse Road and its classic panoramas. We then arc around the horseshoe of Branstree, Harter Fell, Mardale Ill Bell, High Street and Kidsty Pike which hold the spectacular southern half of Haweswater and its tarns in their grasp. Long Stile and the gentle west and north shores of Haweswater bring this journey to a close.

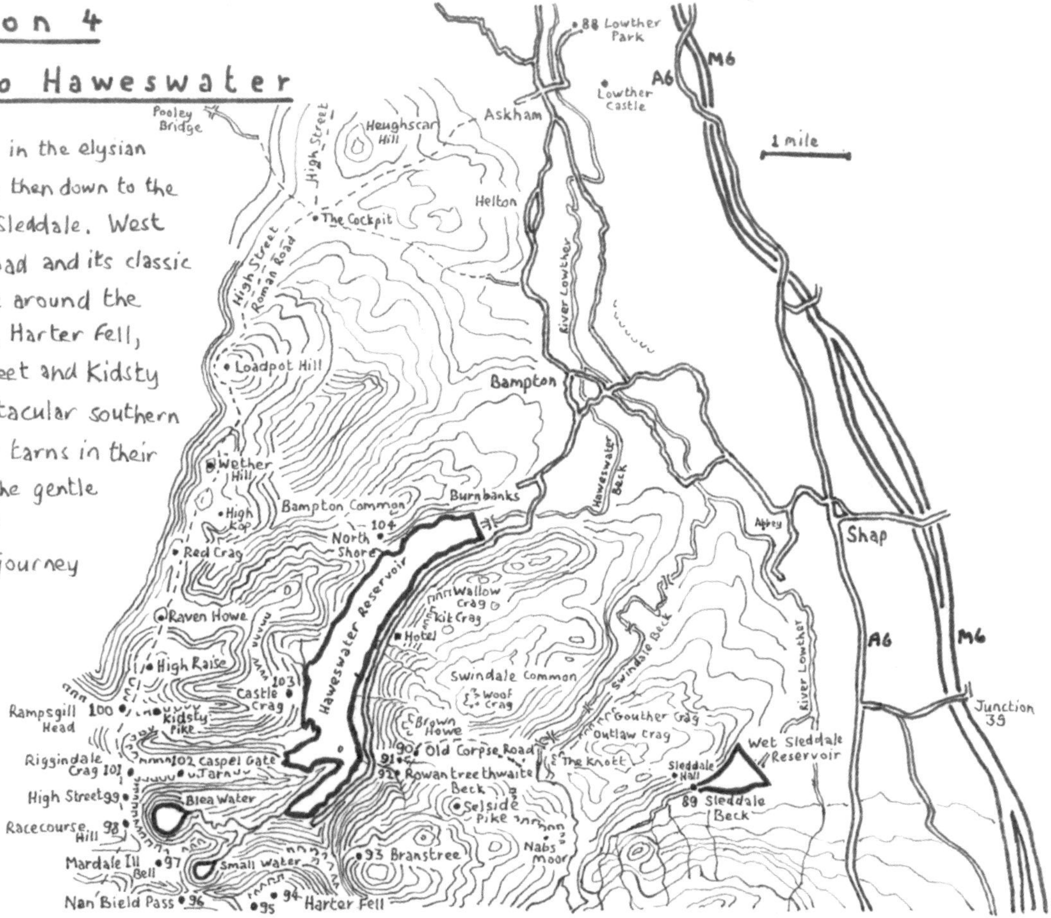

The Lowther Story

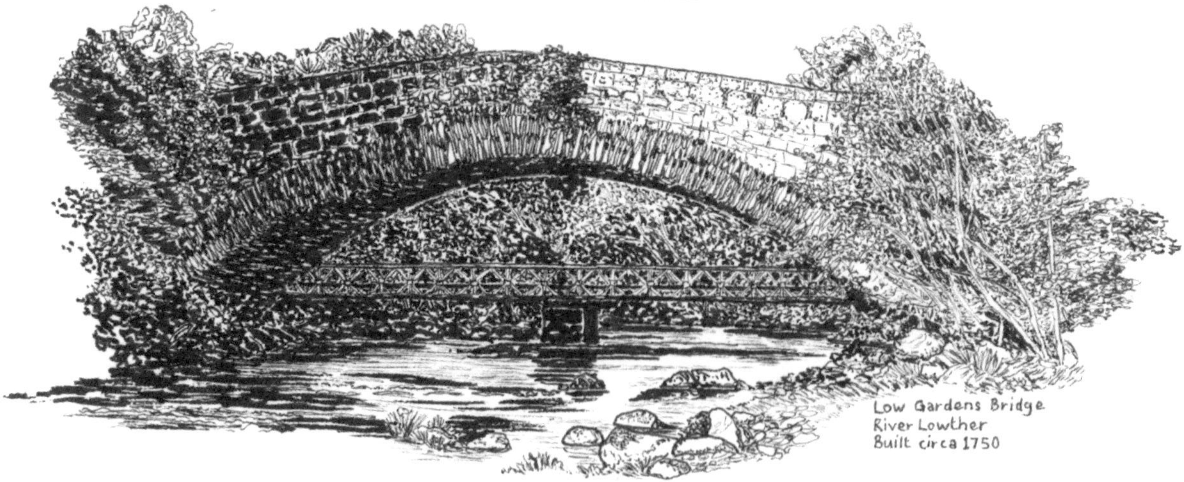

Low Gardens Bridge
River Lowther
Built circa 1750

The Lowther family have been major landowners in Cumbria for a thousand years. The spectacular Disneyesque Lowther Castle was built in 1814; it was said that you could walk across Cumbria and never leave Lowther land. William Wordsworth's father was a land agent for the Lowthers, living in Cockermouth, he died when William was twelve or thirteen. The Lowther's owed the Wordsworth's over £4,000 in unpaid commission, they didn't settle it for over 20 years, forcing the Wordsworths into poverty and to breaking up their family.

The 'Yellow Earl', Hugh Lowther the 5th Earl of Lonsdale was the most flamboyant and reckless of the lineage. He entertained the Kings of Portugal and Italy, and Kaiser Wilhelm II of Germany between 1895 and 1910. His footmen wore yellow, he was the first President of the Automobile Association - hence its yellow logo; also he was the first President of the International Horse Show, the founder of boxings' Lonsdale Belts and in 1936 Chairman of Arsenal F.C.. By this time the family fortune was blown and he had to abandon the castle.

Lowther Park

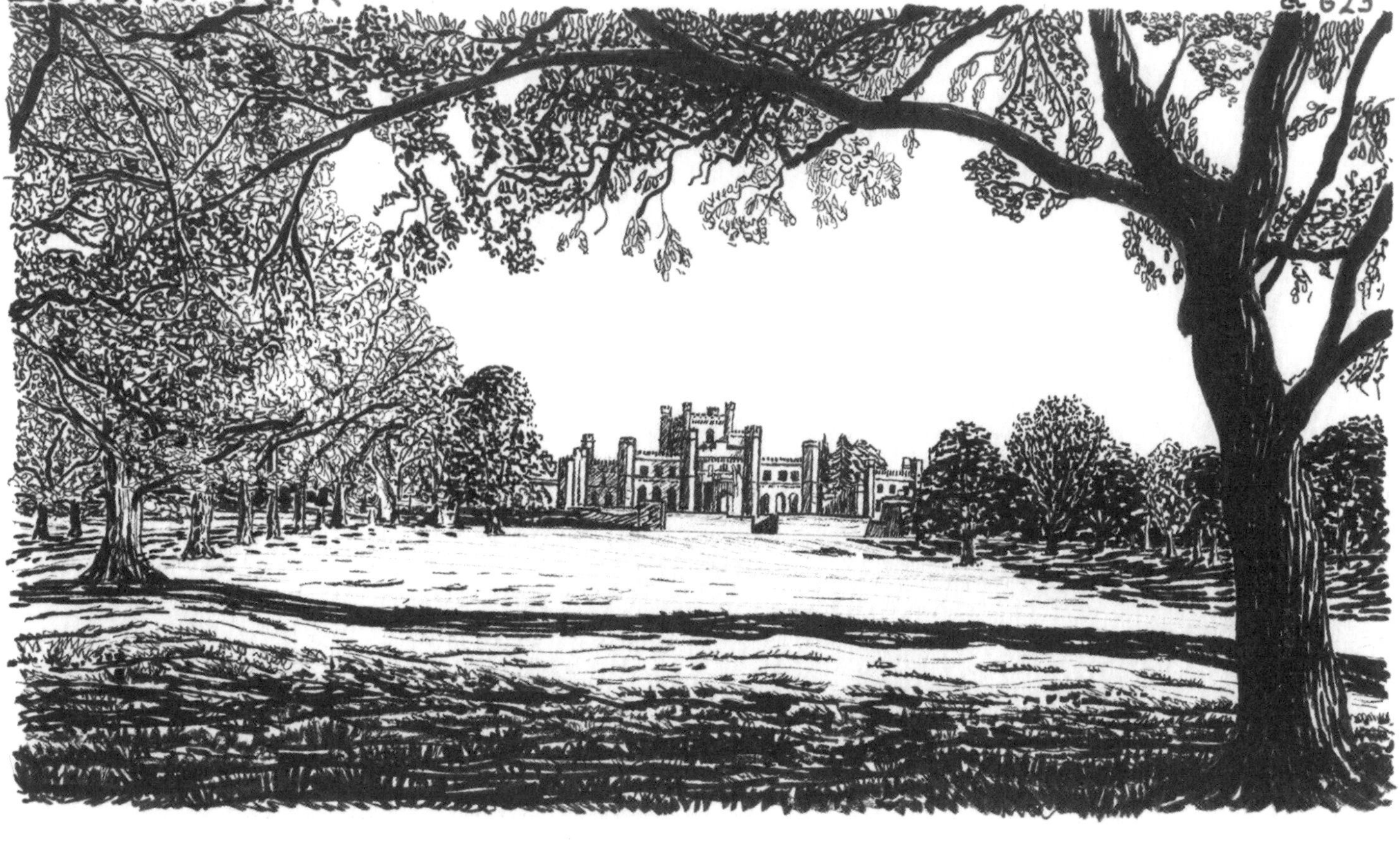

Sledddale Beck - Wet Sleddale

721'

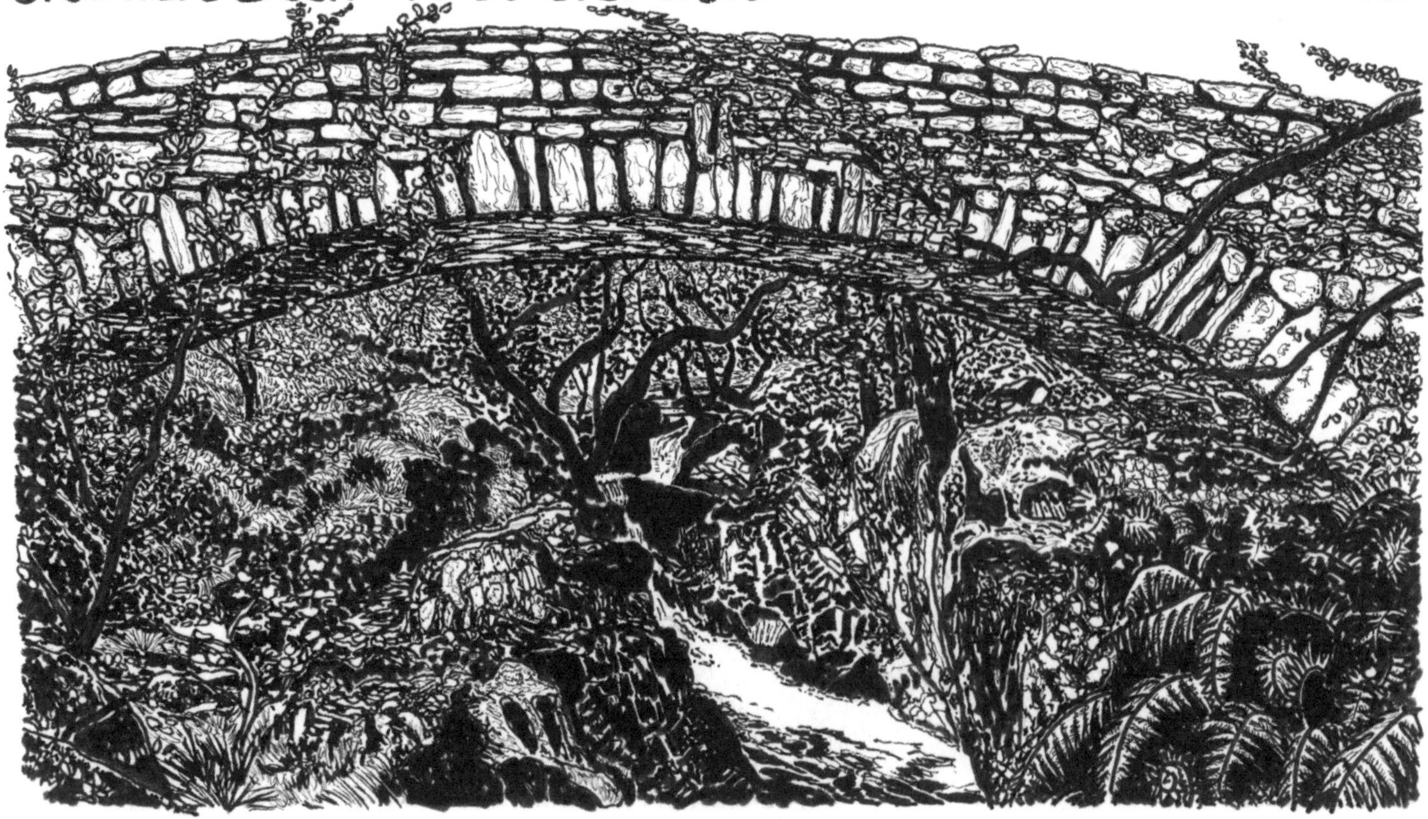

Wet Sleddale

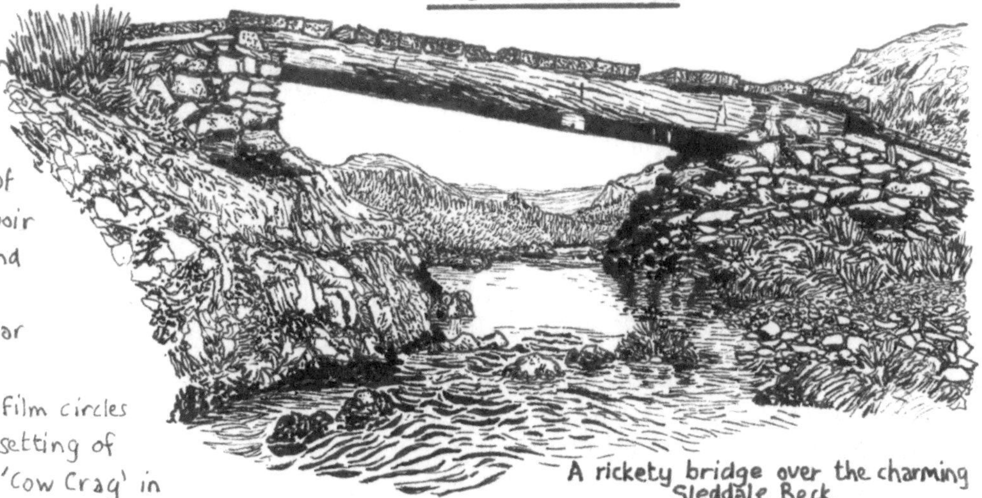

A rickety bridge over the charming Sleddale Beck

The 600 yards long dam retaining Wet Sleddale reservoir was completed in 1966; it feeds into Haweswater via a series of tunnels. Aside from the reservoir it is a beautifully rugged and wild valley with the winding Sleddale Beck being a particular highlight.

The area is now famous in film circles for Sleddale Hall being the setting of Uncle Monty's holiday home, 'Cow Crag' in the 1986 cult black comedy 'Withnail and I' starring Richard E. Grant and Paul McGann. The film is routinely in the 'best ever' lists of British films, and is most celebrated for its one liner delivered in a 'Penrith cafe'; "we want the finest wines available to humanity, we want them here, and we want them now." Presently there is an annual outdoor screening of the film in the grounds of the Hall every summer.

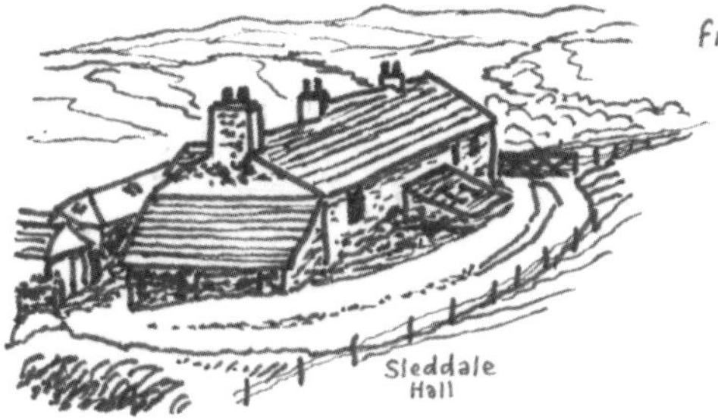

Sleddale Hall

Several shots of a lake feature in the film, these were taken from the Old Corpse Road overlooking Haweswater, and can be seen on the following two pages.

The Old Corpse Road - Haweswater

1344′

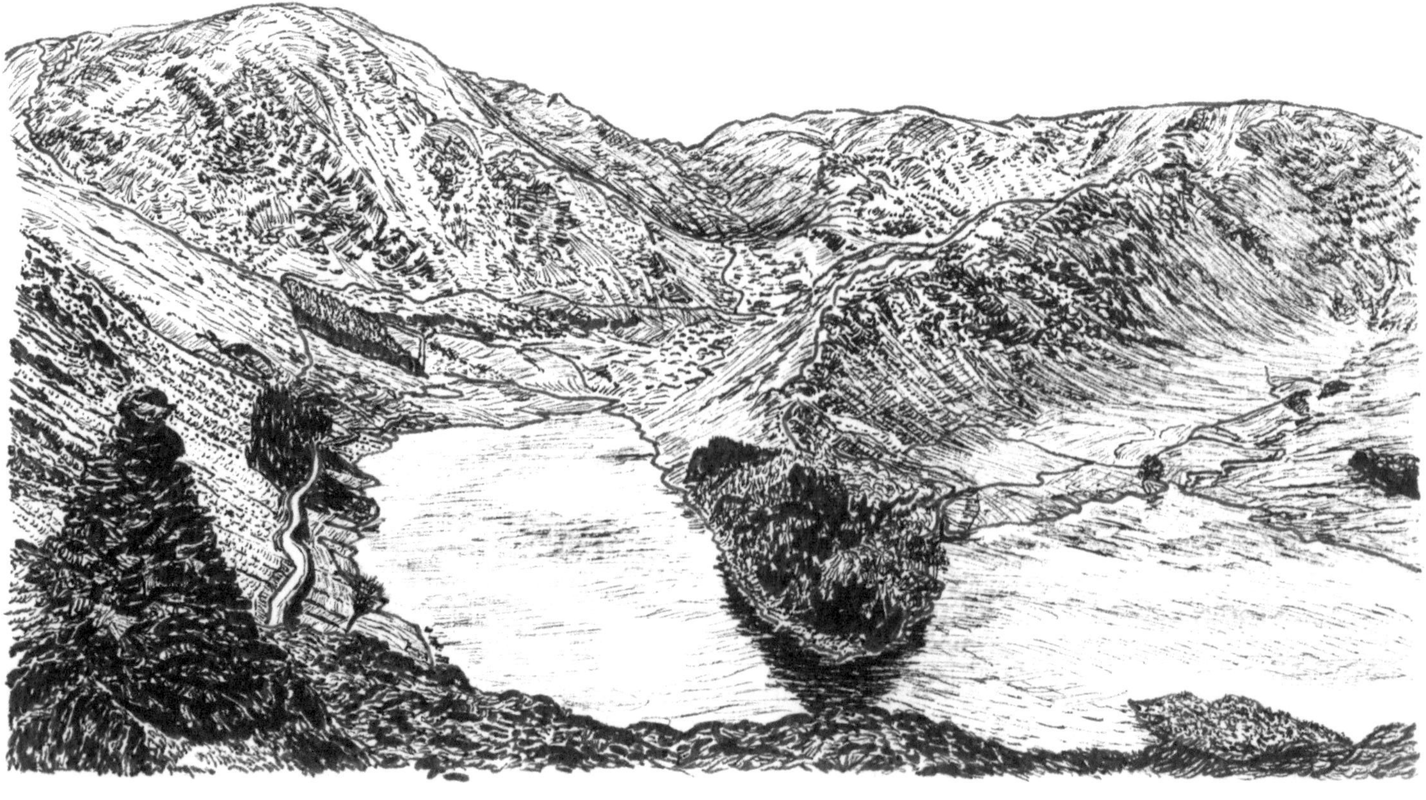

Haweswater - Old Corpse Road

951′

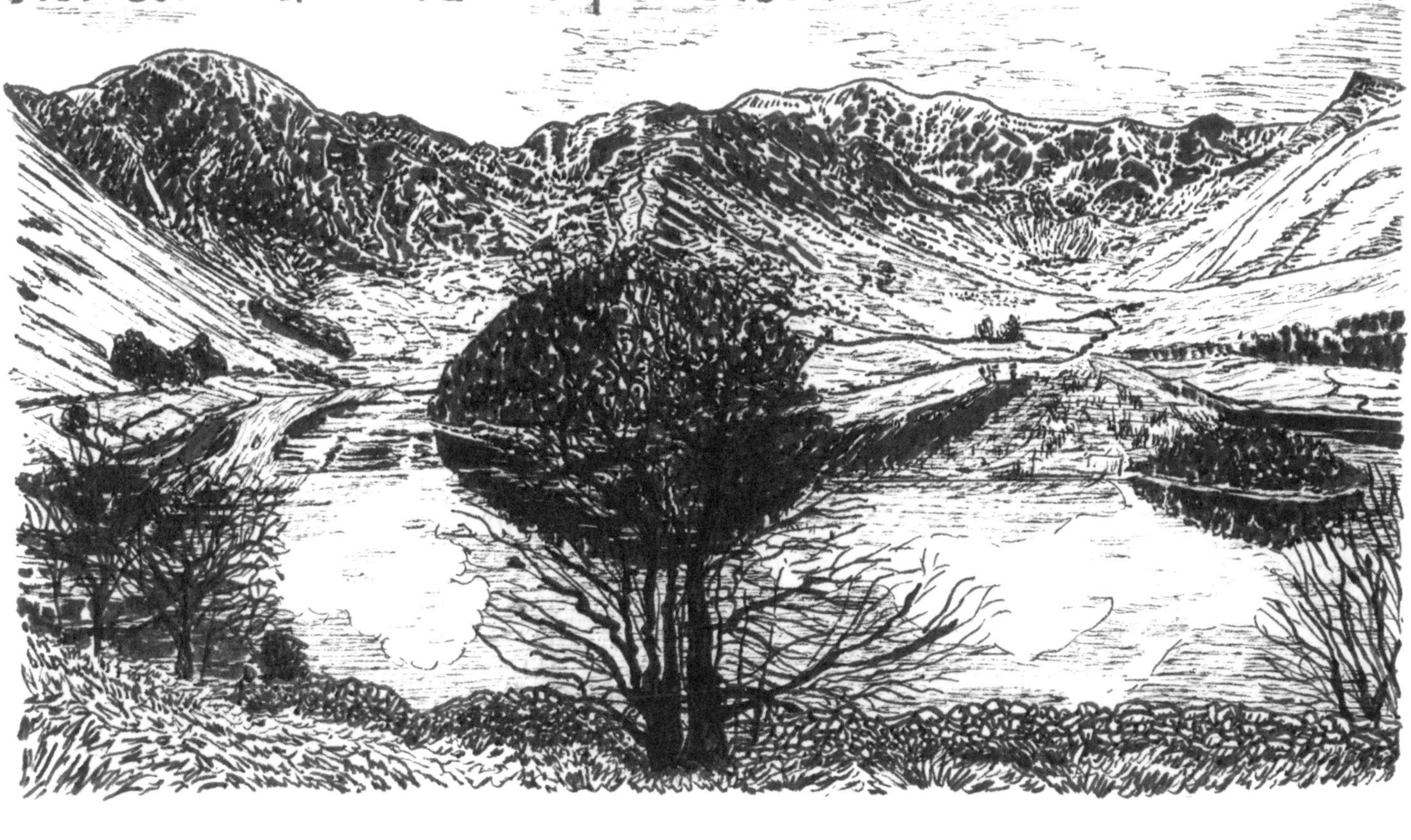

Mardale Valley

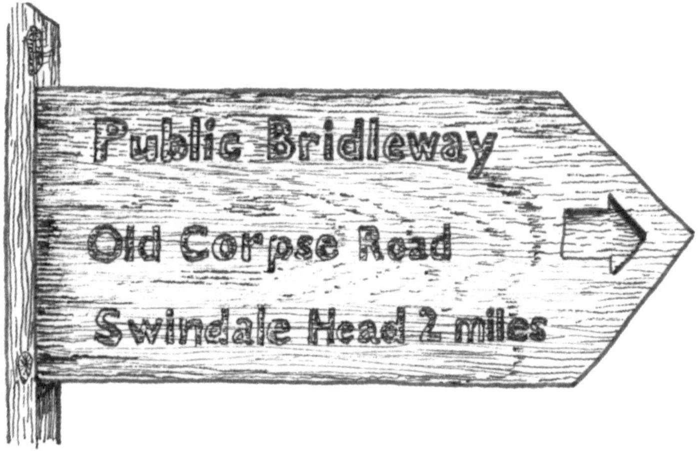

Mankind lived continuously in Mardale Valley from the Bronze Age 5,000 years ago until 1933 when all the properties were compulsorily purchased by Manchester Corporation Water Works (M.C.W.W.). The valley was rich in deer and fish, Bronze Age man used the natural fortification of Castle Crag on the west shore to defend the valley head. Originally Haweswater was 2½ miles long and nearly split into two (named High and Low Water) by a spit of land created by Measand Beck. There were two settlements; Mardale Green at the valley head with the Dun Bull Inn, a church and tiny school and a handful of farms, and Measand with several farms also. The monks of Shap Abbey built an oratory in Mardale Green in the 1300's, this was superceded by Holy Trinity Church in the 1600's, a broad low construct, with walls 3 feet thick and a tower just 29½ feet high.

Before 1728 all of the dead from the valley were taken by packhorse up the steep east side, 8 miles, via Swindale on the Old Corpse Road to the mother church at Shap. The final service at Holy Trinity Church took place on August 18th 1935. Seventy tickets were issued, and loudspeakers installed outside relaying the service to the thousands clogging the valley roads. One of the last hymns was "I will lift up mine eyes unto the hills"; the Bishop thanked the congregation for the sacrifice they were making helping the large urban population 100 miles away.

Holy Trinity Church

Virtually all of the Church was recycled and reused before the valley was submerged. The bell and many furnishings went to St. Barnabas in Carlisle; some pews were made into seats for the new Haweswater Hotel; the pulpit to Rosthwaite Church in Borrowdale, and the masonry and windows went into the Intake Tower on the East shore of Haweswater. Lastly the 97 bodies buried from 1728 to 1930 were disinterred and mostly re-buried at Shap.

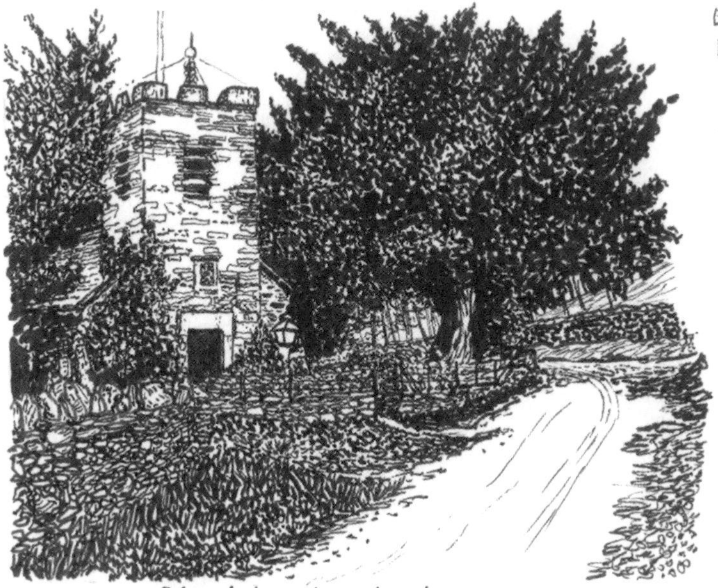

Mardale Church circa 1910

Mardale Green

Originally the Dun Bull Inn was Greenhead Farm, dating from the 1600's; in 1827 it became an Inn. Positioned at the head of the remotest valley in lakeland, it was the last stop on two ancient packhorse routes; east was Gatesgarth Pass leading to Longsleddale; and south Nan Bield Pass to Kendal and Kentmere, with access to High Street making Penrith or Ambleside reachable on a full day's walk. Two tarns lie in the valley head; Blea Water at over 200 feet deep, is the deepest Lake District tarn; Small Water sports a shingle beach and numerous single berth stone shelters. From the very steep slopes west of Branstree's summit (see a few pages ahead) a rare scene in Lakeland can be spied of two tarns beside each other.

Throughout the 1700's on July 12th every year a fair was held on Racecourse Hill, High Street, with wrestling, hound trails, horse racing, and a sociable way of returning sheep which had strayed into the wrong valleys. The last fair was held in 1835, the annual shepherds' meet then transferred to the Dun Bull Inn on the third week in November for the next century. Since 1935 the shepherds meet has been held in Bampton.

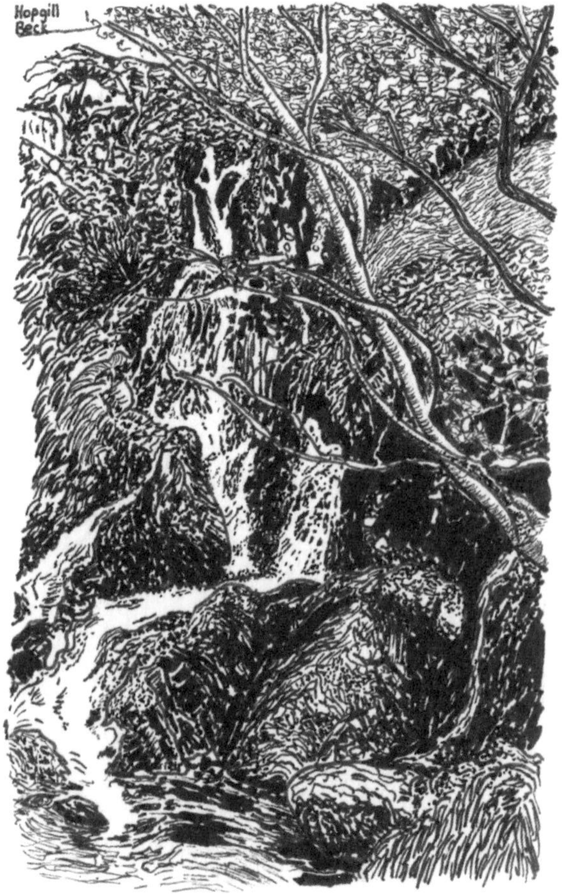

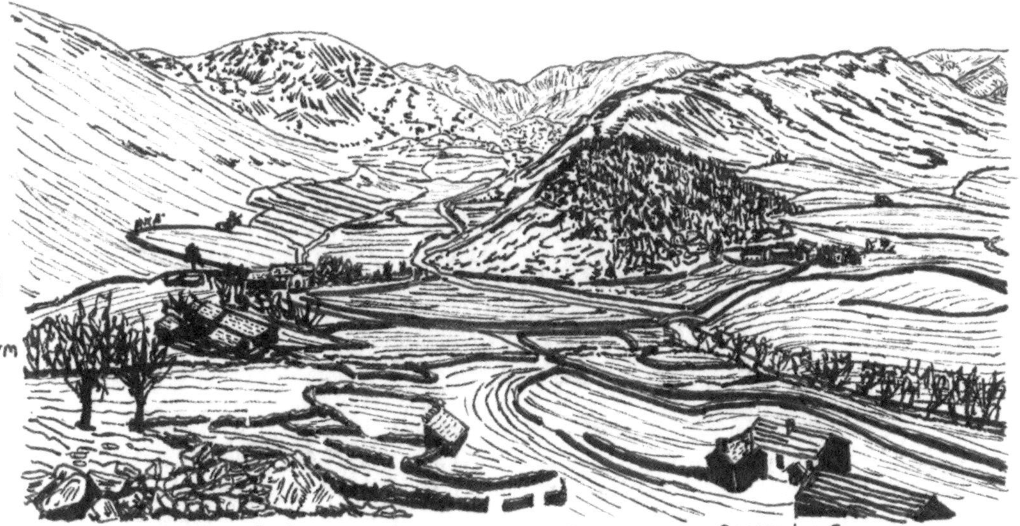

Mardale in the early 1900's

This picture is based on a postcard posted in 1920, printed by Reeds of Penrith.

Rowantreethwaite Beck ~ Haweswater

984′

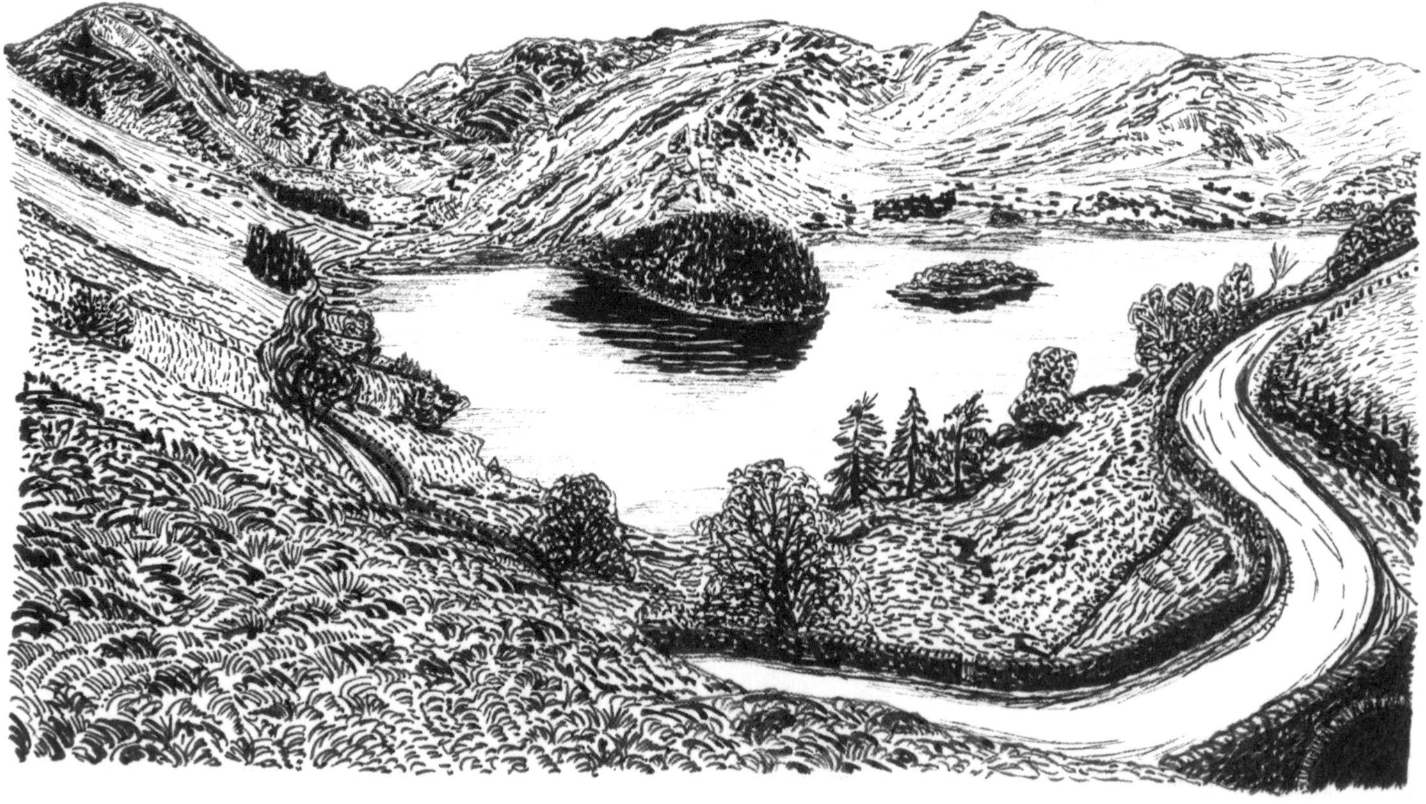

Branstree - West of Summit

2131´

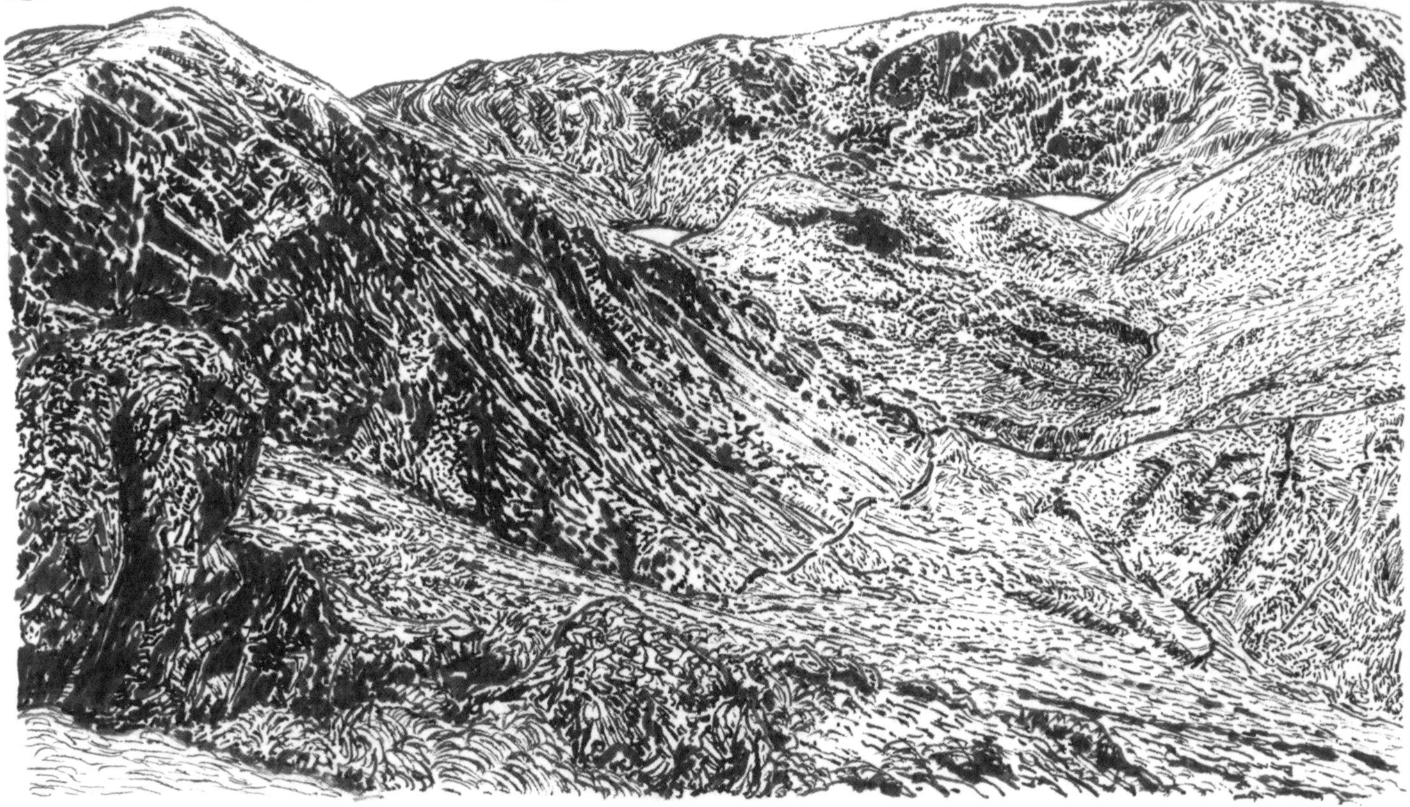

Haweswater

From the passing of the Thirlmere Act in 1878 to the end of World War One in 1918, Manchester's needs exhausted Thirlmere as its population doubled to 700,000. Economic recovery was the countrywide priority.

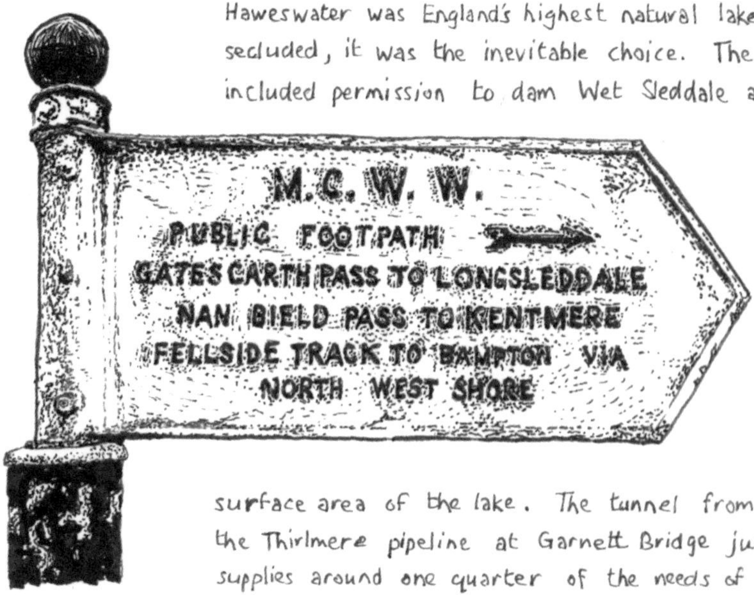

Haweswater was England's highest natural lake at 691' above sea level, and the most secluded, it was the inevitable choice. The Haweswater Act 1919 was passed and included permission to dam Wet Sleddale and Swindale also. In 1929 Burnbanks model village was built to house the workforce and work began on the 1550' wide dam. It was the world's first hollow buttress dam; any movement of the structure is monitored by a huge vertical plumb bomb; when the dam first overflowed in 1942 the plumb bomb moved by 1/20 of an inch. The water level was raised by 96 feet, tripling the surface area of the lake. The tunnel from Haweswater goes south, meeting the Thirlmere pipeline at Garnett Bridge just north of Kendal; Haweswater now supplies around one quarter of the needs of the Northwest of England.

The new valley road on the east side was considered too big and ugly for traffic needs of the time; these days it presents as a normal two lane road. Many locals wanted a replacement for the Dun Bull Inn to be built at the valley head, in a traditional low whitewashed design. Manchester Corporation Water Works had other ideas and built a modern, elevated hotel on the east side.

Haweswater

Forty years later Wainwright agreed with the local sentiment of the time about the hotels' location, "a cardinal sin has been made from the walker's point of view: much more convenient would have been a rebuilt Dun Bull at the head of the valley ..... however the new road gives splendid access to the heart of the Fells."
(A Coast to Coast Walk 1972)

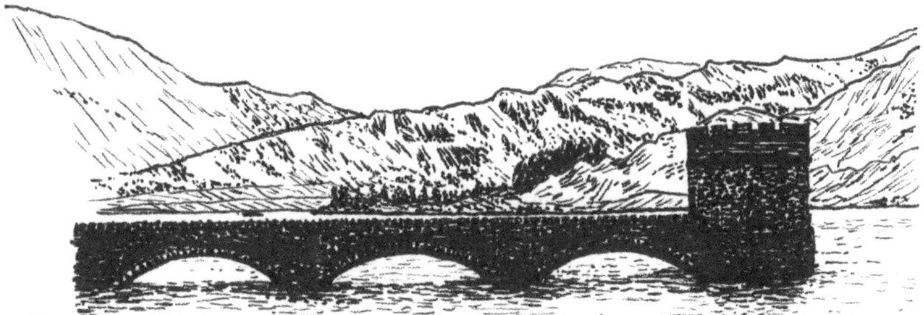

The Draw Off Tower built using stone from Mardale Church

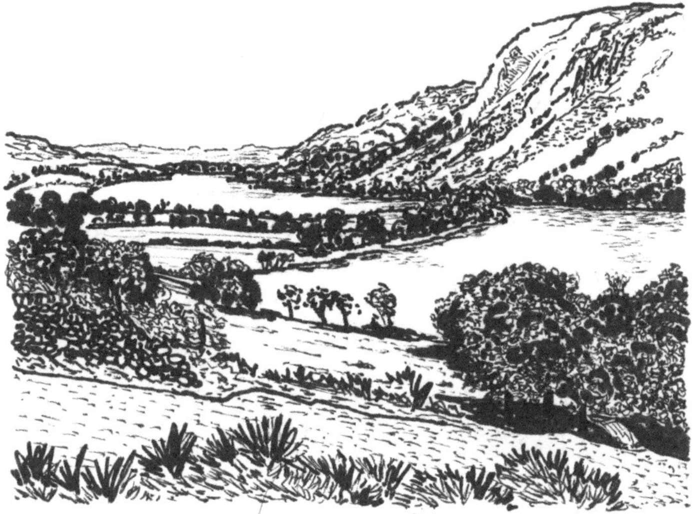

The delta formed by Measand Beck nearly splitting Haweswater in two is shown here before it was submerged.

A century on from Mardale's drowning, nature has had time to soften the hard edges of the flooded valley. The southern half of the reservoir is home to tremendous, stimulating walking with some of the finest passes, tarns, ridge walks and panoramic views taking in nearly the whole of Cumbria. In the northern half of Haweswater man's influence retains the upper hand with the steep inaccessible unnatural shores dominant.

Harter Fell

2539′

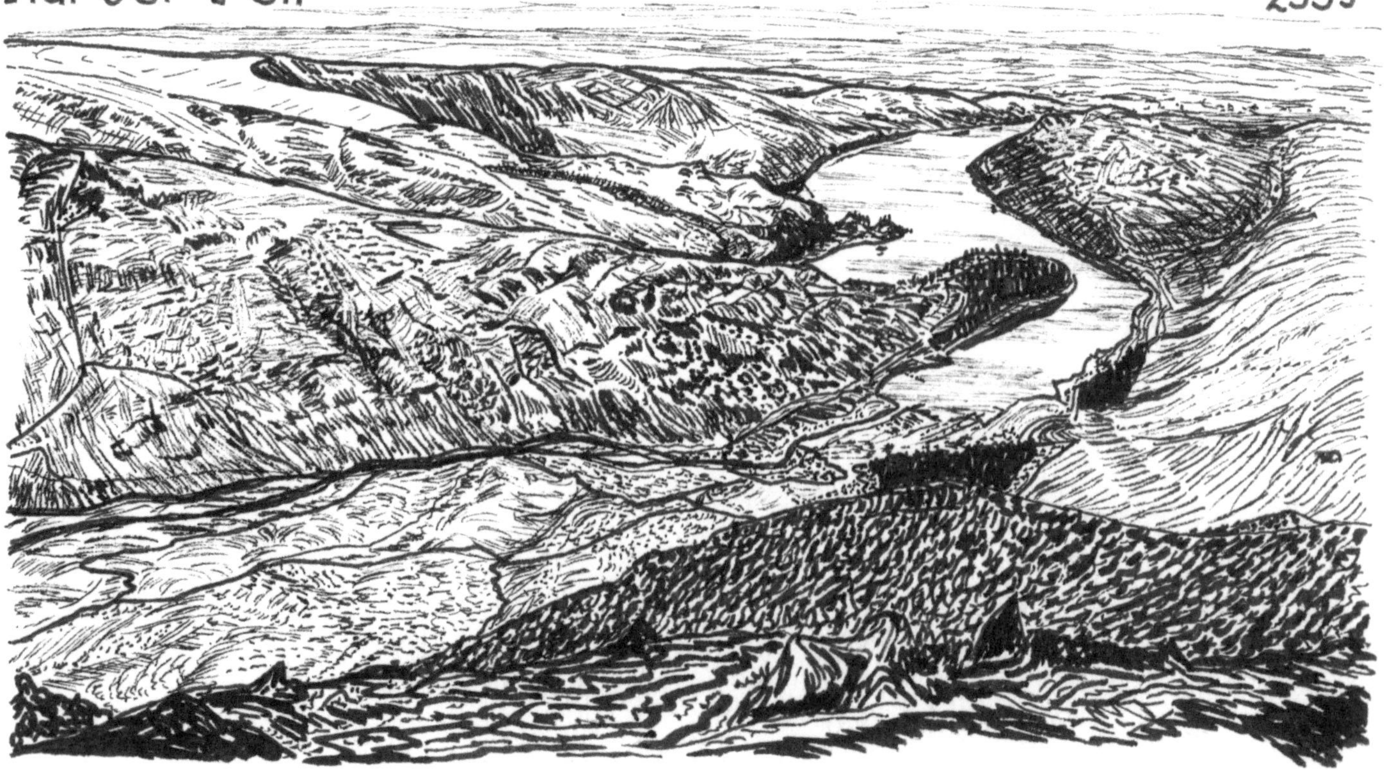

Nan Bield Pass - west flank Harter Fell 2295'

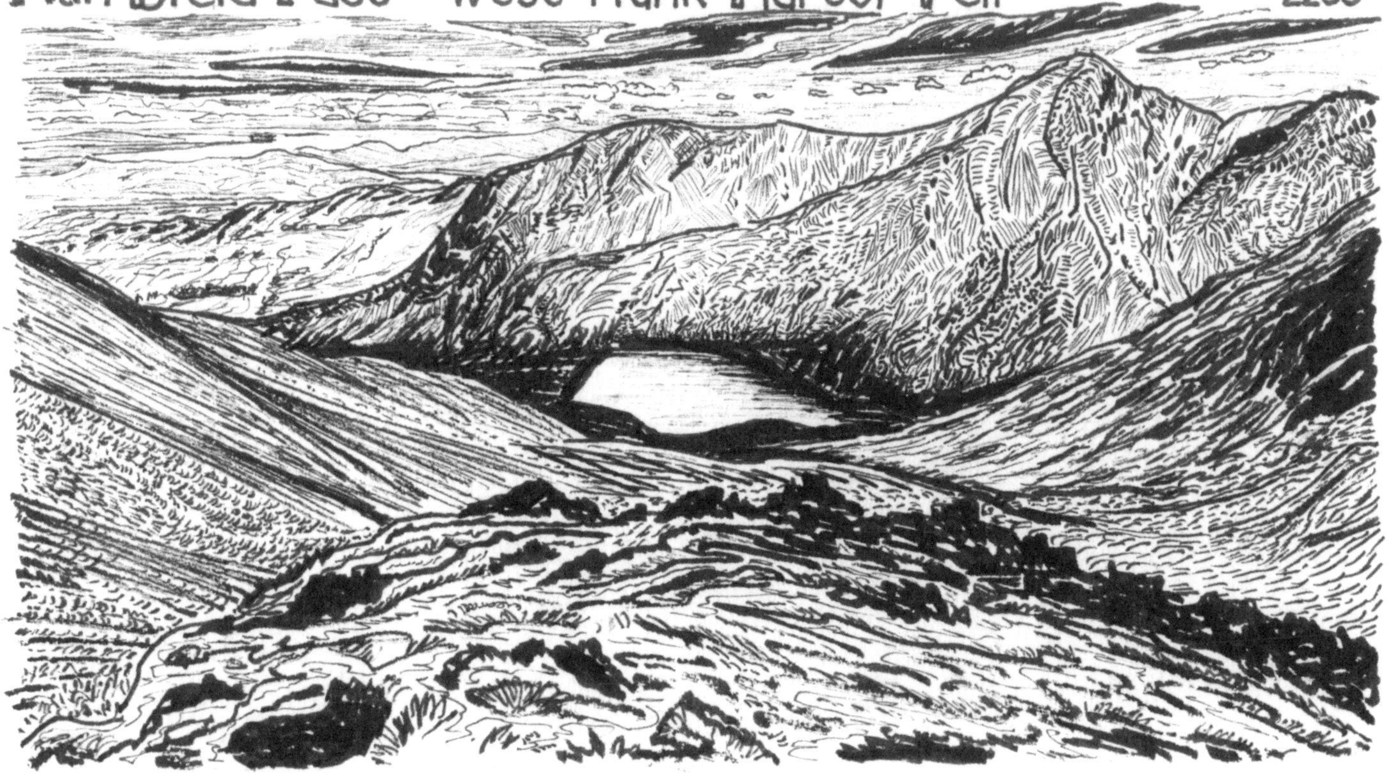

Nan Bield Pass, High Street, Castle Crag

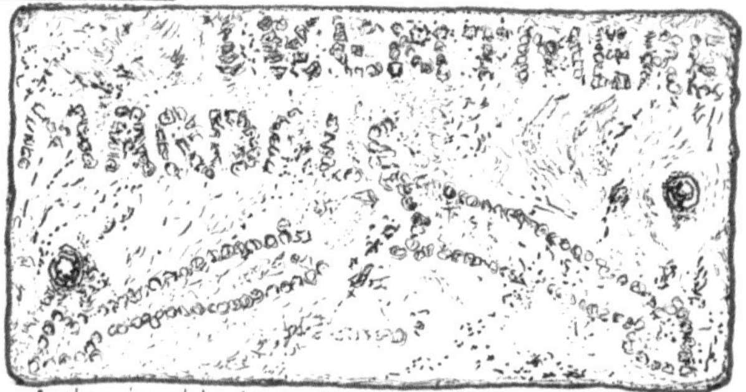

A charming slate sign on the Nan Bield Pass shelter

The drawing opposite features the magnificent stone shelter on the crossroads of the Nan Bield Pass. To the north is the Mardale Valley, to the south Kentmere, east is Harter Fell, and High Street is up to the west. The view from High Street on a clear day is unfettered and finite only to the limit of the human eye; nearly every Lakeland peak can be seen as well as the hinterlands beyond them in every direction. The hills of Dumfries and Galloway across the Solway Firth, the Pennines stretching from Northumberland down to the Yorkshire Dales, and the glistening waters of Windermere guiding the eye south to Morecambe Bay and beyond.

The High Street range with its gentle slopes and flat summit plateau was chosen by the Roman road builders as the safest and best route between Brocavum (Brougham) and Galava (Ambleside) forts rather than the densely forested valleys with trees up to 2000′ high on their flanks.

The swooping glacial valley of Riggindale made the perfect habitat for England's only Golden Eagles from 1969 to 2015; the male is thought to have died having spent his last twelve years without a mate.

Castle Crag guards the northern entrance to Riggindale and historically was the only route to Mardale Valley head. This trading route was frequented by the Border Rievers, these were the 'Debatable Lands' from 1400 onwards for three centuries. Once, the Kendal Bowmen had advanced warning of an imminent Scottish raid and laid their trap, posting archers on the high ground around Castle Crag. It is legend that not a single raider survived; all were buried where they fell.

Nan Bield Pass Shelter

1967'

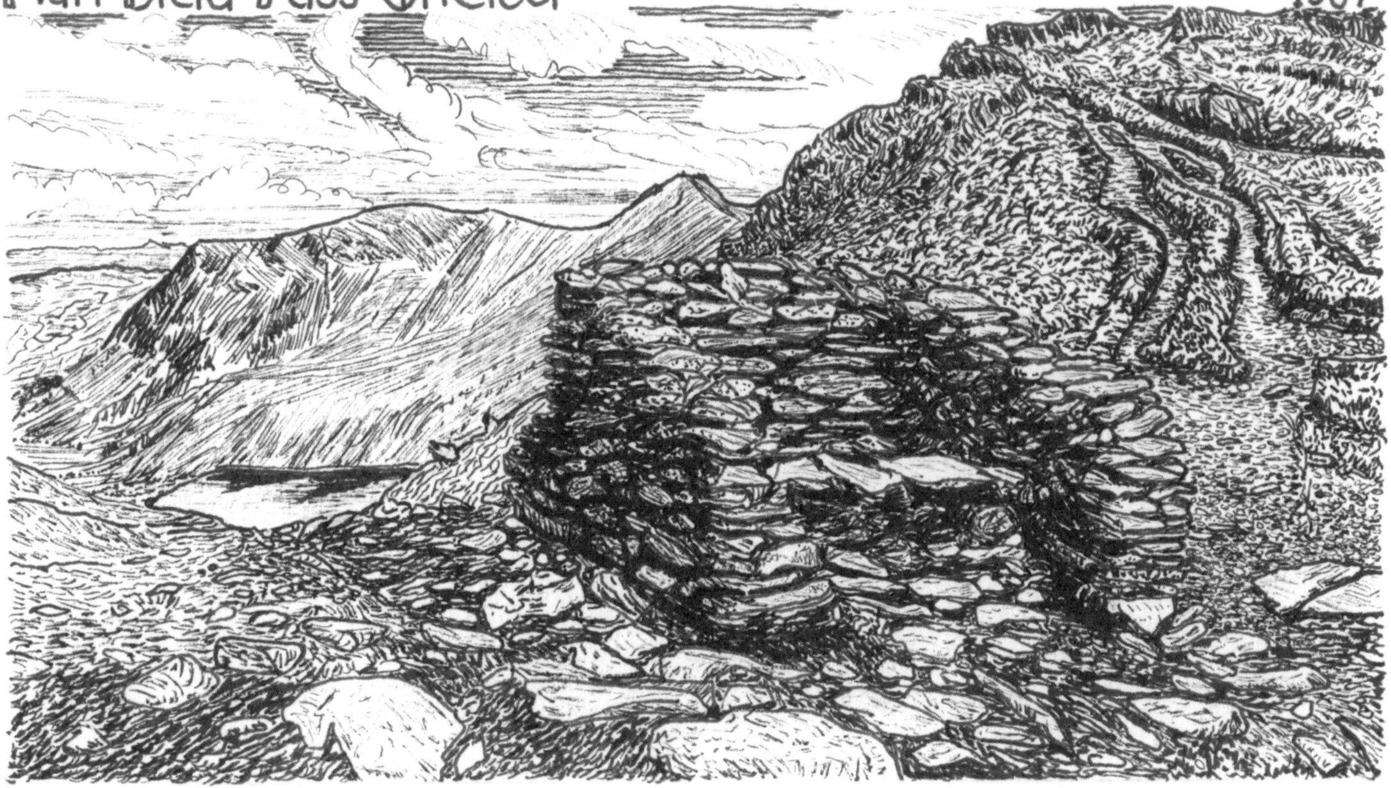

Mardale Ill Bell

2492′

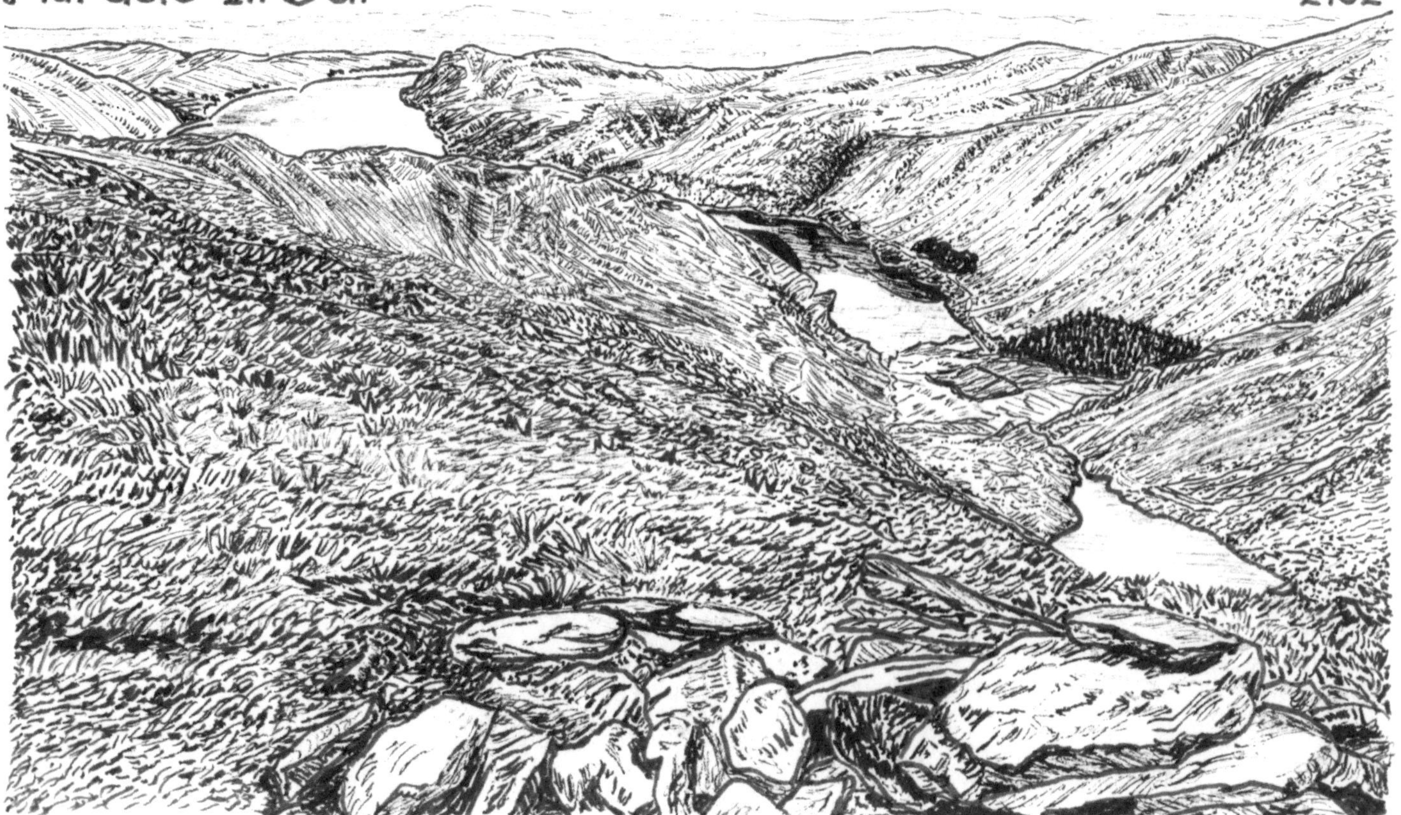

High Street - Racecourse Hill 2692′

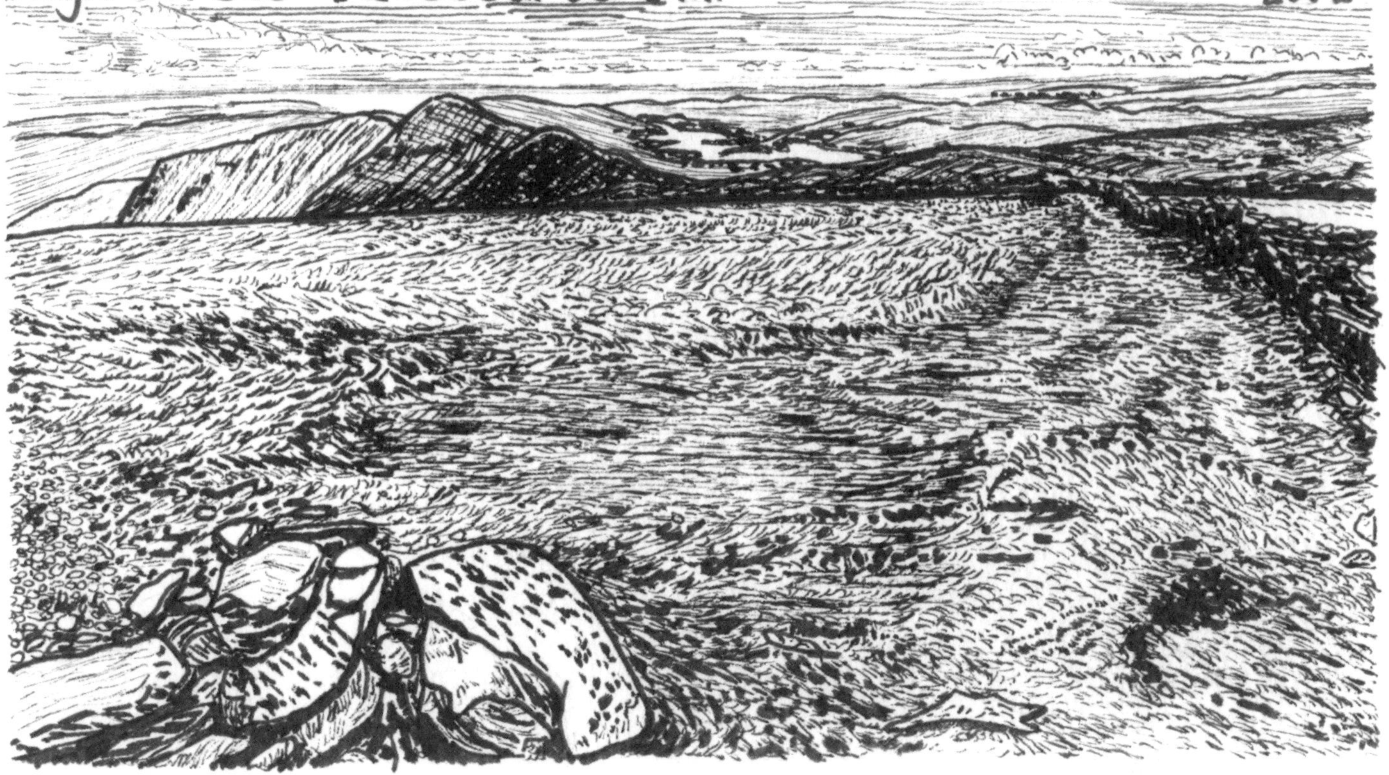

High Street - East of Trig Point

2623´

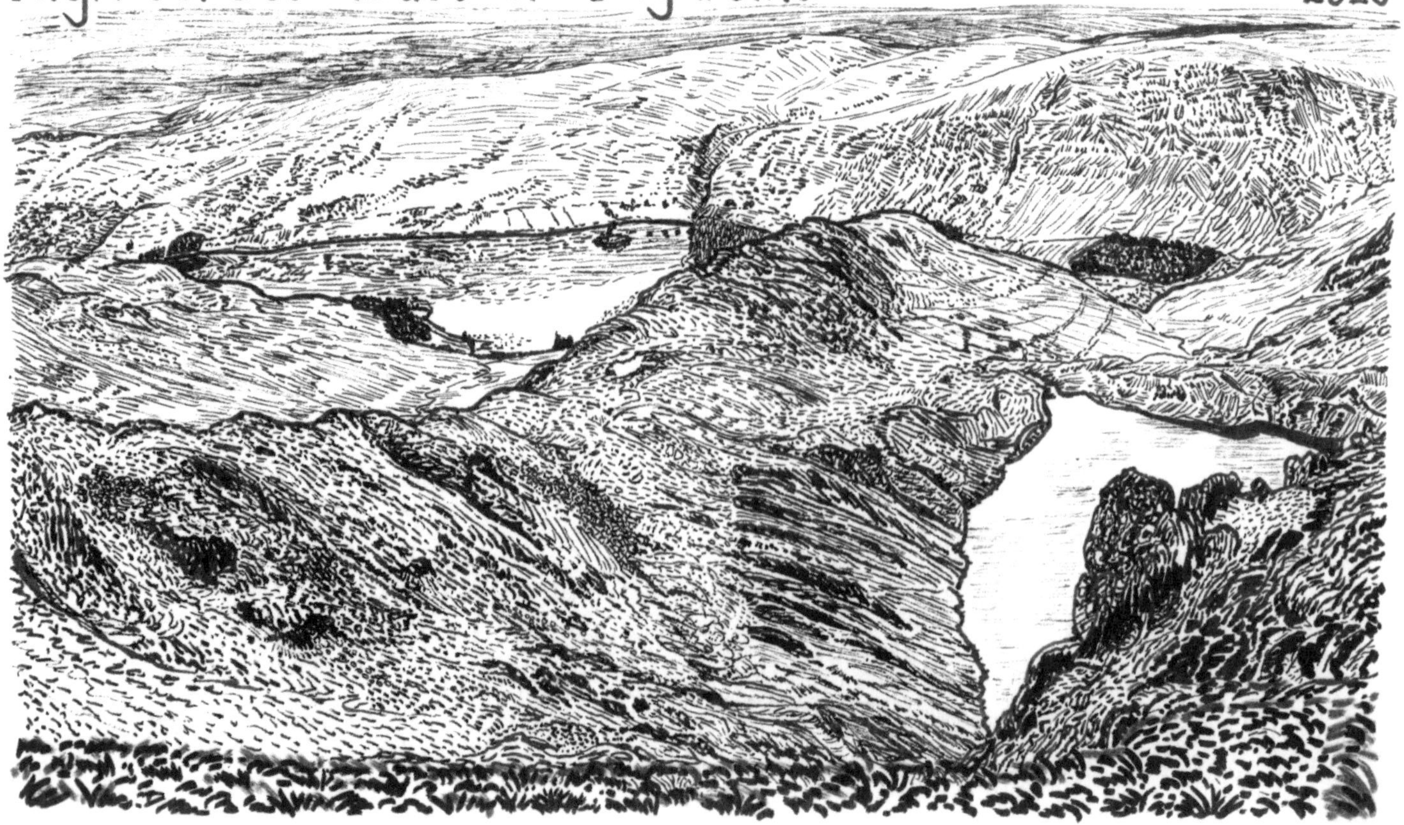

Rampsgill Head

2543′

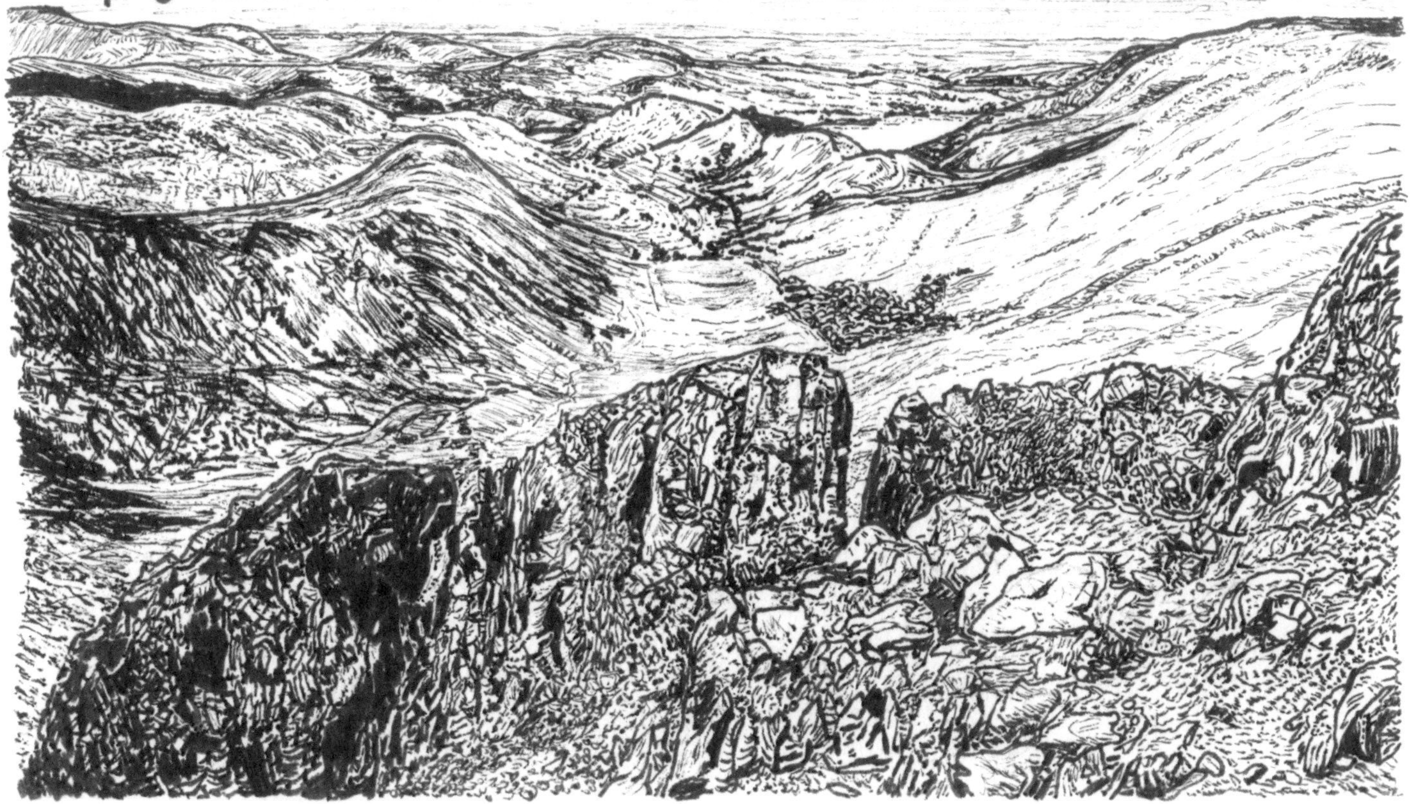

High St. - Riggindale Crag

2656′

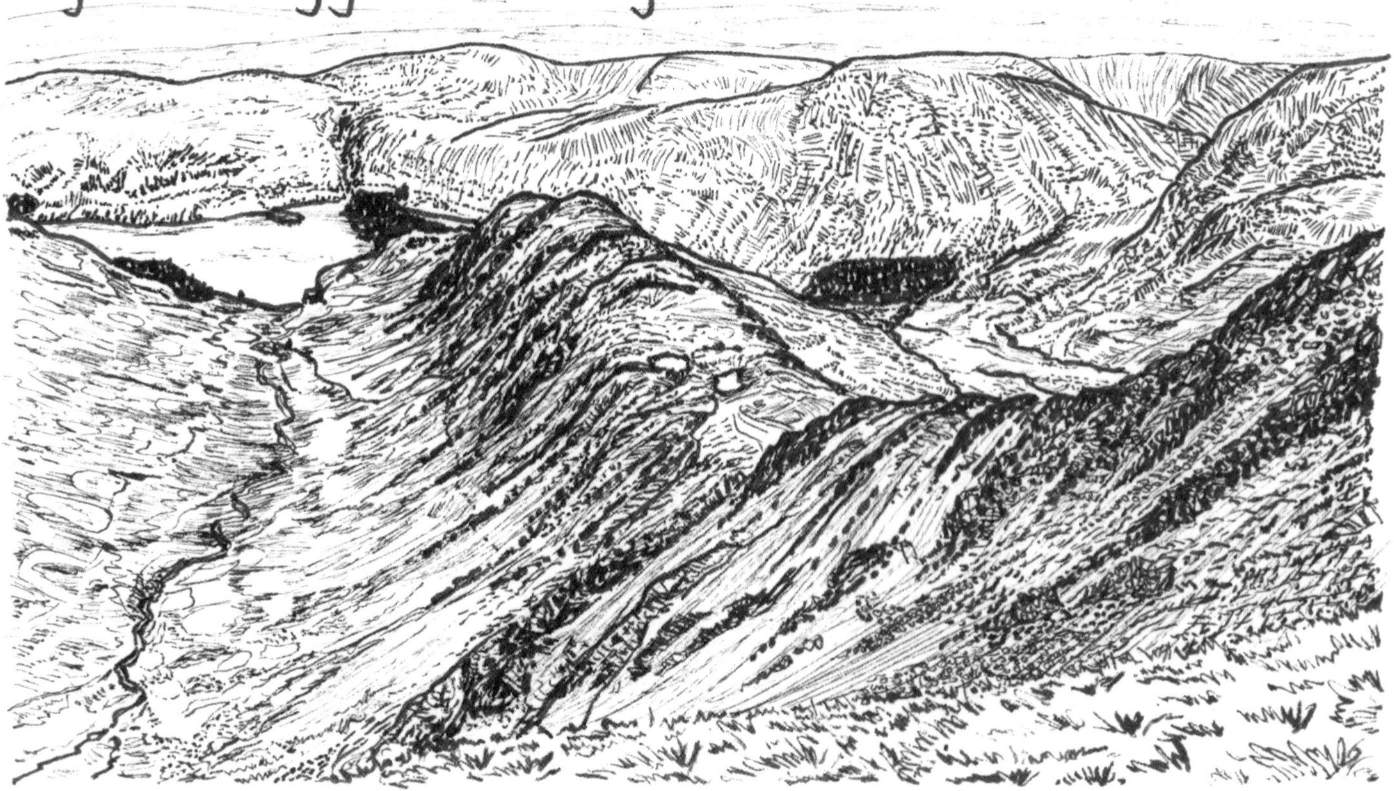

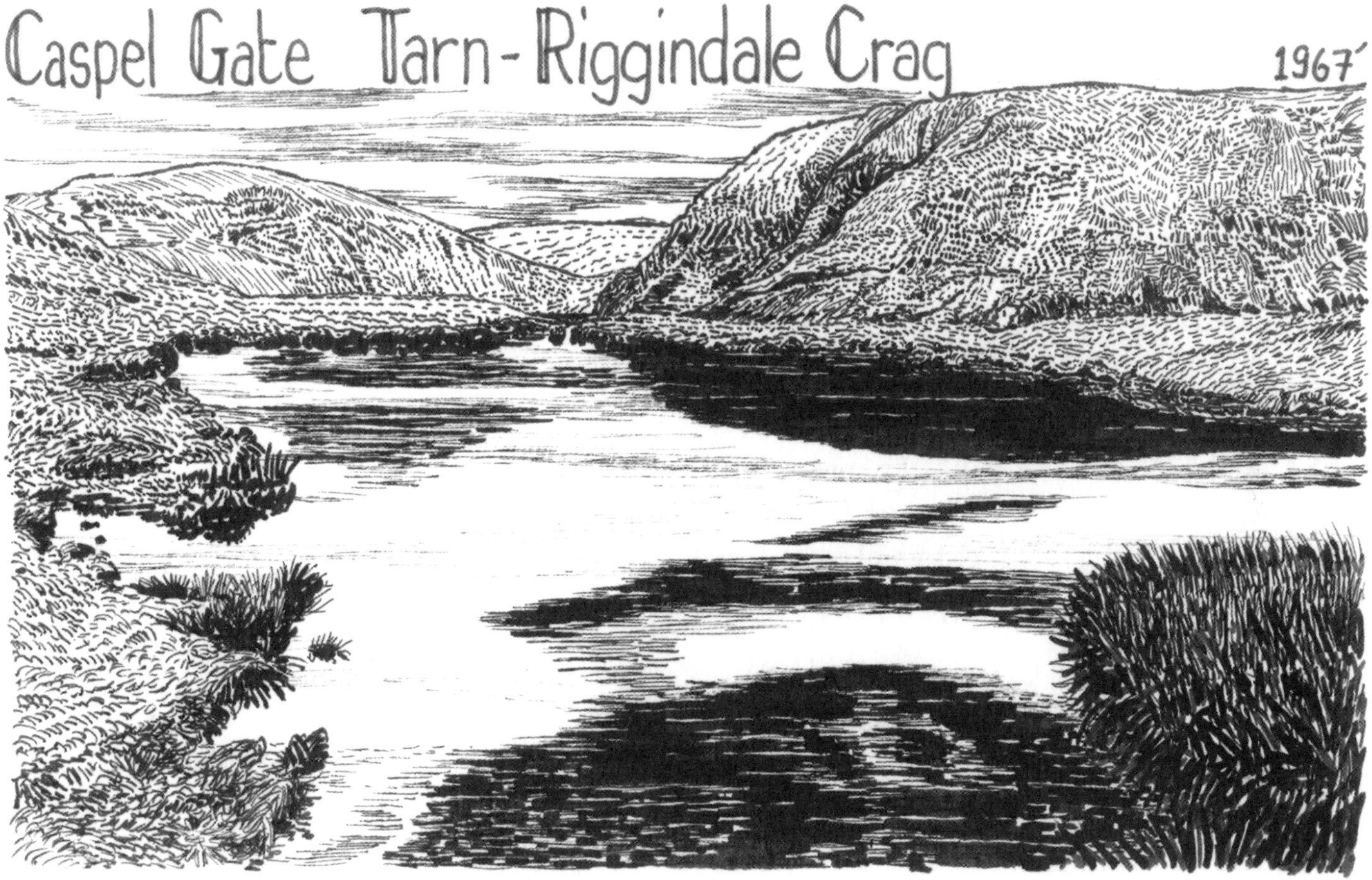
Caspel Gate Tarn - Riggindale Crag
1967'

Castle Crag - Haweswater

984'

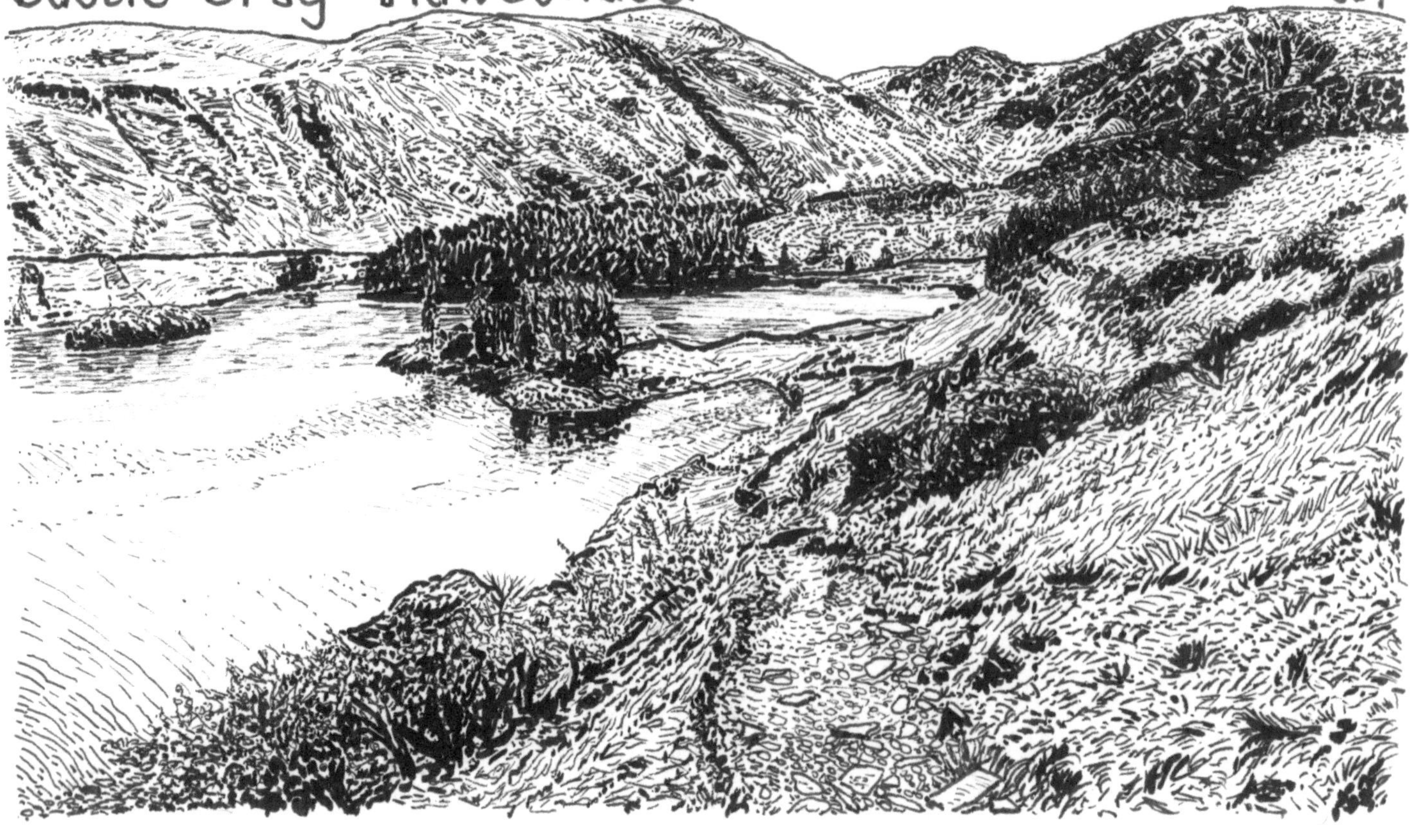

Haweswater - North Shore

967'

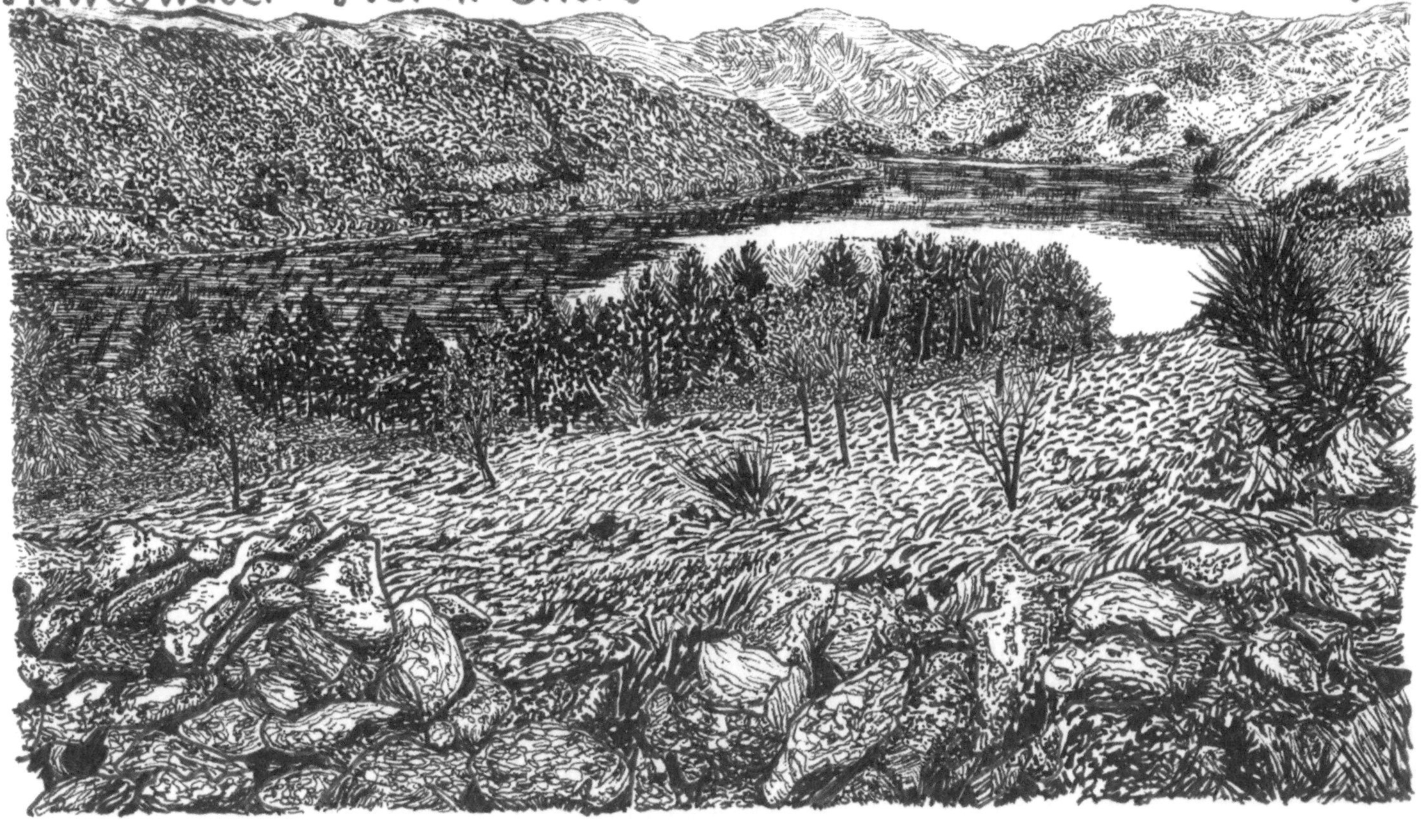

Herdwicks

There are approximately 50,000 Herdwick sheep in the world; nearly all of them are farmed in the Lake District. They have been a dominant breed in Lakeland since the 1100's; their bristly fleeces enabling them to survive the harshest Cumbrian Winters; some have lived through several days of snowdrifts by eating their own wool. Most spend the winter from December to April independently grazing on the common fells, they are hefted; attached to one area of the hills, passing on this knowledge and behaviour to the next generation. The rough and difficult to dye fleeces historically were made into a cloth, Kendal Green, in 1390 it was described as the "worst wool in the realm". Beatrix Potter became a dedicated Herdwick farmer, and stipulated that the farms she gifted to the National Trust must continue with the breed. A unique culture and language has evolved amongst Lakeland shepherds, with the ancient Brittonnic Celtic system for counting sheep still in use; one to ten goes like this: Yan, Tan, Tethera, Methera, Pimp, Sethera, Lethera, Hovera, Dovera, Dick. The farmers I have met are amongst the happiest most fulfilled people on earth, absolutely loving their lives and what they do. Shepherding has been a major factor in shaping the look of this cultural landscape. The pristine, picturesque, verdant stone walled pastures of the valley bottoms were created in the 1700's, and have been maintained ever since for managing the flocks. Matterdale farmer and author of 'The Shepherd's Life' James Rebanks, "landscapes like ours are the culmination and sum total of a million little unseen jobs.... those who work in it don't see it as landscape or romanticise it, its the cleared meadows growing hay to feed the sheep in winter when they come down from the fells.... its the maintained stone walls that keep the sheep sheltered and rotated.... we have to see and understand the indigenous culture that the landscape represents'.

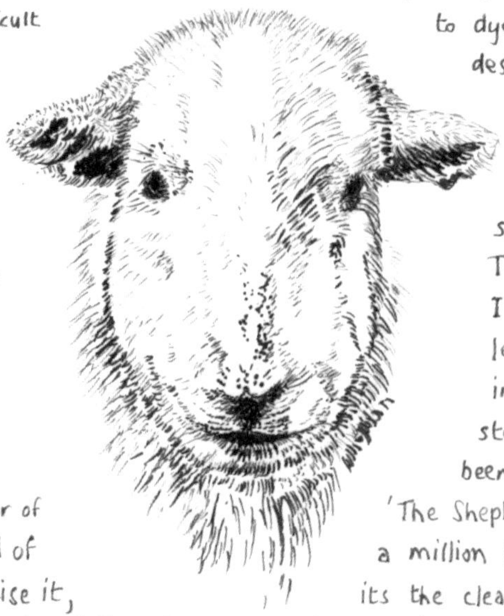

Sheepwrecked

A reflex reaction after World War Two was for Britain to become more self-sufficient in food production, so farmers were rewarded for increasing the size of their flocks. This had consequences: overgrazing of the fells, treeless fell tops as sheep nibble on every sapling, a decrease in biodiversity, soil compaction reducing the absorption of the ground, increasing water run off and flooding. Environmentalist George Monbiot coined the 'sheepwrecked' phrase, "entire fell tops have been reduced to a treeless waste of cropped turf, exposed soil, and bare rock. Almost all the bird, mammal and insect species you would expect to find in a National Park are suppressed or absent...... sheep nibbling out tree seedlings and other edible species are a fully automated system for ecological destruction...... spend two hours in any suburban garden and you are more likely to see more species than walking five miles across any British upland...... the countryside has been sheepwrecked."

Since 2003 flock numbers have decreased as farmers are rewarded more for environmental stewardship; however, 2005, 2009 and 2015 saw Cumbria suffering three "one in a hundred year" flood events in ten years, devastating many homes and lives. Flood prevention measures are already having some impact and will continue to be rolled out; upland tree planting, which makes the soil sixtyseven times more absorbent than turfed ground, and the snaking of rivers slowing the pace at which rain reaches the valley bottoms, to name but two.

None of us alive today have seen Lakeland valleys treelined as they once were up to two thousand feet high; so all of our memories, strongest from our childhoods are of bare topped fells. Hopefully this will slowly change in the decades to come and a balance can be found where the culture and practise of Herdwick shepherding can flourish too.

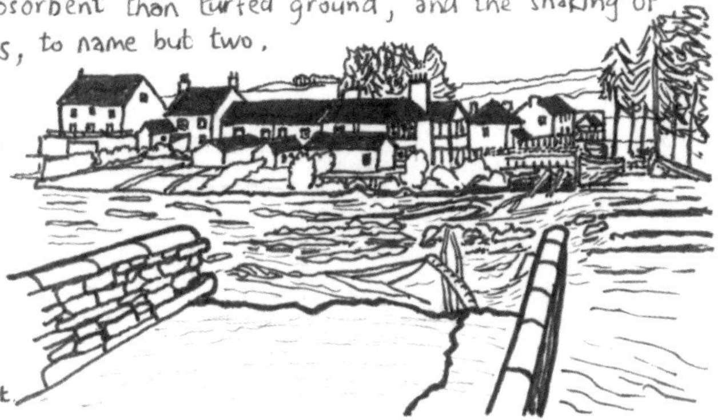

Pooley Bridge
December 2015
Washed away by
Storm Desmond
Ullswater rose by 12 Feet.

The M6

On August 1st 2016 the Lake District National Park was extended east by 27 square miles and the Yorkshire Dales National Park west by a quarter making the M6 through the Lune gorge the boundary between the two. A mile south of Tebay you can come off the A685 and go under the M6 and the West Coast Mainline Railway and cross a pack horse bridge; when you turn around and look up 100' to the rail viaduct, then another 100' to the M6 flyover you really do get a sense of the last 200 years of the development of our world. The completion of the M6 in 1971, running parallel north/south to the Lake District was the most significant transport development in the county since the arrival of the railway at Birthwaite in 1847. It brought 14 million people within a three hour drive of the Lakes; at times now the roads and car parks are overwhelmed. Whatever the Lake District National Park Authority do, they can't ban cars, and they can never do enough to accommodate cars, there simply isn't the space.

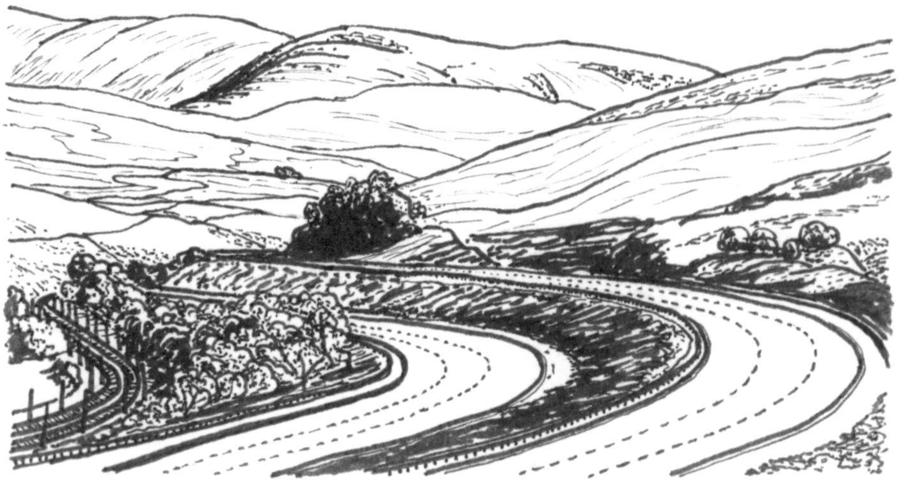

The Lune Gorge section of the M6 overlooked by the cushion like Howgills is the most spectacular scenery to be found on any motorway in England, it makes for a worthy boundary between two wonderful, world class National Parks.

In our lifetimes...

The Lake District is England and Wales largest and most popular National Park, with around twenty million visits every year. In our lifetimes, since 1955, Wainwright's Guides, extending the A66 from Penrith to Cockermouth, the M6, increased leisure time and car ownership; improved facilities, equipment and clothing, fabulous restaurants, Peter Rabbit and his worldwide appeal have all played their part in enabling and encouraging the world to enjoy the delights of the district.

The National Park Authority (with lots of volunteer help) maintains over 1900 miles of footpaths, green lanes and bridleways; mountain path erosion is repaired by charities such as Fix the Fells; the National Trust helps maintain the farming tradition as well as its wonderful lakeshore lands; Friends of the Lake District create their own campaigns and act as an independent voice; these plus countless other charities and voluntary acts have one thing in common - a love of the Lakes. It is this love, affection and deep bond with this place, through the efforts of those that have gone before us, that it is heavily protected in law ensuring that its future is safe.

However as the old adage goes; 'change is the only constant in life' and we don't know where that change will take us. It is the job of scientists, artists, writers, critics and activists to add insight and understanding to the world around us, all seeking out the truth... their success needs imagination, the ability as Einstein said, not just to observe, but to "feel into things".

I hope these pages have helped you see and feel the love of this land.

In conclusion, some personal notes

If you've come along this far with me, thanks, I hope you've experienced some of the joy, marvel, wonder and awe that I have around this glorious district. There are few more satisfying feelings in life than the well earned cup of tea and cake, or a pint after a days walking and exploration. The aching muscles are resting, the boots are loosened or off, and the soul is rejuvenated by a day of fresh air, freedom and exhilerating exercise. My favourite afterglow memory is sat in the early evening summer sunshine in the garden of the Patterdale Hotel after walking with Karen from Pooley Bridge to Howtown, up Fusedale valley and along the Roman Road to Rampsgill Head, then around to The Knott and onto Angle Tarn, descending into Patterdale with just enough time for one golden pint before the last bus back to Pooley. Then there's the bus ride weaving through the wooded shores of Ullswater, arcing around Glencoyne Bay, and the road becomes more gentle as you are released from the Helvellyn massif toward the pastures of Pooley Bridge ... the closing lines from Van Morrisons 'Coney Island' fills my head, "I look at the side of your face as the sunlight comes streaming through the window ... And all the time I'm thinking ... wouldn't it be great if it was like this all the time".

Finishing this book has been like walking up Loadpot Hill from Pooley Bridge, a seemingly endless series of false hopes. If I'd never been to a particular area my mind told me it couldn't be as good as the sensational places I'd already been to ... I was wrong. The Ullswater, Brotherswater and Haweswater valleys just kept on giving. I've loved it all, every second, and love the prospect of the next three books as they give me the purpose and permission to absolutely explore and to see new places.

My thoughts and energy turn to Book Two and the delights of Windermere, Coniston, Grasmere and Rydal Water, I shall not miss Ullswater and its surrounds as I am fortunate to call it my home and my workplace. My childhood was filled with trailer tent and caravan holidays mostly at Coniston and Pooley Bridge, they made a deep imprint. Later in life with a young family and living overseas I felt compelled and drawn back to the area, there was nowhere else I wanted to be and for my children to grow up in.

I am a lucky man, blessed with health, love and the Lake District in my life.

Until the next one...

[signature], August 2020

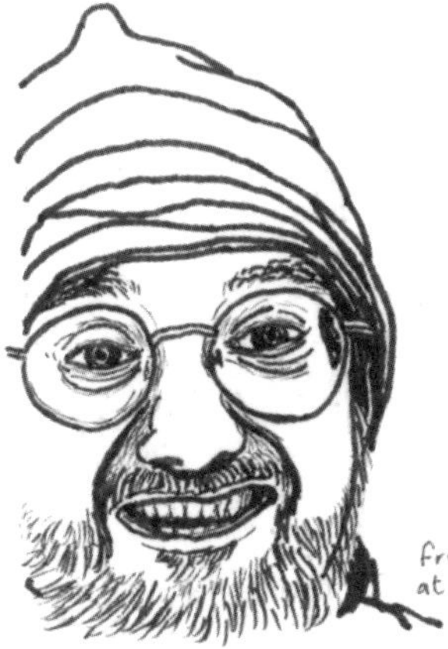

from a selfie taken at Angle Tarn in December 2019

With special thanks for your support, encouragement and help in the making of this book:

Karen Donnelly, Harry, Hannah and Hazel Hindle, Anne and Mark Vause, Mr and Mrs Donaldo, Dave and Gill Bealt, Craig and Bin Ballop, Megster and Webster, Sam Bunting, Peter Moran and Steve Duckworth. Also to Dan, Sarah, Nic and the team for making it possible for me to escape from our wonderful tea rooms. LH.